CAPE HORN

Cape Horn

A Maritime History

Robin Knox-Johnston

Hodder & Stoughton

British Library Cataloguing in Publication Data

Knox-Johnston, Robin
Cape Horn
I. Title
918.304 [F]

ISBN 0-340-41527-4

Typeset by Avon Dataset Ltd, Bidford-on-Avon

Printed and bound in Great Britain by
Mackays of Chatham PLC, Chatham, Kent

Hodder and Stoughton Ltd
A division of Hodder Headline PLC
338 Euston Road
London NW1 3BH

Contents

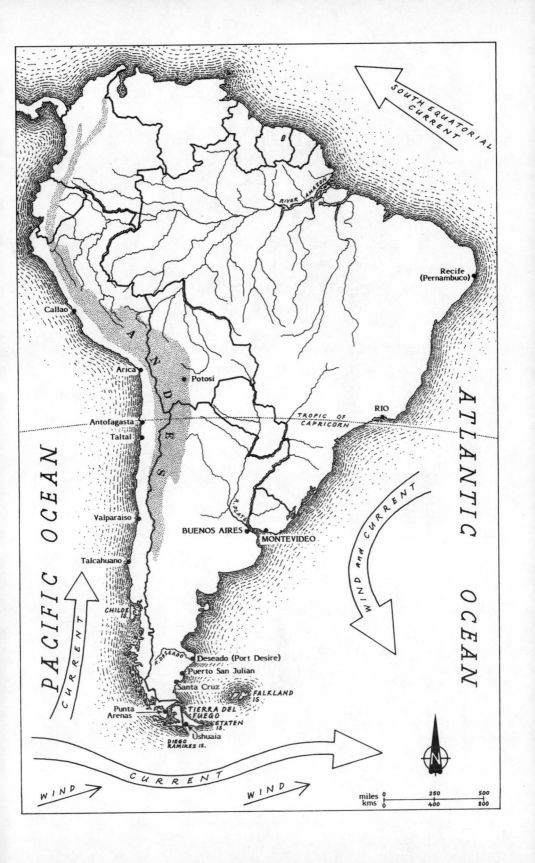

SOUTH EQUATORIAL CURRENT

RIVER AMAZON

Recife
(Pernambuco)

Callao

ANDES

Arica

Potosi

Antofagasta

RIO

TROPIC OF
CAPRICORN

Taltal

PACIFIC OCEAN

ATLANTIC OCEAN

CURRENT

Valparaiso

R. PLATE

WIND and CURRENT

Talcahuano

BUENOS AIRES

MONTEVIDEO

CHILOE
IS.

R. DESEADO

Deseado (Port Desire)

Puerto San Julian

Santa Cruz

FALKLAND
IS.

Punta
Arenas

TIERRA DEL
FUEGO

STATEN
IS.

Ushuaia

DIEGO
RAMIREZ IS.

WIND

CURRENT

WIND

N

miles 0   250   500
kms 0   400   800

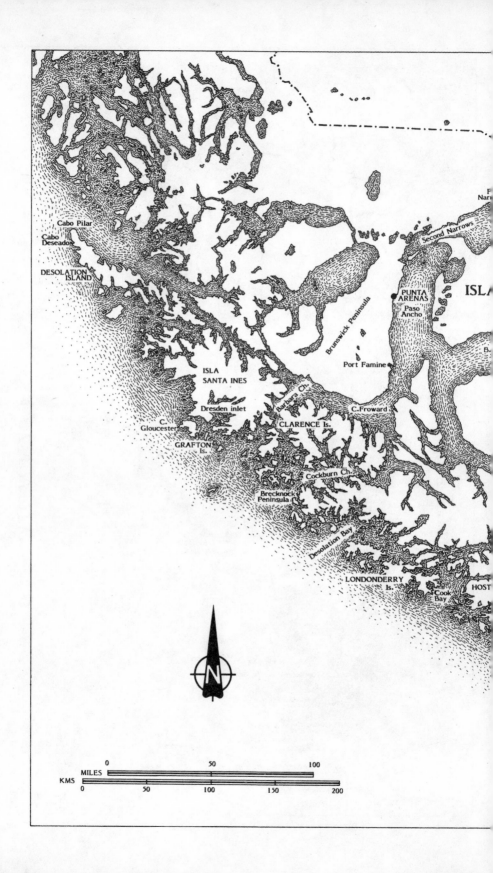

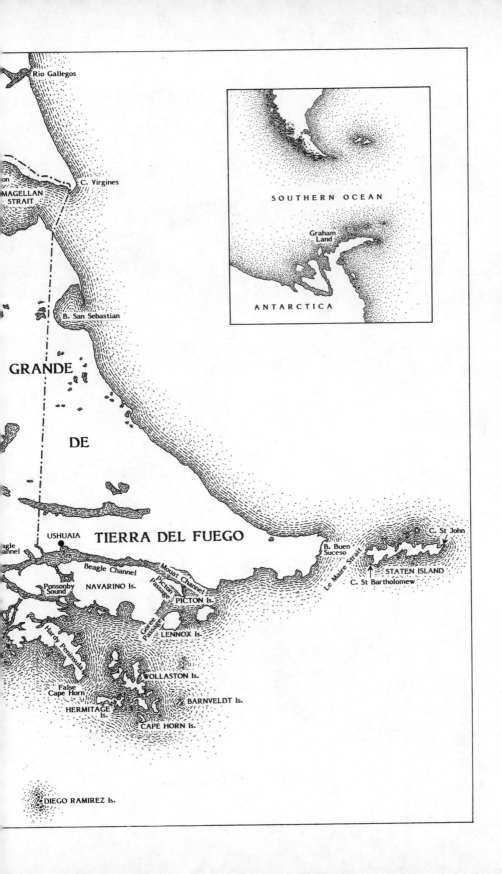

1

A Land of Fire

The Patagonian archipelagos – The numerous islands fringing the western coast of the mainland, between Magellan's Strait and the Penas Gulf form the Patagonian archipelagos; these, like the southern and western parts of the Archipelago de Tierra del Fuego, are about as inhospitable as anywhere on the globe. The land is mountainous, presenting an alternation of impenetrable forest, bare rock, and deep bogs, and is cut up by deep channels into peninsulas and islands, as yet very imperfectly known. Drenching rains, varied by snow and sleet, prevail throughout the year, whilst furious westerly gales succeed each other with rapidity. The scenery is magnificently stern, but is seldom seen to advantage, the clouds and mists usually screening the higher peaks and snow fields; glaciers, however, extend in many places nearly, or quite, to the level of the sea. In such a climate life is scarce.

The Admiralty South America Pilot – Volume 11

Cape Horn is the most famous and feared of all the world's capes. Its position at the southernmost point of South America protrudes nearly 1,000 miles into the Southern Ocean. Of all the oceans of the world, none is more desolate or ferocious than this one, which girdles the globe, filling the space between the continents of Africa, South America and Australia, and ice-covered

Antarctica. Nowhere else on our planet does an ocean have free passage all around the world. An almost continuous succession of easterly moving depressions, uninterrupted as elsewhere in the Northern Hemisphere, generate enormous waves, sometimes as much as 120 feet in height, which are the largest natural dynamic force on the earth's surface.

The consistency of these westerly winds provided the reliable driving force for exploration and trade in the days before vessels were powered by engines. A voyage to Australia or New Zealand from Europe could be predicted because the westerly winds were always there to propel the vessels from the Atlantic eastwards. The homeward voyage was considered the more hazardous as it involved a dive southwards deep into the Southern Ocean to get around Cape Horn. The price for the reliability of this route around the world was paid in lives by the seamen and passengers who had to brave the force of the winds and size of the waves.

These huge waves have an unrestricted passage nearly two thousand miles wide as they roll ponderously eastwards. They brush past Africa and Australia and the southern parts of the Atlantic, Indian and Pacific Oceans, but at one point they find themselves confined. Where South America reaches southwards at Cape Horn, a similar finger of land juts northward towards it from Antarctica. At this point the mighty ocean is forced to squeeze itself through a space only 600 miles wide and is further restricted by the shallowing of the sea bed. The effect is to increase the eastward flow of the current and force the waves to heap up. As if this were not sufficient the winds are similarly squeezed southwards by the Andes mountains and accelerate through the gap. These larger, steeper waves and more violent winds are the reason for Cape Horn's fearsome reputation.

The Cape itself lies at the southern extremity of a group of islands which form the Tierra del Fuego archipelago, separated by Magellan's Strait from the tip of South America. Until about 130 million years ago, South America was a part of a huge land mass we call Gondwanaland, but then a split occurred, and 100 million years ago South America and Africa began to move apart, and Antarctica commenced its gradual movement to the south. The oceans grew as the gap widened, small narrow seas to begin with, but increasing year by year as the lithospheric plates continued their drift, until they formed the mighty expanses we know today.

For millions of years the waves, wind and drenching rain coming in from the Pacific Ocean have battered the land. Exposed soft rock in the west was ruthlessly worn away, and even the hard granite that survives shows the scars of constant battering. Rain, sleet, hail and snow, borne by the winds that frequently blow from Antarctica, have joined in the weathering, and although the snow line in summer rises to 700 metres, glaciers, which descend to the water's edge in places, have assisted in opening and exploiting huge chasms, creating a maze of intricate channels and islands. Icebergs, some from the glaciers and some that have drifted in from the pack ice to the south-west, are occasionally found amongst the islands.

In the exposed west the rocks are bare, for nothing but the hardiest of lichens can cling to their surface, but the land changes gradually to the east, becoming less desolate and providing conditions that will allow trees to survive, until on the Atlantic coast grass and forests flourish. In summer the temperature will occasionally rise above 20° centigrade, but this can be misleading and at Ushuaia, on the southern end of the largest island, the mean temperature for the year is only 6° centigrade. Not surprisingly, the Admiralty Sailing Directions concludes its description of the Patagonian archipelago by saying, 'In such a climate life is scarce.'

And yet when Europeans first arrived they found a comparatively large population of dark-skinned people who survived as near-naked hunters throughout the archipelago. They showed some racial similarities with the Patagonians on the mainland, and were probably driven across the Magellan Strait by the migration of other tribes southwards in a similar manner to the western retreat of the Iberian peoples in Europe. The migration cannot have been easy, as the spring tidal streams, particularly in some of the narrower channels on the eastern side of the Tierra del Fuego, can reach a rate of 12 knots. Quite when the Fuegian peoples arrived is unknown, but the size of the middens in their camping areas indicates that they had lived there for many hundreds, and perhaps thousands of years. The evidence is scanty and the dating imprecise because these people were not builders of anything except small wigwams and retaining walls for catching fish, and did not congregate in large numbers except at special ceremonies such as the initiation of youngsters. They had no tribal leaders and no tribal headquarters were ever built. Families were the main unit, and these would join with other groups of their own tribe, which was really a loose-knit federation of families for defence and for hunting expeditions after large prey such as whales. The only flimsy evidence of early habitation in the area comes in the Yahgan word for an isthmus at Ushuaia, Yaiyuashaga. Ashaga in their language means a channel in the water, not a neck of land, but such a channel would only have existed when the sea level fell during the last ice age about 12,000 years ago.

These Fuegians are pertinent to our story since early sailors who explored the Straits found them both thieves and allies and those who were shipwrecked, right up to the end of the great age of sail when shipwrecks became less frequent, could be shown great kindness, although this was not always the case. That the Fuegians could save lives is shown by the experience of the crew of the *Glencairn*.

The ship was outward bound for Seattle from Rochester in 1907 and had passed east of Staten Island and then set a course to clear Cape Horn by five miles. Conditions were misty and the ship was not aware of the strong north-easterly current frequently found in this vicinity which pushed her towards the land where she grounded west of the Wollaston Islands. Knowing that the ship would not survive for long if a big swell developed, the crew launched one of the lifeboats, which capsized almost immediately, drowning two. The ship then freed herself and began to drift towards the Le Maire Strait, but since she was taking water forward, the crew attempted to edge her towards Tierra del Fuego with the object of beaching her. After a number of days drifting the *Glencairn* grounded again and the crew took to the three remaining boats. A long cold night ensued during which the boats were separated and two men died of exposure but the next day the survivors in the captain's gig saw smoke ashore and rowed in its direction. They managed to get through the surf safely and came to a beach where some natives were waiting. Apparently the Fuegians, who were from the Ona tribe, had been watching the *Glencairn* for some time, had seen the ship's boat, and lit a fire to guide them towards smooth water near Cape San Pablo. The crews of the other two boats eventually joined their captain.

Although they had survived, their boats had been smashed to pieces on the shore, so they planned to head for Ushuaia which lay several days away and over wintry mountains. But the Ona told them of a ranch which lay nearer and guided them to Viamonte where the rancher, the Englishman Lucas Bridges, immediately organised a rescue.

As a postscript, it is revealed that the natives, who usually went without clothes, had dressed themselves as they awaited the arrival of the captain's gig in order not to frighten the strangers. All the survivors of the crew returned home by steamer with the exception of the steward and his wife, who took up employment with Mr Bridges.

In stark contrast, the *Porcupine* of Liverpool grounded in the Strait in 1853 and was attacked by Fuegians in a fleet of canoes. They were beaten back but the vessel had to abandon her voyage and return to the Falklands. Nine years later the *Anne and Eliza* of Boston was similarly attacked and lost eight men, and in 1871 four crew from the British *Propontis* were attacked and killed whilst ashore collecting firewood near Port Gallant.

The Indians were divided into three main and one subsidiary tribe when the Europeans first arrived, although it was a long time before it was appreciated that there was any difference. In the north of Isla Grande were a tribe called the Ona, and in the east, a section of the Ona known as the Aush. In the south were the Yahgan and on the western side the Alakaluf. The Alakaluf and Yahgan were probably the oldest inhabitants of the area. They mixed and intermarried a little, but both were frightened of the Ona and avoided them.

The Yahgan and Alakaluf were largely canoe hunters, but rarely went far from the coast. Their canoes were usually made either of bark or dug out from whole trees, some of the latter being as much as 29 feet in length. The Alakaluf also built some planked canoes, rather on the lines of the Polynesians, but they were a local development. Both used fire, and shared the only source of ignition, iron pyrites, which was found in the area at Mercury Sound on Clarence Island. These workings show signs of having been used for many centuries. Once a fire was lighted every effort was made to keep it alight and it was even taken in a canoe if the family were going away hunting. Fire was also used to warn members of a tribe that a stranger was approaching. Green branches were piled on the fire to produce smoke as a signal for everyone to return to camp. Early explorers wrote of the many smoking fires they saw as their ships passed the coast, and this is the reason why the whole area was given the name Tierra del Fuego, Land of Fire, by the members of Magellan's expedition.

The Alakaluf hunted birds, fish, limpets and seals. Their boundary with the Yahgan was roughly along a line from the Brecknock Peninsula to London and Sydney Islands. The Yahgan were the most southerly inhabitants of the earth, but had a more varied diet of fungus, otters, seal, the occasional guanaco, foxes, fish and birds. Their own name for themselves, Yahgashaga, came from their title for the Murray Narrows which lay in about the middle of the area they occupied, but was shortened to Yahgan by the Rev. Thomas Bridges. They kept largely to the coast to avoid the Ona tribe. Small in stature, they were only five feet two inches tall on average; they were nevertheless very strong, and Captain Fitzroy of the *Beagle* is reputed to have forbidden his very tough sailors to wrestle with them as the Yahgan inevitably won and he felt that this might lead them to despise the white man.

Amongst the Yahgan the women did most of the canoe work and were expert swimmers, something which few of the men mastered. When camping at night off cliffs or rocks where there was no beach to haul the canoe ashore, the women, having first landed the men, would moor the canoe to the kelp weed that fringes the coast, and then swim ashore, even in icy conditions. Young girls were taken out swimming with their mothers to get them used to this task. Whilst the women were so engaged, the men would be gathering fuel for the fire or pursuing any possible source of food ashore.

Both the Alakaluf and Yahgan would eat whale meat when it was available, but hunting fully grown whales appears to have been beyond their capabilities. They needed a large number of canoes to have any hope of harpooning even small whales. Occasionally however, fish traps were built of stone and brushwood across small tidal creeks. Up to a ton of fish could be caught in these in a method similar to that used by other Stone Age tribes elsewhere in the world.

The Ona were by far the most ferocious of the tribes. Their language was different to the Yahgan and Alakaluf, and showed a link with that of the tall, well-built Tehuelche people of Southern Patagonia from where they must have migrated some time in the past. They were nomadic land hunters, using bows and arrows, and their main prey was the guanaco, a wild form of the llama but larger in size. This animal gave them some rough clothing but usually little more than a loin-cloth or cape. They were to be found in the interior of the main island and its northern and eastern coast, but were known to wander occasionally into Yahgan land at the eastern end of the Beagle Channel. Prior to Magellan they had been pushing southward on Isla Grande, and this migration increased as settlers moved into the northern part of the island. The southern movement of the Ona forced the Aush or Haush, a much smaller tribe, to move to the south-east. By the time of European settlement, the Aush were becoming much reduced in numbers owing to attacks by the Ona whom they greatly feared.

Neither the Aush nor the Ona had any traditions of having come from further north, which indicates that they must have crossed Magellan's Strait some considerable time before Europeans came on the scene. They did however share an interesting belief in a strange creature which was half animal and half bird. It had the hind legs of a guanaco, and forelegs like wings and laid enormous eggs. The description is reasonably close to the Patagonian ostrich or rhea which is not known in Tierra del Fuego in modern times, but may have existed there before it was hunted to extinction.

Another social activity when families would band together was the hunting of the guanaco, particularly in the winter when the snow made hunting difficult. The method used was to release dogs to chase the guanaco which would run uphill until the snow became too deep and then turn and race downhill, pursued by the dogs until they either found themselves trapped on a promontory, or escaped by running uphill again. When trapped, the guanaco often took to the water to swim to a neighbouring area, but here the Indians would wait for them with spears or clubs.

When Darwin first set eyes on the Yahgan he estimated their number at 3,000 but by 1884 they had been reduced to about 1,000. Although incredibly hardy and strongly built, able to withstand the cold and wounds that would have incapacitated any European, the native Indians had no resistance to European diseases. That year an Argentine government expedition arrived in Ushuaia to set up a sub-prefecture and a small party of men was left behind to establish the base. An attack of measles brought in by this party, though not particularly serious to the Europeans, proved absolutely fatal to the Indians, and within a short time more than half the inhabitants of the town and its outlying area had died and another quarter died through reduced vitality in the next two years.

The discovery of gold in the gravel beds of Tierra del Fuego in the 1880s brought the inevitable flock of prospectors, who introduced further diseases to which the natives had no resistance. Meanwhile the expansion of farming, particularly the breeding of sheep and cattle, brought in settlers to compete for the land, and many Indians, particularly Ona, were exterminated with impunity as dangerous animals. They stood little chance with their bows and arrows against men mounted on horseback and carrying repeater rifles; but the white men quickly learned to be very cautious if they followed any Ona into the woods.

The Indians were unable to compete with the rush of settlers and pastoral agriculture, which slowly deprived them of their hunting grounds. Some of the Ona were saved and taken to a mission established by Silesian Fathers in both the Chilean and Argentine parts of Isla Grande, where they were clothed and put to work. At one time there were more than 700 confined in this way, but for a man used to his freedom in the wild, this Mission seemed more like a prison than a place of refuge. Many took work in the new sheep farms, and their skill as shepherds was much admired, but they could not build up an immunity to the successive measles epidemics. By 1947 only 150 pure-bred Indians from all four tribes were left, together with a few half-breeds who had inherited from their white parents an immunity to this simple illness.

The way that the Indians were able to survive and prosper until the arrival of Europeans in their desolate country was amazing to all who came to know them. They were excellent trackers and had immense powers of observation, none more so than the Ona, who, being land hunters, had developed tracking to a very fine art. A young Ona boy of sixteen, sent to help find an escaped convict from Ushuaia was given one of the prisoner's boots and spent a week searching round the town, travelling as far as ten miles out to check every path for the footprint he wanted. Eventually he came back to the governor and reported that the convict had not escaped. Not surprisingly the governor did not believe him, but shortly afterwards the fugitive was found close to the convict station living in the middle of a pile of logs. The Ona boy had been right all along.

No incontrovertible evidence has come to light to suggest that there were any other visitors to Tierra del Fuego before the Europeans, but it is possible that the Mochica people, and their successors the Incas, may have progressed south to the region of Cape Horn on their balsa rafts. Although the source of balsa is Ecuador, these craft, capable of taking up to fifty men and three horses, were found carrying on a well-developed coasting trade by the Spanish invaders, who were much impressed by both their seaworthiness and their ability to tack to windward. They encountered them beating against the wind and the Nino current, carrying twenty tons of cargo and a crew of thirty. The course was controlled solely by the use of a number of strategically placed *guara*, or hardwood dagger boards inserted between the balsa logs of the raft. The Spanish particularly noted the cotton sails and herequen rope which they said were superior to their own. The Spanish were given sailing instructions by the Incas for the voyage to Easter Island which proved to be remarkably accurate, and indicate that the Incas had not only been able to sail to this island, but sail back to the mainland as well. The balsa rafts were fully investigated by two Spanish naval officers in 1750, who reported, 'that the great singularity of the floating vehicle is that it sails, tacks, and works as well in contrary winds as ships with a keel, and makes very little leeway.' Thor Heyerdahl, in his Kon Tiki expedition of 1947, showed convincingly that the so-called primitive balsa rafts were capable of safe oceanic voyages of more than 4,000 miles, and in 1953 he carried out experiments which confirmed the Spanish officers' findings. Such craft, expertly handled, would have been capable of voyages to the south, but if they ever made them they would have found nothing there that could have possibly attracted them in that cold and windswept region.

It was a desire for an alternative trade route to the Cape of Good Hope from Europe to the Indies that first brought visitors in the form of European explorers to Tierra del Fuego. None of these explorers stayed willingly. There was little to attract sailors to use the area for replenishment or rest as there was at the Cape of Good Hope. From the earliest times sailors have heaved a sigh of thankfulness as they rounded the Horn and shaped a course northward.

2

The Age of Discovery

The discovery of Cape Horn by Europeans was an inevitable part of the exploration of America. When Columbus failed to find the Indies on his second voyage, fresh expeditions were authorised to search for a passage through the new lands to the west. Four were dispatched in 1499, the most significant being headed by Alonso de Ojeda, who was accompanied by a Florentine, Amerigo Vespucci, the Medici representative in Seville. Vespucci broke away from the main fleet and with two caravels sailed south-east as far as the river Amazon. Although Vespucci's voyage made a modest profit the Spanish, perhaps aggravated by his habit of writing lengthy reports to his masters in Florence, introduced a decree which banned foreigners from involvement in their voyages of exploration thereafter.

Whilst Vespucci sought support elsewhere for another voyage, two expeditions sailed in 1500 which advanced knowledge of the land lying south of the Amazon. A small Spanish fleet, led by Alonso Velez de Mendoza, departed to trade in the Caribbean but was forced off course and made a landfall south of Cape São Roque. From there it continued south to a point beyond Cape São Agostinho before returning to Spain with a cargo of slaves. The second expedition, under Pedro Alvares Cabral, was the first Portuguese fleet to follow Vasco da Gama's voyage to India. Cabral made his departure from the Cape Verde Islands and, having crossed the Doldrums, went hard on port tack into the South Atlantic. Ships of that time were unable to point very close to the wind which south of the Equator are the south-east trade winds. Moreoever the trades vary slightly in direction, particularly towards the Brazilian coast, and as a result Cabral was pushed further west than he probably intended. This mischance lead to Brazil being a Portuguese-speaking country today as Cabral sighted the mountain of Monte Pascoal at a latitude of about 17° south, approximately 200 miles south of the modern port of Bahia. He spent only a few days at anchor in a place he called Porto Seguro, but, as was the custom, left behind two convicts to explore the area. If the ships returned, these unfortunates would provide useful knowledge of the geography, any natives and the potential for trade in return for a pardon. If the men died or no ships returned to collect them, the official view was that nothing had been lost as they were condemned anyway. Cabral sailed eastwards to India but sent one of his storeships home with the news that he had found a large area of land to the west of the South Atlantic which was well south of the Spanish discoveries.

Spain and Portugal had subdivided the world between them under the Treaty of Tordesillas in 1494. Anything east of a line drawn 370 leagues west (1,950 km) of the Cape Verde Islands was Portugal's, whilst to the west all the territory was to be Spanish. The indications were that Cabral's discovery was east of the line and King Manoel of Portugal was quick to claim his rights, mounting an expedition of three caravels under Gonsalvo Coelho which sailed from Lisbon in May 1501. Among the crew was Amerigo Vespucci, who reported as follows:

> From the Cape Verde Islands we sailed south-south-west, close-hauled, until after sixty-four days we came to a new land which, for many reasons to be given later, we judge to be mainland. We coasted this land for 800 leagues, always sailing south-west, a quarter west . . . We sailed so far is those seas that we entered the torrid zone and passed south of the Equator and the Tropic of Capricorn, until the South Pole was fifty degrees above the horizon, and this was my latitude from the Equator. We navigated four months and twenty-seven days without seeing the Arctic Pole nor the Great nor Little Bear; but I discovered opposite them in those southern skies many beautiful constellations invisible in the north, noted their wonderful movements and splendour and measured their positions . . .

Vespucci's description presents us with a puzzle. The latitude of 50° south is well into Patagonia and beyond the estuary of the River Plate which he does not mention, but which is far too prominent to be ignored. So either they did not sail as far south as he thought, or they did, but out of sight of land at this point. The Portuguese records show that the Coelho/Vespucci expedition went as far south as 35° which is north of the River Plate and the Portuguese are to be believed, as they had developed the necessary tables to calculate their latitude, using the sun, more than seventeen years before. What cannot be explained, however, is how the Caneiro map of 1502–04 does show a large river called the Giordan at the approximate location of the River Plate. It is quite unmistakable. But whatever the truth about the year of the River Plate's discovery, information currently available was still insufficient for any explorer or cosmographer to define the new land accurately. Most remained convinced that it was an outlying peninsula of Asia, and it was not yet realised that a completely new continent had been discovered.

Vespucci wrote two accounts of his voyages to the Americas, *Mundus Novus* published in 1504 in Augsburg, and *Lettera di Amerigo Vespucci delle isole nouvamente trovate in quattri suoi viaggi,* which was written in 1504 after his second voyage, and published in Italy in 1505. Although the *Lettera* describes four voyages to the New World, there is considerable doubt as to whether he actually undertook more than two, and the others may have been invented to place him on a par with Columbus who did lead four voyages. Whatever the truth, Vespucci's reports attracted enormous interest throughout Europe, and when Waldseemüller produced his famous map of the world in 1507, he called all the southern part of the new world America, the feminine form of Americus, after Vespucci. Although Waldseemüller dropped this from his 1513 chart, the name stuck, and when Mercator created a world chart fifty years later, he extended the title to include the northern part of the new world. Poor Columbus, who never fully recovered his health after his fourth voyage during which he was shipwrecked for a year in Jamaica (Don Christopher's Cove), arrived back in Spain in November 1504. He died on 20th May 1506 and perhaps fortunately did not live to receive the final insult of his discoveries being named after someone else.

Further exploration southwards ceased until 1513 as the Spanish were concentrating their efforts on searching central America for gold, pearls and other treasures. Then in 1513 Cristobal de Haro, who had previously made a fortune in the Indies spice trade, sailed from Lisbon to the River Plate and a small Spanish expedition led by Juan Diaz de Solis also reached the estuary at about the same time, but shortly afterwards de Solis was killed by natives and his expeditions collapsed. It was de Solis, however, who is said to have thought of the enduring name for the River Plate which was so calm when he first sighted it that it looked like a sheet of silver.

When Haro returned from this South American voyage he moved to Seville in 1516. Here he became acquainted with Juan Fonseca, the influential bishop of Burgos, and convinced him that a western route to the Indies must exist if they continued exploring to the south. They were joined by two like-minded Portuguese defectors, Ferdinand Magellan, an experienced soldier, and Rui Faleiro, an astrologer, cartographer and mathematician. Together they set about organising a two-pronged expedition to find a way through or round the new land. One, led by Gil Gonzales, was intended to sail to Panama, cross the isthmus and explore to the north-west. This expedition succeeded in reaching the Gulf of Fonseca in what is now Honduras. The other, led by Ferdinand Magellan, planned to sail down the eastern coast of South America until it discovered a break in the land.

Ferdinand Magellan led the second most significant voyage in history after Columbus, during which he not only found a route round America, but the survivors also completed the first circumnavigation of the world. He was born, the son of a nobleman, in 1480 at Sabrosa in the Traz-os-Montes province of Portugal. Until the age of fifteen he served as a page to Queen Leonor, consort of King João II, and on João's death entered the service of his successor King Manoel. At the age of twenty-five he sailed as a volunteer with the expedition under the first Viceroy of the Indies, Francisco de Almeida, and was in the thick of the action that within ten years gave Portugal domination of trade in the Indian Ocean. Promoted to the rank of captain, Magellan returned to Portugal in 1512, but almost immediately joined an expedition against Azamor in Morocco which fell in 1513. In a subsequent sortie, Magellan was wounded in the leg, which left him lame for the rest of his life. On his return to Portugal he was accused of trading with the Moors, and although the accusation was dropped the King informed Magellan that he would not receive further employment. Disillusioned, Magellan renounced his nationality, and went to Spain, where he teamed up with Faleiro.

Charles I of Spain (shortly to be elected Holy Roman Emperor as Charles V), whose support was crucial, gave the scheme his blessing, and having settled the terms under which Magellan and Faleiro, as joint Captains General, would share one-twentieth of the clear profits, and have the right for themselves or their heirs to govern any territory discovered, preparations for the voyage were put in hand. It is interesting that apart from the share being reduced from a tenth to a twentieth these terms are very similar to those offered to Columbus.

It was Magellan's stated intention to proceed beyond the River Plate to latitude 75° south if necessary to find a channel connecting the Atlantic with the South Sea, sail to the Moluccas and return by retracing the outward route. The most accurate chronicler of the voyage, Antonio Pigafetta, a gentleman volunteer from Lombardy, says that Magellan had seen a chart whilst in the service of the King of Portugal on which was marked a secret channel drawn by Martin Behaim. However the only surviving work of Martin Behaim is a globe drawn in 1492, which shows a channel between the largest peninsula of Asia and an island called Seilan, which might be Borneo or Sumatra. The theory that southern America was a peninsula of Asia remained strong when Magellan sailed, but it may be that Behaim had drawn another chart after Columbus discovered the West Indies. There is also some evidence to suggest that the Portuguese made more voyages than catalogued, but since many of their records were subsequently destroyed, no one knows whether Magellan did possess information from a previous voyage. He certainly exuded confidence and had twenty-three special charts prepared which would have included all the latest data.

Five ships were purchased, the *Trinidade,* the flagship of 110 tons, *San Antonio,* the largest ship in the fleet at 120 tons, *Vittoria*, 85 tons, *Concepción,* 90 tons, and *Santiago*, the smallest at 75 tons. None of these were caravels, which had been the standard vessels for exploratory voyages, and the two largest were referred to as great ships or *naos,* the largest class then employed for trading. Portuguese spies reported to Lisbon that the ships were rotten, but this was wishful thinking. Magellan does not appear as the sort of man who would have accepted inferior ships, and in any case their performance on the actual voyage gives the lie to the rumour.

The ships were not particularly good sailers by today's standards. The nearest a square-rigged ship could sail to the wind was probably about seven points (almost 80°) and then there was leeway, in other words sideways drift through the water, so the actual course made good was rarely better than 90° to the wind. Compared with a modern yacht which can easily make good a course of 45°, one realises the problems facing sailors of this period. However, as they had never known anything better, they planned manoeuvres to take the poor windward performance into account.

Obtaining crews was difficult. Few men volunteered from Seville itself, perhaps because they remembered what happened to de Solis, but men came from other ports and countries. For example the master gunner aboard the flagship was an Englishman who died of scurvy later in the voyage. About thirty of the crew were Portuguese but significantly these included all the pilots or navigators. When the fleet finally sailed, the total number of crew spread between all five ships was around 270. It was an effectively armed armada, with over eighty cannon, and well stocked with trading items, not only the beads and bells that were so popular with natives, but also with more sophisticated items such as looking glasses, quicksilver and velvet, which were in demand in the Indies.

The fleet sailed from San Lucar de Barrameda in Spain on 20th September 1519, and after calling at Tenerife at the end of the month, crossed the Atlantic to Cape St Augustine, about latitude 8° south near Pernambuco, which they sighted on 29th November. On 13th December they anchored in what is today Rio de Janeiro, the country of Verzin, which was on the King of Portugal's side of the demarcation line, and spent thirteen days refilling water casks and obtaining fresh provisions before continuing southwards. On 11th January 1520 the ships arrived at the River Plate and Magellan remained in this area until 13th February trying to locate a channel to the Mar del Sur (the South Sea). It is hard to believe that surrounded by so many able Portuguese navigators, Magellan really hoped such a large area of fresh water could possibly connect with another ocean, but he did satisfy himself eventually that it was only a river, seventeen leagues (89 km) wide at the mouth. Pigafetta states that no one knew what lay beyond Cape St Mary, so Vespucci's earlier claims seem to have had little contemporary credence.

Travelling southward again along the coast, they explored the Gulf of San Matías on 24th February, and three days later came across two islands with seals and penguins in residence. There is only one place which fits this description and is on its own off the Rio Deseado in latitude 47° 40' south and is still called Islas Pinguino. Many penguins were killed to supplement food supplies and then the voyage continued, ships and crews surviving a serious storm which was the first European exposure to the ferocious *Pamperos*. They sailed into Puerto San Julián in latitude 49° 30' south on 31st March and, realising that winter was coming, Magellan decided to stay put until the southern spring.

Within a day the disagreements which had been festering between the Portuguese and the Spaniards in the fleet came to a head. Magellan had already put Captain de Cartagena of the *San Antonio* in irons for lack of respect and on arrival at San Julián replaced him with his relative Alvaro de Mesquita. This, plus the fact that no sign of a channel had been found after nearly six months of voyaging and Magellan had everyone on short rations to conserve provisions, was bound to cause trouble. De Cartagena was released, but immediately plotted with other Spanish leaders and headed a party from the *Concepción* which captured the *Vittoria* and the *San Antonio*. They sent a message to Magellan demanding that he obey their interpretation of the King's orders and return to Spain. Magellan was in a tricky position as all the senior Spaniards had rebelled, whereas he was only a recent citizen of the country. If he could not quell the mutiny and the rebels sailed for home the loss of three-fifths of his fleet would effectively put paid to the expedition. However it is at such times of crisis that a great leader demonstrates his true qualities. Magellan declined to talk to the mutineers and sent a boat load of trusted sailors to the *Vittoria* where he knew there were many loyal to him. The mutinous captain died in a short scuffle and the rest of the crew quickly swore loyalty to their admiral again. Now the mutineers were outnumbered. Magellan blocked the entrance to the bay so that when the *San Antonio* attempted to escape she was overwhelmed, at which point the *Concepción* surrendered. A court martial was held, but although many of the mutineers were sentenced to death only one man was executed, and de Cartagena, together with a priest who had supported the revolt, was banished ashore and never heard of again. One senior officer who had joined in the mutiny, Juan Sebastian del Cano, was forgiven and spared to play a prominent part in the voyage, but Magellan not surprisingly felt at the time that he could no longer trust the Spanish officers and appointed Portuguese to command all the ships.

The fleet settled down for the winter, but the smallest ship, the *Santiago*, was dispatched to survey southwards. She was wrecked about twenty-five leagues (148 km) south of Port St Julian, but miraculously none of the crew was lost and all managed to return safely across country. Native inhabitants were scarce but one was sighted from the ships in Port St Julian, and Magellan went ashore to meet him. He was a Tehuelche and the Europeans were impressed by his size and the fact that he was naked in spite of the cold climate. Magellan is reputed to have christened these natives Patagonians because of their large feet, *pata* being foot in Spanish. However, a more probable derivation is found in the romance *Primaleon of Greece*, which was published in Spain in 1512. This concerns the adventures of a knight, Primaleon, who sails to a remote island where he meets a primitive cannibalistic people. In the interior lives a giant monster, with the head of a dog and the feet of a hart, called Patagon. Since the Tehuelche Indians were very tall and fast runners, it is more likely that Magellan remembered the book, and named them and their country accordingly. Magellan made a number of attempts to capture Patagonians to take them back to Spain. He was finally successful when his men tricked two of them into having fetters placed on their ankles. When they realised what was happening the Patagonians made a huge fuss but it was too late to extricate themselves. Others who had been enticed aboard escaped, their fleetness of foot and strength particularly impressing the Spaniards.

Whilst sitting out the winter, Magellan had all the ships careened to recaulk and pitch their bottoms. As much of the cargo, stores and armament as possible would be offloaded, the vessels hauled up onto a beach at high tide, and then tilted over by means of tackles from the masts to strong points ashore. After the growth of weed was removed from the ships' bottoms and any caulking or other repairs had been carried out, the whole was coated with tar, or sometimes a mixture of lime and fish oil. Since neither product was particularly effective as an anti-foulant, careening was required at frequent intervals and captains were always on the lookout for a hard but smooth beach, free of obstacles and where the crew could defend themselves against aggressors whilst their ship was out of action. Whilst the vessels were emptied, all the provisions were examined so that rotten supplies could be condemned and those left fit to eat could be redistributed evenly amongst the fleet. This was when the expedition discovered they had been given considerably less than the requested eighteen months' worth of stores. In order to try and make up some of the deficiency Magellan set the crews to catching fish, seabirds and wild llamas which could be salted and preserved.

The four ships left Port St Julian on 24th August 1520 and sailed to a small bay, Puerto Santa Cruz, which had been noted by the *Santiago*. Finding the weather still very cold and the winds stormy, the fleet anchored here for nearly three months. When they sailed on 18th October they hugged the coast, shortening sail at night so they would not miss the channel in the dark. Three days later, on the festival of St Ursula and her Eleven Thousand Virgins they reached a cape in latitude 52° 20' south.

Beyond Cabo Vírgenes (Cape Virgins), the coast encouragingly turned westwards. High land could be seen to the south but, unlike that of the great opening of the River Plate, this time the water was salt and there was a high range of tide, a further heartening indication of a large area of sea to the west. Not wishing to risk all his ships, Magellan anchored the *Trinidade* and *Vittoria* in Bahía Lomas, and sent the other two, the *San Antonio* and the *Concepción*, to explore westwards.

It was probably whilst he waited for these two ships to return that Magellan and the remainder of the crews noticed the fires burning all over the land to the south and gave it the name we still use today, Tierra del Fuego, the land of fire.

The advance party ran into a strong storm almost immediately, and the ships passed the night sailing back and forth across the bay as the anchors would not hold on the sandy shoals. It was a terrifying predicament, being constantly on lookout, with the crew standing by to tack or wear the instant danger was sighted, knowing that even a short delay could lead to their ship being wrecked and to their deaths by drowning if they could not reach the

shore, and probably from starvation or exposure if they could. Pigafetta
states that the two ships due to sail west turned back to rejoin the admiral,
but, finding themselves surrounded by shoals, headed for a small creek,
perhaps intending to run the ships aground and thus save lives. In fact the
creek, and by creek perhaps Pigafetta means a channel, led them to open
water further west. This was the Primera Angostura (First Narrows).
Encouraged, they passed through the Segunda Angostura (Second Narrows)
and out into a bay. This is the Paso Ancho (Broad Reach), forty miles long
and between fourteen and eighteen miles wide. The tides were still strong,
the water still salty and the ships returned to the admiral after two days of
storms that might have destroyed them, with pennants flying and cannons
firing to proclaim the good news.

The whole fleet now advanced together to the Paso Ancho where two
exits faced them, one to the south-east and another to the south-west.
Magellan split his force to speed up the reconnaissance and took the *Vittoria*
and *Trinidade* to check the south-west and ordering the others to explore
the other direction. Magellan cannot have realised the renewed disaffection
amongst his crews by this stage in the voyage or he would never had divided
the ships in this way. During the first night apart, the pilot of the *San Antonio*,
a Portuguese named Estavao Gomes, led a mutiny, wounded the captain
and put him in irons. They then set a course for home. Perhaps the captain,
Magellan's brother, was poor or unjust, or perhaps, as in so many similar
cases, some crews lacked the courage and determination to press onwards
and were less frightened of returning home as deserters than continuing
their voyage. Judging by the lack of punishment meted out at this time to
deserters (Columbus had suffered in a similar fashion a few years before),
the deserters were probably right. They arrived home on 6th May 1521 and
were acquitted of desertion. The unfortunate captain, who had returned in
irons, was kept in prison until the remnants of the expedition returned over
a year later.

Unaware of this desertion, Magellan pressed on. He rounded Cape
Froward, the southernmost mainland point of South America, and shortly
afterwards anchored near a river he called the River of Sardines, where he
decided to await the other two ships. The position of the River of Sardines
is uncertain, but was probably in the vicinity of Port Gallant. His sailors
were now sure the land to the south was composed of islands, not a mainland,
as they could hear the sound of waves breaking on a shore beyond the land
in that direction. Such large waves must be generated in a large expanse of
water. They began to hope they were on the threshold of a great ocean.
Another encouraging factor was that the channel had taken a course to the

north-west. Perhaps they were round the foot of America at last?

Whilst at anchor, Magellan sent away his longboat to investigate the channel ahead. It returned three days later to report that it had sailed to the exit of the channel and seen no land beyond. Here perhaps was what they had been looking for, but restraining his impatience to see for himself, like a good leader Magellan retraced his steps to search for the other two ships. He soon met the *Concepción* but she had no idea of her consort's whereabouts. After they had lost sight of the *San Antonio* they had explored the south-east channel but come to a dead end. It was not another channel but a bay, still known as Bahía Inútil (Useless Bay). Considerable time was wasted looking for the *San Antonio*, the *Vittoria* even went as far as Cape Virgins and left a flag and message for her. They waited for the missing ship near the River of Isles until 22nd November, but of course by then she was already well on the way to Spain.

Eventually concluding the *San Antonio* was lost, the three ships sailed north-west. From Port Gallant to Cabo Pilar, as Magellan christened the cape at the exit from the strait, is about 110 miles, and it took his reduced fleet a week to cover the distance. An average speed of fifteen miles a day must be seen within the context of the need to proceed cautiously in an uncharted area where fierce williwaws whistled off the hills with little warning and could knock a ship flat even with no sails set; freezing rain could reduce visibility to almost zero at short notice; the channel narrowed to a width of about two miles in places and beds of kelp concealed the true shore. Kelp, which can grow to over fifty feet in length and as thick as a man's arm, can be bedded in up to forty feet of water, and is a useful sign of shallows when approaching land. The Portuguese sailors in the fleet were familiar with it, though, from their experience of the Cape of Good Hope where it also flourishes. However, to the novices it must have seemed awesomely large and its appearance, especially after the tall men of Patagonia, would have done little to allay fears that other giant fishes or animals might appear at any moment.

The passage through the entire strait from the first rounding of Cape Virgins, a distance of about 310 miles, had taken a total of thirty-eight days. This is a very creditable time when one considers the caution involved, the difficulties of manoeuvring unwieldy ships in confined waters, the need to explore every small inlet in case it led to the sea and the days lost waiting and searching for the *San Antonio*. The very fast running tidal streams, much too powerful for the ships to sail against, meant that for nearly half the time they had no choice but to anchor or they would be driven backwards. So everyone in the fleet must have heaved a sigh of relief when the channel widened and they could see clear water beyond.

They entered the Pacific on 28th November. Before them lay a vast ocean. Was this perhaps the same one they would know had been sighted by Vasco Nuñez de Balboa on 25th September 1513 from a mountain on the Isthmus of Panama? Alternatively, could it be they had just rounded one of the great Asian peninsulas and this was the vast gulf shown on Ptolemy's map? His choice was to follow the coastline northwards or head off out to sea in the direction of where China and Japan were reputed to lie and he chose the bolder course.

Nothing was known of the Pacific Coast of South America, indeed it was to be another year before Pascual de Andagoya sailed south from Panama and explored the coast of modern Columbia and Pizarro's discovery of the Incas of Peru was still eleven years in the future. Magellan was pretty confident that he still needed to sail further west to reach the longitude of the Spice Islands. The optimists believed that China or the Indies might be only two weeks' sailing away. Indeed everyone must have hoped so, as owing to the cheating suppliers in Spain, they lacked the provisions to sustain a voyage of much greater duration and there had been no attempt, indeed little opportunity, to supplement their food by hunting or fishing whilst in the Strait.

Initially Magellan sailed northwards along the coast until 16th December, when he altered course to the north-west, no doubt assuming the winds in this ocean would reflect the pattern in the southern Atlantic. In fact Pigafetta states that had they sailed due west they would have eventually arrived back at the Cape of Eleven Thousand Virgins which indicates an uncanny insight into the layout of land in the Southern Hemisphere. Pigafetta describes the first European voyage across the Pacific Ocean as follows:

On Wednesday the twenty-eighth of November, one thousand five hundred and twenty, we issued forth from the said strait and entered the Pacific Sea, where we remained three months and twenty days without taking on board provisions or any other refreshment, and we ate only old biscuit turned to powder, all full of worms and stinking of the urine which the rats had made on it, having eaten the good. And we drank water impure and yellow. We ate also ox hides which were very hard because of the sun rain and wind. And we left them four or five days in the sea, then laid them for a short time on embers, and so we ate them. And of the rats which we sold for half an ecu apiece, some of us could not get enough.

Besides the aforesaid troubles, this malady was the worst, namely that the gums of most part of our men swelled above and below so that they could not eat [scurvy]. And in this way they died, inasmuch as twenty-nine of us died and the other giant died [this refers to one of the Patagonians that had been taken on board] and an Indian that had been taken on board in the said country of Verzain [Brazil]. But besides those who died, twenty-five or thirty fell sick of diverse maladies, whether of the arms or legs or other parts of the body, so that there remained very few healthy men. Yet by the grace of our Lord I had no illness.

During these three months and twenty days, we sailed in a gulf where we made a good four thousand leagues across the Pacific Sea, which was rightly so named. For during this time we had no storm, and we saw no land except two small uninhabited islands, where we found only birds and trees. Wherefore we called them the Isles of Misfortune. And they are two hundred leagues distant one from another. And there is no place for anchoring because no bottom could be found. And we saw there a very large kind of fish which they call tiburoni [shark].

The first island is in fifteen degrees of latitude going south, and the other is in nine degrees.[1] By this wind we made each day fifty or sixty leagues or more, sometimes at the stern, at others on the windward side or otherwise.[2] And if our Lord and the Virgin Mother had not aided us by giving good weather to refresh ourselves with provisions and other things we had died in this very great sea. And I believe that nevermore will any man undertake to make such a voyage.

On 6th March 1521, they sighted three islands and sailed towards the largest. As soon as they were close, the natives came out in great strength in canoes and swarmed all over the ships, appropriating anything that took their fancy. The Spaniards were too few and weak to put up much resistance, but when his skiff was stolen, Magellan decided matters were getting out of hand and

---

[1] The first of these islands was discovered on 24th January 1521, St Paul's Day, and named in his honour Albo. It is probably Pukapuka in the Tuamotu Archipelago, latitude 14° 46' south, longitude 138° 48' west. The second was sighted on 4th February, and was probably Flint Island in the Manihiki Archipelago.
[2] The day's runs were between 150-190 miles, a good performance. This would have been calculated by timing objects in the water, if necessary chips of wood thrown from the ship, through a known distance usually marked by notches in the gunwhale. The description of the wind is confusing, but he obviously means the wind was either right astern or from either quarter.

took a party ashore to recover it by force of arms, burning down forty houses and killing seven people in the process. He named these island the Islas de Ladrones or Isles of Thieves (now known as the Marianas). Not wishing to court further trouble the fleet sailed on, and on 16th March they anchored off Samar Island in the Philippines. For the next month, they cruised from island to island, trading a little, and attempting to convert the natives to Christianity. The first sign of the Spice Islands' proximity came when a slave who had travelled in the fleet from Spain found he could understand the local language. Europeans were approaching the Indies for the first time from the east. Sadly Magellan did not live to reap the benefits from his incredible voyage as on 26th April he was killed on the island of Mactan, near Cebu, in a fight on behalf of the local king. Although the voyage was unfinished, Magellan may have circumnavigated the globe before he died as he may well have been east of Cebu during previous service with the Portuguese crown, but without evidence of this, the honour of being the first person to sail around the world goes to an unknown slave born in the Philippines.

Having seen that their leader was not immortal, the King of Cebu now turned upon the Spaniards, inveigled the three captains ashore and murdered them along with twenty-four other members of the expedition. Realising that they lacked the men or the arms to deal with the situation, the survivors took the ships to the island of Bohol, where the *Concepción* was burned as there were no longer sufficient men to crew her. Of the original 270 who departed from Spain only 120 were now left. Some had deserted with the *San Antonio*, of course, but many more had died of scurvy and other diseases during the long Pacific crossing. The two ships continued to the Molucca Islands where the *Trinidade* was judged too rotten for the voyage home via the Cape of Good Hope. The survivors could have jammed themselves into the *Vittoria*, but there were sufficient who felt that it was worth the gamble to try and sail back across the Pacific Ocean and try to find Panama. Fifty sailors agreed to make the attempt but found they could not make progress against the easterly winds and had to return to the Philippines where they were captured by the Portuguese. The *Vittoria*, now captained by the Spaniard Juan Sebastian del Cano, with a crew of forty-seven Europeans and thirteen Indians, set sail for Spain on 21st December 1521. The survivors rounded the Cape of Good Hope between 7th and 16th April 1522, and then headed for the Cape Verde Islands where they anchored on Wednesday, 9th July 1522. However, when they sent a boat ashore, they were amazed to discover that the date there was Thursday 10th July. They had not appreciated that by rounding the globe from east to west, they had lost a day. Whilst they were provisioning at the Cape Verdes, the Portuguese detained one of the ship's boats with thirteen men aboard, at which the remaining eighteen left aboard the *Vittoria*, all that now remained of the sixty or more who had departed from the Philippines, set sail for home. The prisoners were later released by Portugal, but in the meantime the *Vittoria* arrived back at San Lucar on 8th September 1522, thus completing the first circumnavigation of the world. In the process they had uncovered the route around America to the Indies and the vast Pacific Ocean. Cape Horn had evaded them, but with the route to the Pacific now open, its discovery was only a matter of time.

One of the factors raised by Magellan's voyage, and one which would lead to endless squabbles between Spain and Portugal, was exactly where the line of demarcation between the two nations lay in the Indies. In 1524 their representatives met but could reach no conclusion. Part of the difficulty was that the Portuguese were already well established but also neither side could calculate accurately the precise longitude so they were unable to agree on where exactly 180° from the Pope's line in the Atlantic occurred in the east. The Spanish response to the failure of this conference was to organise another Indies armada following Magellan's route.

A soldier, Garcia Jofre de Loaysa, was chosen to command the fleet of seven ships which sailed from Corunna on 24th July 1525. The *Anunciada*, of 170 tons, was blown eastwards of the Strait of Magellan in a terrible storm and tried to reach the Indies via the Cape of Good Hope but was never heard of again. The *San Gabriel*, of 130 tons, was also forced eastwards, but having returned to the strait, she failed to locate her companions and retreated to Spain. The *Santi Spiritus*, commanded by del Cano, a ship of 200 tons, achieved an unwanted place in history by becoming the first vessel to be lost in the strait, and del Cano transferred to the flagship *Santa Maria de la Vittoria*, the 300-ton flagship. She, with two caravels and a pinnace, reached the Pacific Ocean but were soon separated by a storm. One of the caravels and the flagship made the Indies but then the flagship sank at Tidore. The other caravel may have been wrecked on Chaine Island, which is amongst the channels on the south-west coast of Chile, where an unexplained wooden cross was found in 1606. The pinnace eventually arrived in Mexico. Loaysa died during the crossing and del Cano, who succeeded him in command, died five days later whilst the ship was still at sea. The survivors, unable to continue since they had no ship, lived on in the southern Philippines long after their king had ceded the islands to Portugal in 1529, but only a few stragglers ever made their way home to Spain.

Shortly after Loaysa's expedition left Spain, crew members of the *Trinidade* from Magellan's expedition who had been imprisoned by the Portuguese in the Cape Verde Islands, were allowed to return home. Alarmed by the stories of the Portuguese treatment of these men, the King of Spain decided to reinforce Loaysa. An expedition was already being prepared under Sebastian Cabot, (son of John Cabot, the Genoese turned Englishman who is credited with the rediscovery of Newfoundland), to sail to the east and explore for fresh territory. The instructions were changed and Cabot was ordered to proceed with all speed to assist Loaysa.

Cabot sailed in April 1526 with three *naos* and a caravel. He made a landfall in Brazil near Cape St Augustine, but faced with southerly headwinds, called into a small Portuguese settlement at Recife to replenish stores. Whilst here they learnt that survivors from other Spanish expeditions were living with Indians on an island called Catalina and were rumoured to have discovered a rich source of silver. The small fleet sailed to the island, met men from the *San Gabriel* which had turned back when Loaysa's fleet was scattered by a storm and two men who had been shipwrecked from de Solis's fleet in 1516. The marooned sailors were no doubt delighted to see some compatriots and Cabot was no less delighted with their news of large quantities of silver located in the upper reaches of the River Plate. So ignoring his instructions to join Loaysa as quickly as possible, or perhaps believing the chances of Loaysa's fleet actually arriving in the Indies were slim, Cabot decided to investigate the rumours of silver and never reached Magellan's Strait.

The next attempt to pass through Magellan's Strait was initiated by Ferdinand Cortez, the conqueror of Mexico. Two ships and 400 men sailed in this expedition, but failed to negotiate the strait. A few years later, in 1535, another bid was made by Simon de Alcazaba, who had been appointed Governor of New Leon, the southernmost of four regions into which the Spanish had divided South American. Alcazaba headed for southern Chile from Spain intending to sail to his destination via Magellan's Strait in two ships, the *San Pedro* and the *La Madre de Dios*. Not for the first time the expedition was plagued by mutiny shortly after reaching the strait. Alcazaba and many of his officers were killed by the mutineers and only the *San Pedro* eventually returned to Spain with the starving remnants of the expedition.

In 1539 the first attempt to establish regular communication by sea to Chile and Peru via the strait instead of overland via Panama was financed by the Bishop of Plasencia. Three small ships left Spain under the command of Don Alonso de Camargo. One ship was lost in the First Narrows and

Camargo continued in another, whilst the third was separated from her
consorts and wintered on the southern coast of Tierra del Fuego before
returning to Spain in 1541. This unnamed ship thus became the first to
spend a winter in that isolated corner of the earth and only limited details
are known of her adventures. Initially she was driven by squalls down the
coast of Tierra del Fuego and into one of the creeks or fjords of Staten
Island. Here they lost the last anchor, so six cannons were lashed together
as a makeshift substitute, but the bottom of the fjord was foul, so the anchor
rope soon parted and they were forced to sail backwards and forwards,
hoping the weather would ease and allow them to detect a creek where the
ship could be tied to the shore. In the course of the tacks, they sighted an
opening to the south-west, (the Le Maire Strait) and sailed through. Then
they spied what appeared to be a safe inlet and sailed towards it, but as they
came close strong winds forced them to cut away the mainmast and they
entered under headsail alone. This gives some hint of the wind's strength
and their desperation to reach the shore. Cutting away a mast was very
much a last resort since it left the vessel almost impossible to control except
downwind, and making and stepping a new mast was a major undertaking.
Within the inlet they secured the ship with hawsers and cables to suitable
rocks or other firm points ashore so that it was held safely whatever the
wind's direction.

There is little evidence to establish the whereabouts of the haven used by
these men for the next six months. They called it the Haven of Foxes. During
their stay they came across a piece of wreckage from Camargo's flagship
so they knew their admiral and his crew had been wrecked. No effort was
made to look for any survivors and no trace of Camargo and his crew was
ever found. What is surprising is that they do not report meeting any natives,
though Magellan two decades earlier had sighted numerous fires on the
other side of the island. However, they did record there were ducks and
good fishing.

Having endured the winter and its snow, sleet and gale force winds, once
spring appeared and the weather became less boisterous, the crew rigged a
new mainmast from spare spars carried on board and sailed home safely to
Spain. The captain is one of the great unsung heroes of Cape Horn. He
must have been a man of iron will and determination, and sufficiently
inspiring to hold the crew together in those unfamiliar and very uncomfortable
winter quarters on the edge of the world. Had they had time for anything
other than survival and explored just sixty miles to the south-west they
would have been the first people to discover Cape Horn and shown that
Tierra del Fuego was an island, with only a wide ocean to the south. In

typical bureaucratic fashion the captain's report was filed and forgotten for centuries as it contained nothing that was considered useful!

The loss of two out of three ships and the hardships experienced by the survivors would have discouraged further attempts at exploration had not the discovery of the silver mountain at Potosí six years later in 1545 encouraged the governors in South America to retry Magellan's route. There was every incentive. The sea route north from Arica, the nearest port to Potosí, to the Isthmus of Panama was over 2,000 miles, and often involved delays, especially in the wrong season. One expedition sailed from Chile to carry out a more thorough investigation of the strait in 1553, and got to Cape Froward before turning back. They did succeed in exploring the coasts of Chiloe Island and the Chonos Archipelago. Juan Ladrillero set out from Valdivia in southern Chile in 1557 and surveyed right through the strait to Cape Virgins, spending two winters compiling pilotage instructions before returning to Valdivia. When we read the accounts of the suffering of the *Beagle*'s crew nearly three hundred years later in similar circumstances we can only look back with admiration at the achievements of these Spanish seamen who were the first to sail through Magellan's Strait from west to east.

Ladrillero's fate is not known for certain but seventeen years later a letter was sent by a Juan Ladrillero, then living in Mexico, to the King of Spain, offering, although old, to search for a channel to the Pacific in North America. Nevertheless, Ladrillero's expedition produced an excellent set of sailing instructions which are still valid today:

The characteristics by which Cape Deseado (Cabo Pilar) may be recognised are as follows: it is a high, bare mountain, extending a short distance east-south-east with many ravines. There are no other mountains to the south of it because the coast trends south-east. The land [Desolation Island] of which it forms the tip is narrow, not more than five leagues across thirty leagues inside the strait. On the seaward side of the Cape are two high, slender rock stacks, the one nearer the sea lower than the other; the higher one formed of black rock; and seaward of these two stacks lies a low promontory of black rock.

The best order for navigation in the Strait is as follows: those who come from Chile or Peru should arrange to sail from Valdivia in September or early October. As soon as they have a north wind they should proceed twenty or thirty leagues out to sea, and run south-south-west in the open sea as far as 51 degrees south latitude. In that latitude they should close the land and make landfall at Cape San

Francisco. They can find anchorage off La Campana Island, in the bay which Francisco de Ulloa discovered; or else in a harbour about two leagues from the latter, in a channel opening to the south-south-west. Here they can careen if necessary.

Alternatively they can find shelter in the Bay of San Lazaro [Nelson Strait] and if necessary can anchor there, or else on the seaward side of a group of islands further up the same inlet, seven or eight leagues from the sea. To make the entrance to the Strait from either of these two bays they will have to wait for an east or south-east wind. With these winds the navigation is straightforward. They will know when they are approaching the Strait, because from about ten leagues off [thirty miles] the current sets strongly towards the entrance. The east or south-east wind usually holds for two or three days, enough to enable them to reach the Strait and be well inside before the wind changes. Once inside, they should be safe, even if the wind goes round to the north; but if they are caught by a change outside the Strait, they may find themselves in trouble. A norther is often accompanied by dense fog, and there is a string of islands [The Evangelists] near the mouth of the Strait, twelve leagues long and extending four leagues out to sea.

To the ships sailing into the Strait the mountains seem to close in so that it appears to be a dead end, and one would not enter into it without previous knowledge; but when one is sailing out, it appears straight and open like the arm of the sea. One can pass through the Strait from the South Sea to the north in six or seven days, because the prevailing wind is from the north-west and blows directly into the Strait. The best time of year for this passage is in December, January or February, because then the weather is temperate, though even then there may be a cross wind from the north. These northers usually last for a day and a night, but sometimes for two days or more. Whilst they last the visibility is bad with heavy rain.

In winter, though there may be periods of south or south-east wind and of relative calm most of the time, the wind blows with gale force from the north-west, west, or south-west, with freezing temperatures and snow. The days are short, in the Strait in July only about six and a half hours . The gales last eight, ten, or twelve days. A ship going out into the open sea in that area between the middle of March and the end of September is likely to encounter trouble because the coast is broken and rocky, and one can anchor only in sheltered harbours.

Ships coming from Spain and making the passage of the Strait from east to west should enter the Strait at the Atlantic end between

October and February [as Magellan did]. They should pass through making westing with the aid of the tides. When they reach the Pacific end of the Strait they should wait for an east or south-east wind, though this may mean a wait of twenty days or more. They should then sail in the open sea, parallel to the coast, as far as 40 degrees south, which is the latitude of Valdivia. From there on they will find southerly winds and can make their passage north without risk or trouble. If, however, they cannot leave the Strait before the middle of March, they should winter in the Strait and not attempt to put out to sea, because from April onwards, the prevailing wind off the coast of Chile is from the north.

The Strait is the most impressive of all the inlets in that region. It is possible to anchor almost anywhere within it, but it is important to keep clear of the sides where the mountains are covered with snow. The snow may be up to ten fathoms deep [sixty feet], and breaks off in huge lumps a hundred, sometimes a thousand estados across [an *estado* was equal to the height of a man, perhaps five feet six inches at that time]. This snow is as hard as rocks and comes crashing down with a noise like thunder. Because the channels are so deep ships tend to navigate close to the shore, but this can be extremely dangerous. I have seen places where the channel was a league and a half in width, and too deep for sounding, yet so thickly strewn with these lumps that a launch could not thread a way through them. They float in the water like floating islands, often two, three and four estados above the water and an equal depth below. I give this warning at the risk of being disbelieved and ridiculed for the safety of those who navigate the Strait in future.

Although Ladrillero had obviously not realised that there is between eight and ten times as much of an iceberg hidden below the water as shows above, his description is clear and would not disgrace modern pilotage instructions. The Spaniards now had the sea route between the Atlantic and the Pacific well surveyed, but it was dangerous, time-consuming, and had proved expensive in ships. So they continued to give preference to the safer alternative of shipping all cargoes on the west coast north to Panama where they crossed the isthmus by mule train and were then loaded again on ships destined for Spain. No further Spanish voyages were made using the Strait of Magellan for twenty years and the next ships to appear did not fly the banners of Spain but the red cross of St George of England, as Spain's small but increasingly confident Protestant enemy in Europe extended its maritime challenge.

3

Drake's Passage

Drake's Passage, the 600-mile-wide stretch of water that separates South America and Antarctica, owes its name to Sir Francis Drake, the great English maritime adventurer, although he never sailed through it and whether he actually sailed in it is an unanswered question.

Drake was born around 1540 at Crowndale, near Tavistock, the son of a Protestant clergyman. Because of his religious beliefs, his father was forced to flee a Catholic Devon and settled in Kent, where his son grew up and was apprenticed to the captain of a small collier trading out of Whitstable. Drake eventually succeeded the captain when he was twenty-one years old. It was invaluable experience, but he quickly abandoned the coal trade and joined his Hawkins cousins on the more profitable east African trade. During the course of a trading voyage to Africa and central America in 1567 the family fleet was attacked by the Spanish in San Juan de Ulua and suffered a serious loss which Drake tried to recover by peaceable means, but when these failed, resorted to raiding Spanish possessions in America to obtain recompense. It was whilst on one of these voyages in 1573 that he crossed the Isthmus of Panama and was taken up into a tree by a friendly Indian and shown the Pacific Ocean, becoming the first Englishman to view it. He prayed there and then that 'God should give him life and leave to sail once in an English ship upon that sea.'

Drake's inspiration may have been to sail on this ocean but his intention was plunder. The initial objective was to sail through the Magellan Strait, raid the unfortified towns of Chile and Peru, capture large quantities of booty and return home by retracing his outward passage. This was not the task for a single vessel, so he required a reasonable-sized fleet and financial backing. Partial support certainly came from Queen Elizabeth I of England, but this investment was not publicised in order to avoid political embarrassment with Spain. In all five ships were assembled : the *Pelican* of 120 tons, flagship, the *Elizabeth*, a new ship of 80 tons commanded by Thomas Winter, the *Swan*, a flyboat or store ship of 50 tons, the *Marigold*, of 30 tons and a small pinnace named the *Benedict*. The crew in the five ships totalled 164.

The small fleet sailed from Plymouth on 15th November 1577 and as a deception to keep their real destination from Spanish spies, it was announced they were heading for Alexandria. A storm during the first night, however, forced the ships to shelter in Falmouth, where the *Pelican*'s mast was cut away to save the ship, and the *Marigold* was driven ashore. The battered ships returned to Plymouth for repairs and departed again on 13th December, their objective no longer a secret. The route was the standard one: down the west African coast to the Cape Verde Islands, taking a number of prizes on the way and more importantly, some pilots as prisoners. Amongst these was the Portuguese Nuño da Silva, who kept a log during his time with Drake which has only come to light this century in the Spanish Archives of the Indies in Seville.

The fleet crossed the southern Atlantic to make a landfall north of the River Plate at about latitude 33° south in April. Drake obviously had some knowledge of Magellan's route, which he augmented with information from Da Silva but he spent time coasting and exploring, reconnoitring for a safe haven to shelter his ships throughout the winter. He eventually put into Port St Julian on 20th June, and noted a gallows still standing from Magellan's sojourn.

There were always people who found grievances as the length of already long voyages increased. The enforced stopover for the winter had given Magellan problems in this place, and Drake soon had troubles of his own. Thomas Doughty and his brother John, both with a higher social standing than Drake and with good connections at Court, had apparently felt bitter about taking orders from a man they considered to be their inferior. Potentially more dangerous was their habit of voicing their opinions to the crew. Drake, a practical person, who knew his ships and men probably better that most, appreciated only too well the influence that gentlemen of the Doughtys' standing could exert on others. A weak man would have left the matter alone, hoping it would go away, but Drake was far from weak and he was aware that if the threat to his authority was not checked quickly, people would start taking sides and threaten the whole venture. When faced with a problem his inclination was to treat it as a threat and react aggressively and this is exactly what he did now. He had Thomas Doughty arrested and brought to trial.

The jury, consisting of crew members, found Doughty guilty but the matter of punishment raised a difficulty. On small ships such as these there was no place to confine a prisoner where he could be prevented from having contact with the crew and stirring discontent or worse, earning sympathy. So Doughty was offered the choice of being executed or marooned. He opted for execution and was beheaded. Having lanced the boil, Drake's next task was to raise morale and boost the team spirit for the next stage of the voyage. It was at this point that he made his famous statement, one that was to influence the British Navy through the years: 'The gentlemen shall hale and draw with the mariner, and the mariner with the gentlemen.' This was a revolutionary idea at a time when seamen were considered to be at the bottom of the pecking order, and the gentlemen's role was to share in the proceeds, help to discipline the seamen and lead in the fighting, but in no way to become involved in the actual working of the ship. Drake, however, was short of manpower, but even more important, by making the gentlemen work instead of sitting around idly, he shrewdly removed the opportunity for them to foment further trouble.

After a stay of fifty-eight days the fleet, which was now reduced to three ships, the *Pelican,* the *Elizabeth,* and the *Marigold,* plus the little pinnace sailed from Port St Julian on 17th August 1578, and arrived off Cape Virgins on the 20th. On this day Drake changed the *Pelican*'s name to the *Golden Hinde,* the crest of Sir Christopher Hatton, a close personal friend. Nuño da Silva stated in his subsequent examination by the Inquisition in Mexico that Drake waited until the 23rd for favourable winds before sailing into the strait, which sounds likely. An adverse wind was the only matter that could have delayed him since he was brimful of confidence and considered what a Spaniard could do without knowledge was well within his own capabilities. They found the winds very strong, often contrary, and after the third day they anchored frequently, to rest the crews and await advantageous winds and tidal streams. They saw fires ashore and met natives with whom they had friendly relations, but these contacts were brief as Drake was not prepared to be sidetracked from his purpose of reaching the Pacific as quickly as possible. They passed Cape Deseado and entered the Pacific Ocean on 6th September, a passage time through the strait of seventeen days, nearly half that taken by Magellan, but then Drake did not lose time looking for a missing vessel.

In fact Drake was not the first Englishman to sail on the Pacific. Captain John Oxenham, one of the men who accompanied Drake when he sighted the Pacific in 1573, had made a subsequent raid across the Isthmus of Panama and captured two Peruvian treasure ships in 1575. He did not get this booty home as the Spanish mounted a hot pursuit and captured him and his men. He was executed as a pirate, a fate that would await Drake if he was caught.

With the strait behind him, Drake set a course to the north-west. The motive for this is unclear as it took him away from the land and the towns he wished to raid. However, he may have wanted to gain sea room or perhaps avoid the risk of being seen and reported before he could descend on his prey. In these water Nuño da Silva would have been of little assistance because although the Portuguese had an idea of the shape of South America, only those in the Spanish service such as Magellan had actually sailed there. According to San Juan de Anton, a Spanish captain captured later and subsequently released, Drake had a huge chart on board measuring eleven yards in length that had been especially made for him in Lisbon. This is almost certainly bluff on Drake's part, as none of his crew reported seeing it, but he was quite capable of pretending he had special intelligence in order to trick the Spaniard into giving away information.

Drake's movements over the next seven weeks are given in greater detail because although we can plot his courses and distances sailed it cannot be proved beyond doubt whether or not he was the first person to sight and even round Cape Horn. The day after they cleared the Magellan Strait, on 7th September, they ran into a gale which allegedly lasted until 28th October. It should not be imagined that the wind blew at a full gale force throughout the fifty-two days, but it is quite feasible, knowing the weather in the area, that a series of gales swept in from the Southern Ocean (I have experienced six in ten days). The seas would have had no opportunity to quieten in between the gales and in the vessels of that time high waves made manoeuvring very awkward. The English ships, although probably the most seaworthy then produced in Europe, were not good sailers compared with later designs. They could only make good a course of six to seven points ($67°$ to $78°$) to the wind, and in heavy weather this would be worse. Beating off a lee shore in a gale, in other words trying to sail away from danger into the directions from which the wind was blowing, was a very ticklish problem. When I sailed on the modern replica of the *Golden Hinde* we found that we pointed about $80°$ to the wind, but managed to improve this when we slackened the leeward shrouds so the yards could be braced round further.

Even so, we only pointed up to 70° with anything like efficiency.

The fleet was swept 200 leagues to the west (about 14° of longitude, to about 89° west) and a degree to the south of the strait. This would indicate a north or easterly wind direction. Drake did manage to get a meridian altitude of the sun which gave him the latitude of 57° and a tierce south. During the course of these gales, the *Marigold* was engulfed by a wave and her crew of twenty-nine drowned.[1] The wind must have changed direction as the two remaining ships were now driven by a westerly gale towards the land. They managed to sail into a bay between rocks somewhere around 51° south. However the wind changed within a few hours, and the ships lost their anchors and were again forced out to sea. At this point the *Elizabeth* strayed from the flagship, and sailed back inside Cape Deseado. Captain Winter could have earned himself everlasting fame and fortune had he proceeded with the voyage independently, but he was not made of the same stern stuff as Drake and after waiting for three weeks he returned through the Strait and sailed back to England.

Meanwhile Drake had been pushed to the south. On 14th October he anchored around three leagues off the coast in fifty fathoms of water at about latitude 54½°, probably in the vicinity of the Cockburn Channel. Three hundred feet is a considerable depth and no seaman would have been happy with this sort of anchorage, especially with the frail rope anchor cables of that time. By now too they must have been aware of the risk of another westerly gale coming along, so this deep anchorage suggests that the crew were desperately in need of a rest. They did not rest long as the next day we learn that they weighed anchor and moved to a more sheltered position, although we do not know where. Here Drake lost his pinnace, the *Benedict*. Although he was unable to recover any of the men at the time and believed they had all perished, seven survived, one of whom was a Peter Carder who miraculously made his way back to England seven years later. On 17th October a change in the wind direction caused them to seek another haven and they anchored again amongst some islands the next day. This may have been in the lee of Londonderry Island but from the expedition's

---

[1] Folklore in the Falkland Islands maintains that the wreck of an Elizabethan ship, said to be from Drake's expedition, lies high and dry on Jason West Cay, the westernmost island of the group. In 1982 Ewan Southby-Tailyour visited the cay during the British tidying-up operation after the Falklands war, and saw part of a wooden wreck about sixty by twenty-five feet above high water mark. A sample was analysed and found to be hamtrack, a North American timber regularly employed for shipbuilding in the nineteenth century. This was no Elizabethan vessel and certainly not one of Drake's, as all his are accounted for.

point of view the significance was that this was where they first met the
Fuegians. Four days later another wind change parted the anchor cable;
they must have carried a large supply of anchors, because the following day
they anchored off an island which Da Silva puts at 57° south. They remained
for a further four days exploring, gathering wood for the galley fire and
catching seals and penguins to supplement rations.

It was whilst here that Drake is reported to have noted: 'The Uttermost
Cape or headland of all these islands stands near 56 degrees, without which
there is no main island to be seen to the southwards but that the Atlantic
Ocean and the South Sea meet in a most large and free scope.' This was the
first realisation that Tierra del Fuego was a group of islands and that an
alternative route to the Magellan Strait existed. Certainly on his return to
England he told his kinsman Sir Richard Hawkins that he had gone ashore
with a compass and found the southernmost part of the island, and this land
was further south than any man had ever seen. Chaplain Fletcher, not a
friend of Drake, records that he landed and discovered that this place, which
they called Elizabeth Island, was three parts of a degree to the south of any
other islands. Horn Island is in latitude 55° 58' south, very close to Drake's
position, but Nuño da Silva claimed that the island was in 57° south, the
same figure quoted by Chaplain Fletcher. Da Silva was a seaman and a
navigator. We have no means of knowing what instruments, if any, he was
allowed to use but he obviously believed that the southernmost island was
in 57° when interrogated by the Spanish after he left Drake in 1579. As far
as the Chaplain's account is concerned, it does not surface until thirty
 years after the voyage, and as Fletcher was no navigator his opinion is
hearsay.

One fact is clear from all the accounts, the island had nothing visible to
the south and this leaves only two possible choices, Horn Island and the
Diego Ramirez group in 56° 31' south, fifty-six miles west-south-west of
Cape Horn. These islands do have water but no trees. A translation of Da
Silva's testimony states that when leaving on 28th October, a course was
set to the north-north-east and north, which is impossible from Cape Horn
unless the ship sailed into the islands of Tierra del Fuego. So this leaves
only the Diego Ramirez Islands which coincide more closely with the reported
latitude. Latitude could be assessed with a reasonable degree of precision,
and indeed Drake's latitudes for the Capes Virgins and Deseado, which
were calculated from sun observations using a cross-staff, are very good. In
1974 Christopher St J. Daniel took a cross-staff on a voyage across the
Atlantic in a replica of the *Golden Hinde* and ascertained that the instrument
was accurate to within about twenty minutes of latitude or twenty miles

north or south. However, as he admits, he had the advantage of far superior tables to aid his calculations.

A theory has been advanced that the Pactolus Bank, which now is covered by sixty-seven fathoms of water, may have existed as an island in Drake's time, but been worn away by the sea and icebergs since and this was the original Elizabeth Island. Retracing Drake's reported course does not assist us, as although we can guess this, without any observations of the longitude we can never be certain, and it was not possible to measure longitude for another 180 years.

So although Drake deserves the credit for discovering that Tierra del Fuego was not the northern tip of a great southern continent and that another large expanse of ocean extended to the south, we will never know if he actually saw or landed on Cape Horn. However, discovery of another route around America had considerable strategic significance, as it meant the Spanish could not simply garrison Magellan's Strait to discourage rivals and enemies. The news was kept secret for a while, both by the English and the Spanish, but inevitably the open sea between Cape Horn and Graham Land 600 miles to the south subsequently became known as Drake's Passage.

Drake's subsequent adventures do not concern Cape Horn. Suffice to say that he sailed slowly up the coasts of Chile and Peru towards central America, or New Spain as it was then called, capturing ships and looting towns. Nuño da Silva was put ashore, unharmed, at Guatulco in Mexico along with other prisoners taken during the voyage. Although Drake had treated him well and restored most of Da Silva's possessions to him, the poor man suffered considerably when he returned to the Spanish. He was thoroughly examined, in particular with regard to Drake's future plans. Unfortunately Da Silva could tell them little so he was handed over to the Inquisition and tortured. On his release he was rumoured to have settled in England under the name of Sylvester. A *Statement* of his time with Drake was published soon afterwards by Hakluyt, and the survivors of Drake's crew confirmed the accuracy of his notes.

Drake cruised in Mexican waters until he captured the Spanish Manilla Galleon, the name given to the large vessel aboard which all the Spanish annual profit from the Philippines was collected and sailed across the Pacific to Panama – a prize worth trying for. The Spanish found the Pacific route safer than the alternative around the Cape of Good Hope. The *Cacafuego* (Spitfire) yielded over eighty pounds of gold and no less than twenty-six tons of silver. It is said that Drake removed his stone ballast and replaced it with the silver ingots as the haul was so great. He then sailed into a bay in California where he careened and prepared the *Golden Hinde* for the homeward voyage. Whilst here he made the momentous decision to return to England via the western route probably reasoning it was too risky to retrace his tracks through Magellan's Strait with the possibility of Spanish ships searching for him. So he sailed across the Pacific Ocean to the Spice Islands where he dallied until intelligence reached him of another large ship in the vicinity. Not wishing to risk his booty he weighed anchor and headed for home. He left Java on 26th March 1580 and made a passage round the Cape of Good Hope, stopping only at Sierra Leone en route to Plymouth, which he reached on 3rd November 1580. The voyage was only the second circumnavigation of the world and the first by an Englishman. To this day it rings down over the centuries as one of the greatest maritime adventures of all time.

Drake had been right to take the long route home as the Spanish reacted quickly to the shock of his invasion of what they had come to see as their private preserve. Armed ships were gathered and sent to pursue him, but by the time this fleet reached Panama, he was already in California. They assumed, incorrectly, that he would return the way he had come via Magellan's Strait, so ships were sent down there to lie in ambush. They were commanded by Pedro Sarmiento de Gamboa, an experienced sailor, who was also instructed to explore the southern coast of Chile and search for suitable sites for fortifications that could seal Magellan's Strait. The Spanish Pacific trade was now too important to be left unguarded. Reports of Drake's exploits were certain to attract others and the simplest way to prevent a repetition of these raids was to build a fort and block the strait against enemies.

Sarmiento sailed from Callao in October 1579, and took two months exploring the coast of Chile before entering the strait in late January. He made a very thorough examination and noted a number of potential sites where effective defences could be established. Although he was separated from his consort, he completed the work and sailed back to Spain to report. Philip II responded by organising an armada under Diego Flores de Valdez with twenty-three ships and 3,500 men. A force of 500 men under Sarmiento were to remain in the strait and provide its defence, others were to garrison towns in Chile and Peru and the remainder were to sail on to the Philippines to consolidate Spain's position in the area.

Of all the expeditions that set out for Tierra del Fuego, few suffered as much as this one and few leaders showed as much determination as Sarmiento. The expedition had an inauspicious start when it ran into equinoctial gales and lost five ships with all hands. It returned to Cadiz for repairs. When it sailed again they only reached Rio de Janeiro before taking up winter quarters for six months and did not head south for the strait until November 1580, the same month that Drake got home. Off the River Plate a ship sank in a gale. De Valdez retreated northwards with the main part of the fleet, changing his mind and rejoining Sarmiento when he heard that English ships were in the vicinity. Sarmiento had in the meantime lost his own flagship and transferred to another vessel. At this point General Sotomayor, the commander of the troops intended for Chile and Peru, lost faith in the sailors. He demanded that he and his soldiers be landed and when this had been accomplished, marched them overland to their destination. The fleet, by now reduced to five ships, thereupon returned to Rio for another winter. The following year they made a further attempt and reached the First Narrows, but strong headwinds here discouraged de Valdez, he turned for home and this time kept going.

Back in Rio de Janeiro Sarmiento found four ships with further supplies waiting for him and he returned at once to the strait. One of these ships grounded on the mainland somewhere between Cape Virgins and the First Narrows and the second-in-command of the expedition put 400 men and thirty women ashore to salvage what they could. Having relieved himself of this burden he then sailed back to Spain with the other three ships, leaving Sarmiento with just a pinnace and eight months' of provisions. To add to his difficulties some 200 Patagonians were quickly on the scene and began to help themselves. The arrival of soldiers brought some respite but the threat remained. Leaving a Lieutenant Viedma in charge of the bulk of the survivors at what he now called Ciudad del Nombre de Jesus, Sarmiento had the pinnace loaded with all it could hold and then leading 100 men, set off along the coast to the west. They marched for 130 miles until they reached Anna Point, just a few miles east of Cape Froward, where they built a city named after the King of Spain, Ciudad del rey Felipe, at what is now Port Famine. His choice was sound as far as shipping is concerned, as this is the last safe anchorage for vessels sailing west before Cape Froward. The fort Sarmiento built at Ciudad del rey Felipe was strong and armed with cannons from the wrecked ship, but the backbreaking labour of construction led to a mutiny fomented by a priest. Drastic measures were necessary and Sarmiento impaled the three temporal ringleaders, the priest merely being clapped in irons on account of his cloth.

With the fort ready it was time to unite the force, so he set off to collect the remainder of his party in the pinnace. Unfortunately strong winds blew him out clear of the strait and prevented his re-entering it. Running short of food Sarmiento was forced to head north to obtain more supplies. He requisitioned one ship he came across, loaded her with stores and dispatched her to the settlement, but she never arrived as her crew no doubt altered course for Spain as soon as they thought they were safe. Sarmiento's pinnace was wrecked shortly afterwards but he managed to get ashore and requisition yet another. The comparative ease with which Sarmiento had found vessels up to now is an indication of how quickly trade and colonisation had gone ahead in South America in less than fifty years. His latest acquisition proved unsuitable for her task and he looked round for another but word had got out concerning the dangers and no captains were prepared to volunteer their vessels. In desperation, with no ready means of getting back to the settlement, Sarmiento decided to return to Spain and obtain support from the King. Even in this he was unlucky as off the Azores he was captured by an English ship and taken to London. Freed by Queen Elizabeth once she heard his full tale, Sarmiento was arrested by the French on his way from England to Spain, and so did not return home until eight years after the expedition had departed.

In the meantime the leader of the settlers left behind at the wreck had marched his party to the fort, though this did little to improve their lot as the fort was not large enough to accommodate everyone, nor were there sufficient food supplies to feed them for very long. With a ruthlessness common to the age 200 men were turned out and told to move away from the area and fend for themselves as neither the fort not the surrounding countryside could support such numbers.

The fate of these men is unknown and they probably perished during the winter through cold, starvation or at the hands of the Patagonians. However until quite recently it was rumoured there was a city hidden in the Andes which housed their white-skinned descendants. The prospects for those who stayed behind in the fort were only marginally improved by this decimation as, when spring came, only fifteen men and three women remained alive. The expedition cost over a thousand lives and twenty ships and the strait was as open to invaders as ever. The only memorials to this gallant band are the subsequent name given to the settlement, Port Famine, and the name of the highest mountain in Tierra del Fuego, Mount Sarmiento.

Spanish fears of further raids were justified before the unlucky Sarmiento eventually got home to Spain. Encouraged by Drake's triumphs, a second English expedition sailed in 1582, led by Edward Fenton, with instructions to trade with India and China, as well as look for the western entrance to the North-West Passage, but quarrels amongst the crew caused it to turn round in Brazil. Another English ship, the *Floris*, made an equally unsuccessful attempt to get through the strait at about the same time. Either of these expeditions could have been the English ships whose presence so discouraged de Valdez.

Four years later, in 1586, a Suffolk gentleman, Thomas Cavendish (Candish in early accounts), also set off to emulate Drake. He mortgaged his estates to build two ships, the *Desire,* of 120 tons, and the *Content,* of sixty tons, to which was added a supply ship, the *Hugh Gallant.* The expedition attracted 126 men, including some of Drake's veterans.

They sailed from Plymouth on 21st July 1586 and after an inconclusive fight off Cape Finisterre with five Biscayan vessels returning from the Grand Banks, put into Sierra Leone for food and water. They stopped again near Rio de Janeiro in November to service the ships and assemble a pinnace they carried in pieces on board. Drake too always took good care of his ships and this attention to the state of the vessels by the English is in marked contrast to the Spanish and Portuguese at the time. The basic difference lay with the choice of commanders. The Spanish and Portuguese nearly always put noblemen in charge of fleets, regardless of their maritime skills, the most senior seaman on board usually being the pilot. The care of the ship was the responsibility of the boatswain. On English expeditions the leader was usually a man of considerable seagoing experience and one who therefore appreciated the need to ensure the ships were well found.

The fleet sailed down the coast to about 48° south where they entered a bay called Port Desire. Here the ships were cleaned again and whilst hunting for water, a small party was attacked by Indians and two of the crew were injured by arrows. During the stay at Port Desire penguins were given their modern name by a Welshman in the crew, '*Pen gwyn*', the Welsh for white head. Proceeding along the coast, they reached Cape Virgins on 3rd January, ran into a gale which lasted for three days and then sailed into the Magellan Strait. On 7th January they encountered a wandering Spaniard, who said he was one of only twenty-three survivors, including two women, from Sarmiento's settlers. Cavendish took these poor wretches on board his ships. Since this number is greater than the numbers who are reported to have survived the first winter at the town, perhaps this party included some of those who were turned out to fend for themselves the first winter. The Spaniard showed them a wreck in the First Narrows which they thought was the barque *John Thomas*, but to whom it had belonged is not known.

Cavendish stopped at Sarmiento's city:

The ninth day we departed from Penguin Island, and ran south-south-west to King Philip's City, which the Spaniards had built; which town or city had four forts, and every fort had in it one cast piece, which pieces were buried in the ground, the carriages were standing in their places unburied: we digged for them and had them all. They had contrived their

city well, and seated it in the best place of the Straits for food and water.
They had built up their churches by themselves: they had laws very severe
among themselves, for they had erected a gibbet, whereon they had done
execution upon some of their company. It seemed to us that the whole
living for a great space was altogether upon mussels and limpets, for
there was not anything else to be had, except some deer which came out
of the mountains down to the fresh rivers to drink. These Spaniards which
were there, were only come to fortify the Straits, to the end that no other
nation should have passage through into the South Sea, saving only their
own; but as it appeared it was not God's will so to have it. For during the
time that they were there, which was two years at the least, they could
never have anything grow or in anywise prosper. And on the other side
the Indians oftentimes preyed upon them, until their victuals grew so
short, their store being spent which they had brought with them out of
Spain, and having no means to renew the same, they died like dogs in
their houses, and in their clothes, wherein we found them at our coming;
until that in the end the town being wonderfully tainted with the smell
and savour of the dead people, the rest which remained alive were driven
to bury such things as they had there in their town either for provision or
for furniture, and so to forsake the town, and go along the sea-side, and
seek their victuals to preserve them from starving, taking nothing with
them, but every man his arquebus and his furniture that was able to carry
it and so lived for the space of a year and a more with roots, leaves, and
sometimes a fowl which they might kill with their piece. To conclude,
they were determined to have travelled towards the River Plate.

A very dismal picture and it is hardly surprising that Cavendish re-christened
it Port Famine.

Cavendish made quite a slow passage through the straits as he did not
clear Cape Deseado until 24th February 1587. He anchored whenever the
wind was contrary and on one occasion met up with some natives with
whom he had a fight. It was noted that these natives, who were said to be
cannibals, possessed a number of Spanish weapons, presumably taken from
the wanderers from Port Famine. A southerly wind became a gale and drove
the ships north, during which time the *Hugh Gallant* temporarily became
separated, but rejoined the *Content* at Mocha Island. Like Drake, Cavendish's
crews had to fight the Arauco Indians who were enslaved by the Spaniards,
but eventually arranged a truce and were led to a Spanish store house from
which they stocked up the ships.

Cavendish raided up the coast as far as Mexico, burning towns and any ships he came across, including quite a large number under construction, before he engaged the Manilla Galleon off Cape St Lucas, the southern extremity of California. This was the *Santa Ana*, of 700 tons, which he took after a prolonged fight. It yielded enough booty to make every man in the entire crew rich for life. With this valuable cargo stowed, Cavendish set sail for England, following the same route as Drake, and came into Plymouth on 9th September 1588. It is said he arrived with sails made of damask and his sailors dressed in silk. Cavendish probably caused more damage to Spain than Drake on his circumnavigation (the third ever) and certainly retained more of the profits, as Drake was obliged to share with a number of shareholders, not least Elizabeth I. The wealth lost by Spain as a result of these two raids was enormous and came at a particularly bad moment for Philip II, who had borrowed heavily to pay for the recently failed armada against England.

Yet another Englishman, John Chidley, sailed into the Magellan Strait in 1589, but the appalling weather prevented him from progressing further than Cape Froward. His crew were struck down by illness and when he arrived home he had only six men left capable of working on deck.

Seduced no doubt by the attention his exploits had attracted at Court, Cavendish quickly spent his money. To repair his fortunes he decided to repeat his earlier success and fitted out another fleet which sailed on 6th August 1591. The men in this expedition were hardened seafarers. Amongst them was John Davis, a veteran of the search for the North-West Passage and probably the finest seaman of his day, who commanded Cavendish's old vessel the *Desire*. Adrian Gilbert, brother of Sir Humphrey, founder of the Virginia colony, commanded a barque, *Dainty*, Cavendish the *Leicester*, Thomas Cocke the *Roebuck*, and there was also a pinnace, the *Black*. They sacked the towns of Santos and St Vincent on the way out, but missed the plunder as the inhabitants had warning of their approach and time to escape. Before they reached Port Desire Adrian Gilbert had grown dissatisfied with Cavendish's leadership and sailed for home. When the remaining four ships entered the Magellan Strait rather late in the season the weather was far more severe than on the previous voyage and it was not until 18th April that they rounded Cape Froward. The fleet then anchored near Crooked Reach until 15th May because of the strength of the wind and during this time many of the crew died of scurvy or exposure to the extreme cold. As the conditions were so inhospitable, Cavendish proposed they should retreat to the Atlantic and make their way via the Cape of Good Hope to the west coast of America – a daring plan. However the fleet no longer had sufficient provisions for so long a voyage and simply headed back towards Port Desire.

Unfortunately only two of the fleet reached Port Desire, the *Desire* and the pinnace. The other two were blown north and lost track of their companions, and when they landed at about 36° south, they lost nearly fifty men killed in fights ashore. The *Roebuck* deserted shortly afterwards, and Cavendish eventually anchored off Ascension Island where he died on 20th May 1592. Before he died, however, he wrote a long report on the voyage in which he charged Davis with desertion. 'The running away of the villain Davis was the death of me, and the decay of the whole action, and his treachery in running from me, the utter ruin of all.' One cannot be sure of Sir Thomas Cavendish's state of mind when he wrote this as the truth was very different and the report, when it reached England, did great damage to Davis's reputation.

In fact Davis showed great loyalty to the adventure. After he lost sight of the admiral in the *Leicester,* Davis sailed to and fro looking for him, and only when damaged by a storm, headed into Port Desire. He refitted the ship but was so short of stores they had to unreave the hawsers and respin them into new ropes. When the ship was ready, and assuming Cavendish must by now have headed back towards the strait, Davis sailed there – not for home as was falsely claimed. On 9th August he was hit by a great storm, and on the 14th found himself 'driven among certain Isles never before discovered by any know relation, lying fiftie leagues or better from the shoare east and northerly from the Streights'. This is the first mention of the Falkland Islands, the bearing is accurate, but the true distance is just over 250 miles, not 160 or better as Davis calculated.

Davis persevered and the *Desire* re-entered Magellan's Strait and slowly worked her way through looking for signs of Cavendish. They cleared Cape Deseado on 2nd October and set a course to follow Drake. However they again ran into a storm lasting several days during which they lost sight of the pinnace, which was never seen again. Davis left an account of the storm which is as inspiring four hundred years later as when written, and shows the determination of the man.

The fifth our forsayle was split, and all to torn; then our master took the mizzen, and brought it to the foremast, to make our ship work, and with our sprit-saile we mended our foresayle, the storm continueing without all reason in fury, with haile, snow, rain and wind such and so mighty, as that in nature it could not possibly be more, the seas such and so lofty, with continuel breach, that many times we were doubtful whether our ship did sink or swim . . .

Our sails had not been half an hour aboard but the footrope of our foresail broke, so that nothing held but the eyelet holes. The seas continually brake over the ship's poop, and flew into the sails with such violence, that we still expected the tearing of our sails or the oversetting of our ship, and withall to our discomfort, we perceived that we fell still more and more to leeward, so that we could not double the Cape; we were now come within half a mile of the Cape, and so near the shore, that the countersurfe of the sea would rebound against the ships side . . .

Being thus at the very pinch of death, the wind and the Seas raging beyond measure, our master veared some of the maine sheate, whether it was by that occasion, or by some current or by God's mercy, the ship quickened her way and shot passed the rock, where we thought we should have shored.

Davis realised the main was sheeted in so tightly that the sail was providing less forward momentum and greater leeway and by easing the sheet he put more power into the sail and lessened its sideways force. The *Desire* now ran back into the strait for about seventy-five miles before they found shelter with the one remaining anchor and lines to the shore. Here they remained for two days whilst the men tried to recuperate, but another williwaw drove them towards the shore and Davis was forced to sail. With little food, an exhausted ship's company and a tired, weatherbeaten ship, he had no recourse but to steer eastwards because if they reached the Pacific they would have been no match for even a weak Spanish vessel. Some idea of the conditions and the crew's state can be gathered by the story that when one of the seamen was blowing his frost-bitten nose, it fell off! They anchored off Penguin Island, near Port Desire, and killed fourteen thousand penguins which were dried , but whilst engaged in this exercise his men were attacked by Patagonians and thirteen were killed. Continuing homewards, they were assaulted again and lost a further thirteen men near Rio de Janeiro where they called in for water. When some pinnaces came out from Rio itself, Davis had to sail quickly, and with the remaining crew ill and desperately short of water, tacked slowly towards Cape Frio. Fortunately, a provident rainsquall revived them, but by now the penguins were going bad and the crew began to suffer from a terrible and fatal swelling which started at the ankles and spread upwards until it reached the chest, whereupon the victim suffocated. The crew was now reduced to sixteen, only five of whom could work, and in this exhausted and putrid condition the ship eventually staggered into Beerhaven in Ireland on 11th June 1593.

Davis never returned to Cape Horn. When he arrived home he discovered his reputation had been ruined by Cavendish's final report, and in addition to losing all his money, he had been deserted by his wife. However, the man who could manage to fight against so many vicissitudes at sea was not to be defeated ashore. He wrote two books, *The Seaman's Secrets,* in 1594 and *The World's Hydrographical Description* the following year. He also invented a double quadrant and improved the backstaff, instruments employed to take sights of the sun, which did much to restore his name and were the most sophisticated navigation instruments available until the Astronomer Royal Halley invented the octant nearly 140 years later.

4

Raiders

Looting Spanish wealth rather than pure exploration and charting had been the incentive for the voyages of Drake, Cavendish and Hawkins, so when the cost became too great, as it did after the failure of Cavendish's last expedition and the capture of Richard Hawkins, English enthusiasm for attacking the King of Spain's Manilla Galleons was dampened for several decades. If there were other expeditions no evidence of them exists. English interest in the route to India shifted eastwards via the Cape of Good Hope and they saw little reason for taking the hazardous route through the Magellan Strait or attempting the possible Drake's Channel around Cape Horn.

The Dutch, however, who like the English were challenging the maritime might of Spain, entered the Indies trade shortly afterwards, and initially used both the Cape of Good Hope and the Magellan's Strait routes. The first Dutch expedition by the western route consisted of five ships and departed from Goree under Admiral Jacob Mahu. The admiral died on the voyage south and was succeeded by Simon de Cordes, who brought the fleet into the strait in April 1598 and wintered until September in a small bay called Bahía Cordes on the north shore of Paso Froward. One hundred and twenty of the fleet's 500 men died during this period and rations ran short, but when spring arrived the survivors were sufficiently fit to continue into the Pacific Ocean. Here the fleet was scattered, and one ship was driven to latitude 64° south, where they came upon a land (Graham Land) burdened under ice and snow. Although they did not go through Drake's Passage this is the first crossing of it and the first recorded sighting of Antarctica. Having worked her way back north, the ship was captured by the Spaniards at Valparaiso. Two others were blown back into the strait, but one managed to sail clear again and reached the Moluccas where the two remaining ships had already arrived. The last of the fleet, the *Faith*, was left behind in the Strait. None of the ships returned to the Netherlands and the expedition was a commercial disaster

However, it must be judged in the context of its times. The inaugural Dutch fleet to the Indies via the Cape of Good Hope consisted of four ships and 250 men when it sailed four years earlier. Three ships and eighty-nine men returned to Texel in August 1597. These losses were considered acceptable because although they brought home only a small cargo of peppers, the value was sufficient to ensure a profit. The appalling loss of seamen's lives was omitted from the profit and loss account, seamen were seen as lowly members of society and thus expendable.

The great era of Dutch expansion in the East was just beginning. Within a few years they replaced the Portuguese as the principal traders in spices and exotic goods from India, China and Japan. In 1601 fourteen rival ventures sailed totalling sixty-five ships, half the size of the invincible armada that had tried to invade England only thirteen years before. The arrival of so many enterprises in the Indies at the same time created a seller's market that raised prices and threatened the profits of the investors and since this benefited nobody one single company was formed in 1602. The United Netherlands Chartered East India Company (VOC), with the enormous capital of six and a half million florins, was at that time and for many years to come the largest company in the world. With many influential investors the new company had no trouble in acquiring a monopoly of trade and navigation to the Indies which included the routes east of the Cape of Good Hope and west via Magellan's Strait for a period of twenty-one years.

But there were risks here too. Vessels separated from their fleets became prey either to the English or the Portuguese and this and other dangers encouraged the Dutch East India Company to experiment again with the South American route. A fleet of six ships under Admiral Joris Spilbergen sailed in August 1614 and arrived at the strait after seven months. On the way, whilst engaged in collecting stores on the Brazilian coast, it was set upon by the Portuguese aided by natives, and Spilbergen took the precaution of capturing a Portuguese barque and distributed her crew around the fleet so as to have hostages if his men were caught again in a similar affray. As on many other early expeditions to South America, Spilbergen had to contend with a mutiny and the punishment he dealt out was no less drastic than his predecessors'. The culprits were flogged mercilessly and their bloody, unconscious bodies flung into the sea. The fleet entered the strait in April 1615 and whilst exploring the coast lost two men to an Indian ambush and two more from another mutiny. On clearing the strait Spilbergen ran into a superior Spanish fleet off the coast of Peru, and after a furious action which lasted all night, forced the Spaniards to surrender. The damaged victors sailed on to the Indies and Spilbergen completed his circumnavigation on board another Company ship, the *Amsterdam*, which he joined in Bantam.

Whilst the shareholders in the Dutch East India Company had every reason to be happy with their monopoly, there were many other in the Netherlands who resented this restriction on free trade and looked for means by which they too could gain access to the profitable business that was making millionaires of many of their more fortunate countrymen. Their only hope lay in finding a route to the Indies not exclusive to the Company. The North-East Passage round the north of Russia and the North-West Passage north of America were considered and rejected, so attention began to focus on one other possibility. In 1589 an English clergyman, Richard Hakluyt, had published the famous book *Hakluyt's Voyages* which contained a report of Drake's circumnavigation. This included a description of the landing made by Drake on Elizabeth Island and his comment that he could see no land to the south. Drake of course never claimed to have found a passage to the south of Magellan's Strait, or if he did, the information was kept secret by the English government. Nevertheless, the account in Hakluyt and the report from the ship in Simon de Cordes' 1598 fleet of open water south of the strait prompted people to speculate about the possibility of bypassing the Dutch East India Company's monopoly.

A small group of merchants led by Isaac le Maire, who had resigned his directorship of the Dutch East India Company, banded together and formed the Compagnie Australe which planned to pioneer a new route. Two ships, the *Eendracht* and the *Hoorn,* of 360 and 110 tons respectively, were fitted out under the command of Willem Schouten, a skilled navigator who had already undertaken three voyages to the Indies. They sailed on 14th June 1615 and after a call into England to recruit a gunner and a carpenter, proceeded to Sierra Leone to trade. The rest of the journey south followed the pattern of earlier voyages except that at a latitude of about 4° south, the *Hoorn* felt a mighty bump. The sails were lowered and the pumps manned although the ship was not leaking, the only clue being a cloud of blood around the ship. It was only later when the ship was careened that the tusk of a narwhale was discovered, which had penetrated through three layers of planking!

The two ships pulled into Port Desire to careen and prepare for the arduous passage ahead of them. The *Hoorn* was beached and as the tide ebbed it was decided to bream her to remove the many months' growth of weed and barnacles on the bottom. Breaming involved lighting fires of brushwood or grass beneath a ship to burn off the growth. Unfortunately the grass burned too fiercely and with an intense heat which rapidly set fire to the pitch on the hull. Within moments the hull was ablaze and it was impossible to save the ship. Schouten salvaged what he could from the hulk and after a further month collecting any available food, set course to the south with both his crews in his remaining vessel.

They sighted the Sebaldine Islands (The Falklands), an indication that they were well clear of the mainland, and then steered to the south-west. The noon altitude of the sun on 20th January 1616 put the ship in latitude 53° south. On the 23rd they found soundings (the name given to a depth of water of less than 100 fathoms) and by nightfall they spotted land to the west and south-west. Sail was reduced for the night, a wise precaution in unexplored waters and at daybreak they saw more land to the south-east but separated from the land to the west by a channel about eight leagues wide. They proceeded towards the channel and at noon latitude was calculated at 54° 46' south. On this day their passage was complicated by enormous shoals of whales and they were also pushed eastwards by a current. The next morning they were close to the north shore of land which they believed was a part of Terra Australis and named it Staten Land – the title has lasted, but Staten Land is in fact an island. The land to the west they called Maurice Land but this has retained its original name of Tierra del Fuego. By noon they were back in the channel, which was christened the Le Maire Strait after their director. Whilst here they obtained a latitude of 55° 36' south which is some forty miles too far south. The centre of the Le Maire Strait, which is only about sixteen miles long, is in latitude 54° 52'. This error is instructive as Schouten was obviously an experienced navigator, so it indicates the difficulties associated with using primitive instruments like astrolabes or cross-staffs from the heaving deck of a ship and explains why explorers preferred to take observations onshore when possible.

On leaving the Le Maire Strait Schouten kept out to sea. He reported losing soundings so he was aware he was back into deep water and no land was visible to the south and west. However the most telling clue that he was clear of land were the huge waves encountered when they cleared the lee of the land. For the next two days the sturdy *Eendracht* beat into a westerly gale, tacking backwards and forwards in an effort to make westing. They were out of sight of land when they calculated their latitude at 57° south, but this position is no more accurate than others taken on board as when running south-west before a north-easter they came to two islands which they reckoned were in the same latitude whereas in reality these are at 55° 55' south. They gave these islands the name Barneveldts after the founder of the Dutch East India Company no doubt because although they were employed by a rival organisation it would be prudent to flatter one of the Netherlands' most powerful men. The ship put in another tack to the south and when she came north again found that the land to the west tended towards the north-west whereas that to the east slanted north-east. With no other land in sight Schouten guessed that this must be the southernmost point of the South American continent. He rounded this southernmost point at 8 p.m. on 29th January 1616, and in honour of his home town called it Cape Hoorn.

Schouten calculated the latitude of Cape Hoorn as being 57° 48' south. The actual position is 55° 58', a discrepancy of 110 miles, larger than his earlier ones but almost certainly due to the prevailing sea conditions. The ship was rolling heavily. For a number of days Schouten beat westwards, his greatest latitude he thought was 58° south, and he hove to when the wind built up the sea to a point when progress was totally impossible. It was not until 12th February that land was resighted, which proved to be Cape Deseado, the final proof that a route through open water existed to the south of Magellan's Strait.

Schouten gave the name Le Maire Strait to the whole passage south of Cape Horn, but sufficient people knew of Drake's report for his name to stick. Today Le Maire's Strait separates Staten Island from Tierra del Fuego, and Drake's Passage is the channel between Cape Horn and Graham Land in Antarctica, 600 miles to south.

It would be pleasant to record that brave Captain Schouten continued the voyage, filled the hold with valuable cargo and returned to the Netherlands a hero. Unfortunately this was not to be, not through mistakes in navigation, nor through contact with the Netherlands' enemies, but due to the selfishness of the Dutch East India Company. Schouten sailed across the Pacific Ocean to the Indies by a more southerly route then was normal. He called at the Juan Fernandez Islands to rest the crew and then traded profitably in the Indies. However, when he sailed the *Eendracht* into Bantam, a Dutch East India Company's harbour, he was hauled before the governor who, advised by Admiral Spilbergen, refused to accept the claim of a passage south of the Magellan's Strait. Might was right this far from the law courts in the Netherlands and the *Eendracht* and her cargo were confiscated and the crew dispersed amongst the Company's ships. Schouten plus two sons of

Le Maire were shipped home with Spilbergen although one of the sons died en route. On arrival Isaac Le Maire was horrified by the expedition's tragedies and determined to obtain justice. First his son's account of the voyage was published, as much to gain sympathy as to prove his case, and then he took the mighty East India Company to court. Two years later he was vindicated and the Company was ordered to repay the entire value of the ship and her confiscated goods, but it was too late to save the Compagnie Australe which had been liquidated in the meantime.

Thanks to Le Maire's book the existence of open sea between the Atlantic and the Pacific Oceans south of Magellan's Strait was confirmed and given wide publicity. This threat to the security of their South American possessions was bad news to Spain and had to be investigated. An expedition was mounted by his Catholic Majesty with all speed.

Two caravels were prepared, named the *Nuestra Señora de Atocha* and the *Nuestra Señora del Buen Suceso,* although whether these were rigged with the lateen rig like the Portuguese caravels, or square rigged on the fore and main masts as was often the case with Spanish caravels is not known. The expedition was commanded by Captain Bartolome Garcia de Nodal and his brother Gonzalo de Nodal was captain of the second vessel. Both were hard, professional sailors, with nearly thirty years of excellent service to the crown behind them. They sailed from Lisbon, then under Spanish control, on 27th September 1618. Less than two months later they were in Rio de Janeiro where, on advice from Flemish and Portuguese pilots, the vessels were modified for the rigours ahead by increasing the freeboards and constructing decks over the exposed holds. Within two weeks they were ready. During part of the stay in Rio the crews were locked in prison to prevent desertions and a mutiny, lead by the steward of Bartolome's vessel, was also put down, the three ringleaders being spared the gallows but sentenced to service in the galleys. Continuing the voyage they landed briefly near Port Desire to kill sea lions for food before sailing to Cape Virgins. Near Possession Bay they paused to examine a wreck, but do not report on its type or nationality. Their next landing was on the Le Maire Strait at a place they called Puerto Buen Suceso (Port of Good Success). At Good Success they met the Haush Indians, but for once there were no hostilities. A gale delayed them in this safe bay until 27th January 1619 when they headed southwards. A very strong tidal stream swept them through the rest of the Le Maire Strait, which they called the São Vincente Strait. They state that although there was no wind they were swept through the strait within three hours, the first report of the very strong tidal streams here that can run at up to 8 knots. As they cleared the south side of the strait they named the south-western point of Staten Island Cape San Bartolome and then started a beat to the south-west against the prevailing winds. On 5th February they came to Cape Horn, which they named Cabo San Ildefonso. Their log reads:

> Between Cabo San Ildefonso and Cabo San Gonzalo[1] there are three islands very like the Berlings.[2] Off the Cape there are two or three lofty rocks, and near them four or five smaller ones, appearing above them close to the Cape and to the south-west, there are the entrances to many bays and ports, all bordered by wooded hills. Cabo San Ildefonso is easy to make out, as the mountains are very high.

Horn Island is indeed 1,391 feet. The Nodals did not land at Cape Horn although they obviously sailed very close to it and corrected its latitude to within a few miles of the true position. A week later when they were south of the Horn, steering south-west with a west-north-westerly wind they discerned another island which they named after their cosmographer, Diego Ramirez. They fixed the island's latitude at 56° 31' south, within two miles of its actual position, another piece of very accurate navigation for the instruments of the time especially as the observations were made from the ships. Intending to land on 13th February, they hove to under easy sail the night before, but a gale sprang up and they were forced south to latitude 58° 30' before eventually clawing their way to the north-west. They were undergoing typical Cape Horn weather of strong gales and heaving seas with the added aggravation of the cold and snow showers. It was not until 25th February that they sighted the Four Evangelists Islands, just to the north of the western entrance to Magellan's Strait where they turned and began to explore back through the strait itself. A month later they were back in the Atlantic Ocean, having completed the first circumnavigation of Tierra del Fuego and made a very thorough survey of the coast. They returned to St Vincent on 7th July 1619 with all the original crew alive and well, the only exceptions being the mutineers left in Rio.

In the annals of Cape Horn exploration, this must rank as one of the most professional expeditions, particularly when seen against the standards of the age in which it took place, and it would be nice to report the two brothers had many years to enjoy their justly deserved fame. Sadly both perished

---

[1] A point twelve miles west of Cabo Buen Suceso on the south coast of Tierra del Fuego eighty-two miles north-east of Cape Horn.
[2] A group of islands about sixty miles north of Lisbon. Schouten had called these three islands the Barneveldts.

on 5th September 1622 when a hurricane struck a fleet returning from Havana to Spain, and their respective commands were lost. However, their signature rightly remains on Cape Horn through the names of many points, rocks and the most prominent peak on the Brunswick Peninsula. Appropriately they are also remembered in the Diego Ramirez group, where the two main islands are called after the brothers, the northern one is Bartolome and the southern, Gonzalo. The mile-wide channel between is known as Canale Nodales.

The Nodals proved that Schouten's account was correct and there was indeed a serious threat to the Spanish South American colonies. They had also found an alternative route for their ships but the Spanish government took no action on the Nodals' report then or later. Their trade continued to pass in ships to the Isthmus of Panama and later an alternative route was developed by land across the Andes from Potosí through Tucumán and down the River Plate. The cost of maintaining a fleet of warships on the west coast of South America sufficient to discourage a marauding expedition was prohibitive and so, remembering Sarmiento's expedition, they preferred to depend upon the weather's fearsome reputation in both Magellan's Strait and Drake's Passage to discourage adventurers. Although another raiding expedition sailed south towards Cape Horn very soon afterwards, there were few more during the next eighty years and it is hard to say that on a purely financial basis the Spanish were wrong.

The Dutch were now at war with Spain and although the Spaniards had the finest and most powerful armies in Europe, at sea the Dutch were more than their match. One method of hurting Spain open to the Dutch therefore was to employ sea power and in 1623 a fleet of eleven ships left Texel under the command of Jacques l'Hermite with the sole purpose of raiding Spanish and Portuguese possessions in Africa and America. Part of this fleet consisted of very large ships for the time, the *Amsterdam* and *Delft* being 800 tons (equivalent to 1,200 tons' displacement today), and over 300 cannons were distributed amongst the ships. The fleet reached Cape Horn on 6th February 1624, but was driven south by bad weather, and although they endeavoured to make westing, when the Cape was next in sight on 14th February, it was still seven leagues to the west. Two days later when they next tacked inshore they had made enough progress for it to be bearing east. They sailed past an island to the west of Cape Horn which was named Isla l'Hermite, after the admiral, and into a channel which they called the Nassau Channel. Here they anchored on the east side of what is now Peninsula Hardy, probably in Orange Bay but possibly in Schapenham Bay, named for their vice-admiral. They had nearly a month exploring, watering and gathering wood, during which time a shore party of nineteen men who were unable to rejoin their ship owing to bad weather were attacked and killed by natives. L'Hermite died at Callao on the voyage northwards harrying the coast of South America, and the fleet finally sailed across the Pacific Ocean to Batavia where is was disbanded. As an attack on Spain it had a nuisance value, but it failed to achieve its expectations since it created no new colonies nor threatened Spain's domination over her own.

The following Dutch attempt was in 1642 when the Spanish colonies of Chile and Peru revolted and the Netherlands States General decided Spanish distractions provided an opportune moment to go on the offensive again. A fleet of five stout ships and 1,800 men under Captain Brouwer was despatched to the Pacific. They were driven back to the north through Le Maire Strait and found shelter in Flinders Bay on Staten Island. On trying to proceed they were again pushed in the wrong direction to the east and came to Cabo San Juan, which they rounded, and headed south-westwards, thus proving that Staten Land was an island. The expedition was a failure. One ship was lost off the Horn, and when Captain Brouwer died, having achieved little as far as aiding the rebellion was concerned in either Peru or Chile, the rest of the fleet turned for home, taking the Cape Horn route which they reported as being surprisingly easy. This was the end of Dutch attempts to gain territory on the west coast of South America and they concentrated instead on trying to capture territory in Brazil. However, the Portuguese revolt against Spain in 1640 saw Britain and France in support of Portuguese independence and the Netherlands eventually resigned her claims in Brazil in 1661, and was left only with small land holdings in Surinam and Esequibo (Dutch Guiana).

The next expedition of note was that of John Narborough, the captain of the *Sweepstakes* in King Charles II of England's Navy, who sailed in 1669 to explore and investigate the trade potential on the west coast of South America. His orders stated that when this was achieved he was to search for the western end of the North-West Passage which was thought to lie at the northern border of the American continent, and then to complete a circumnavigation. The outward voyage to Tierra del Fuego was without incident. He called at Port Desire and measured a Patagonian and found him to be only five feet eleven and a half inches tall; large but not a giant as Pigafetta had claimed. Deserted by his consort, the pink *Bachelor,* he avoided Drake's Passage and sailed through Magellan's Strait relatively easily, charting as he went and finding it totally deserted. Interestingly the master of the *Sweepstakes* was Grenville Collins, who later made the first proper survey of English coasts.

The coast of western South America was still largely unknown to everyone but the Spanish at this time and they jealously guarded their *derroteros* or sailing instructions. These charts and descriptions were placed aboard Spanish ships just prior to departure, and were quickly recovered upon the ship's return. To lose or sell them to a foreigner incurred the death penalty. So lacking hydrographic information Narborough proceeded cautiously northwards. His attempts to establish trading conditions failed and he received a less than friendly welcome, even being compelled to abandon a lieutenant and three men who were taken hostage. Discouraged, he turned for home via Magellan Strait once more and ignored the rest of his orders. The main benefit from this venture was the hydrographic data obtained which gave England at least some intelligence of the Chilean coast.

Further details came into English hands ten years later from the buccaneer Bartholomew Sharp. Sharp served with Henry Morgan during the latter's attack on the Isthmus of Panama, and resolved to repeat the adventure on his own account. Finding few pickings on the Pacific coast of Panama, he stole a number of canoes and with these attacked and captured a Spanish warship which he renamed the *Welcome*. Now armed with a more suitable vessel for his ambitions he set off on a cruise down the South American coast, taking whatever of value came his way. On one of the prizes, the *Rosario*, Sharp seized the *derrotero* before it was thrown overboard. It contained details of all the ports, harbours and anchorages between latitude 15° north and Cape Horn, together with pilotage instructions. Sharp shrewdly took this as part of his share of the loot. He continued the voyage, probably making the first passage around Cape Horn by a British ship. During his rounding of the Cape he confirmed that Staten Land was an island, and also noted that he spent much time navigating through a sea 'gleaming with icebergs'. From Staten Island he sailed, without sighting land, to the West Indies where Sir Henry Morgan was now the Governor of Jamaica. Sir Henry had been given this unlikely appointment in a desperate attempt to suppress piracy, an excellent example of turning a poacher into a gamekeeper. He promptly had Sharp arrested, since Britain and Spain were in the process of signing a peace treaty. However, although Sharp was brought to trial the local courts declined to find him guilty but, realising his position was precarious, Sharp boarded the first boat sailing to England, relying on the captured information to win him a pardon from the King. On arrival he wasted no time in travelling to the Court where he presented the *derrotero* to King Charles II who appreciated its value. The contents were kept a closely guarded secret but a translation was ordered from a Captain Hack. Sharp's gamble in seeking the ear of his sovereign paid off. He was acquitted of the piracy charge and further rewarded by being given a commission as a captain in the King's Navy. However, the life of a respectable captain proved too quiet for a man with such an adventurous spirit, and it was not long before he deserted his ship and sailed with a Dutch vessel, which he captured off Ramsgate, back to the West Indies where he led a group of pirates based at Anguilla.

About fifty of Sharp's crew had quarrelled with him at the Juan Fernandez Islands before the passage round Cape Horn, and they returned across the Isthmus of Panama. One of these was William Dampier who, after two years of cruising in the Gulf of Mexico, joined another pirate expedition in 1683 under Captain John Cook aboard the *Revenge*, a vessel of eight guns and a crew of fifty-two. Whilst off Sierra Leone they captured a Danish forty-gun ship and transferred to her as she was more powerful and suited to their purpose. They exchanged the *Revenge* in Sierra Leone for sixty negro girls, then renamed the Danish prize *Bachelor's Delight* and continued their travels towards the Pacific Ocean. The ship passed to the east of Staten Island, ran into very severe weather and was nearly overwhelmed. Dampier, who was serving as a seaman, described what happened.

In a very violent storm we scudded before the wind and sea some time, with only our bare poles; and the ship, by the mistake of him that con'd, broached too, and lay in the trough of the sea; which then went so high that every wave threaten'd to overwhelm us. And indeed if any of them had broke in on our deck it might have foundered us. The master, whose fault this was, rav'd like a madman and called for an axe to cut the mizan shrouds, and turn the mizan mast overboard; which indeed might have been an expedient to bring her to her course. The Captain was also of this mind. Now our main-yard and fore-yard were lowered upon a port-last, as we call it [a heavy rope topping lift], that is down pretty nigh to the deck, and the wind blew so fierce that we did not dare to show any headsail, for they must have been blown away if we had, neither could all the men in the ship have furled them again; therefore we had no hope of doing it that way. [They were attempting to get the bows of the ship down wind again.] I was at this time on the deck with some others of the men; and among the rest was one Mr John Smallbone, who was the main instrument at that time of saving us. 'Come' said he to me 'let us go a little way up the fore-shrouds, it may be that that may make the ship wear; for I have been doing it before now.' He never tarried for an answer, but ran forward presently, and I followed him. We went up the shrouds half-mast, and there spread the flaps of our coats; presently the ship wore. I think we did not stay up there three minutes before we gain'd our point and came down; but in that time the wind got into our mainsail, and had blown it loose; and tho' the main-yard was down at port-last and our men were got on deck as many as could lie one by another, besides the deck full of men, and all striving to furl the sail, yet could we not do it, but were forced to cut it along by the head-rope and so let it fall down on the deck.

After three weeks' hard sailing in sleet and out of sight of land, the *Bachelor's Delight* rounded the Cape. It is recorded that during this time each man drank three quarts of burnt brandy a day without it having an adverse affect upon their performance! They then proceeded to the Juan Fernandez Islands. Quite how the poor negresses fared is not reported but one hopes they had been put ashore before the ship attempted the Horn. The first ship they encountered in the Pacific was another British buccaneer, the *Nicholas,* commanded by Captain John Eaton. The two ships joined forces, but after achieving only limited fortunes, they split up and headed for the East Indies where most of the men went home by various routes. Cook attracted considerable attention by announcing that during his voyage he had seen a great continent in the south seas – Terra Australis. An account of the voyage, the eighth circumnavigation, was written anonymously by a Cambridge MA, William Cowley, who had been persuaded to join the *Revenge* at the outset of the voyage as navigator, and subsequently transferred to the *Nicholas.* This report was published in 1699 in William Hack's *A Collection of Voyages*.

Dampier reached England in 1691, and in 1699 was given command of the *Roebuck* by the Admiralty and dispatched to investigate Terra Australis. He made a very fast passage, leaving England on 14th January and arrived on the Australian east coast via the Cape Horn route on 26th July. He made a rough survey of this and the west coast and then sailed for home, but lost the ship off Ascension Island. At his subsequent court martial he was found unfit to command a King's ship. Nevertheless, after two voyages around the world, his reputation was securely established and he was given charge of a private raid to the Pacific with two ships, the *St George* and the galley *Cinque Ports* between 1703 and 1707. Bad weather during the passage around the Horn forced them south to 61° latitude. Dissatisfaction amongst the crews with Dampier's leadership led to the desertion of one ship and all but twenty-seven of the men left him before the Juan Fernandez Islands where he marooned the sailing master of the *Cinque Ports*, Alexander Selkirk. His final voyage around the Cape was as pilot for Captain Woodes Rogers' circumnavigation in the *Duke* between 1708 and 1711.

Like many captains at the time Woodes Rogers took the precaution of obtaining a King's Commission to give his voyage a veneer of legality, but the line between this and piracy was very finely drawn. He had two ships, the *Duke* and the *Duchess*. He called at the Falkland Islands which he left on Christmas Day and we are informed that he celebrated New Year's Day 1709 in a fresh west-south-west gale and thick fog, but served up a tub of hot punch with each man receiving about a pint. By 5th January he was well south of the Horn in latitude 61° where he ran into a severe gale. The main course was the last sail to be furled (by lowering the yard to the deck), but on the *Duchess* the lee side of the sail fell overside and then went aback and the weight of wind pushed the ship onto her side. The *Duke* stood by expecting the sail to be rehoisted fully reefed, but the *Duchess* ran off to the south. The *Duke* wore round and followed, but instead of heaving to the *Duchess* continued on her course, causing great concern to Woodes Rogers because of the proximity of ice. At daybreak on the 6th the wind began to ease and the *Duchess* hove to at last, reporting that the sea had smashed the cabin windows and filled the steerage and waist, but apart from the cold and wet, all was well. On the 7th conditions improved sufficiently for the commodore to board the consort which he found festooned with wet clothing hung up to dry and that sensibly the crew had lowered six guns into the hold to gain more stability.

By 15th January Woodes Rogers progressed as far as 79° 58' west although still in latitude 61° 53' south, and he felt confident in setting a course for Juan Fernandez Island. There he found Alexander Selkirk who had been marooned for fifty-two months and offered him a passage on the ship. Time had not healed Selkirk's antipathy for Dampier, because when he saw the pilot he asked to return to his island, but was dissuaded. His adventures excited the interest of Daniel Defoe who used them for the basis of his book *Robinson Crusoe*. The remainder of Woodes Rogers' voyage was highly lucrative as he captured the Spanish treasure galleon *Nuestra Señora de la Encarnación* off the Mexican coast and when the cargo was sold after their circumnavigation, it realised £148,000.

The English and the Dutch were the only foreign raiders entering the Pacific by way of Cape Horn until 1696 when the French pirate de Genes appeared on the scene with six ships. Two years later a more official

expedition sailed in an attempt to open up trade with the Spanish colonies in
Peru and Chile. The two ships, led by Gouin de Beauchesne, sailed through
Magellan's Strait in June 1699 and did not emerge into the Pacific until
January 1700. He claimed the climate was not so very different to France at
the same time of year and colonisation should be possible, but his commercial
intentions were not appreciated by the Spanish authorities who treated him
as a freebooter. However, some merchants advised him to seek a less obvious
anchorage and at Hilo he managed to undertake a considerable amount of
trade away from official eyes. He returned via Cape Horn in January 1701.
This attempt was not repeated.

The next projected raid into the Pacific was in May 1713 when a British
tartan, a small single-masted vessel with a lateen mainsail and bowsprit,
named the *French*, sailed into the maze of islands around Tierra del Fuego.
She initially entered Magellan's Strait, but having rounded Cape Froward,
turned south from the strait through Barbara Channel which lies between
Clarence Island and Isla Santa Ines, and into the Cockburn Channel. This
channel is bounded by steep ice-clad mountains and has tidal streams of up
to 7 knots, probably in excess of the tartan's best sailing speed, so this
would have been a very hard and dangerous passage, particularly as they
were required to survey the channel with great care.

Spurred on by Woodes Rogers' triumphs, two vessels, the *Speedwell*
and the *Success*, sailed for the Pacific in 1718 commanded by Captains
Shelvocke and Clipperton respectively. The *Speedwell* lived up to her name
and was much the faster of the two vessels, which quickly lost contact. In
the Le Maire Strait, the *Speedwell* found the current so strong that she was
driven back to the north. However, when the current turned to the south,
'There arose such a short sea, which at the same time was so lofty, that we
alternately dipped our bowsprit and our poop lanterns into the water.' After
such weather Shelvocke struck down everything unlikely to be required
which was just as well in view of what was approaching.

> We had found it very cold before we came this length, but now began
> to feel the extremity of it. The bleak westerly winds of themselves
> would have been sufficiently piercing; but they were always attended
> either with sleet or snow, which continually beating on our sails and
> rigging, had cased the masts and every rope with ice, and had in a
> manner, made our sails almost useless to us. So much were we
> accustomed to the most severe storms, that we used to think it tolerable
> weather if we could bear a reefed mainsail; for it was common with us
> to be two or three days together lying-to under bare poles, and exposed

to the shocks of prodigious seas, much larger than any I ever saw.[1]

Like Woodes Rogers, Shelvocke was pushed well south, as far as latitude 61° 30' where the mist gave anxieties about colliding with icebergs, and one of the crew fell overboard and was drowned because his hands were so numb with cold that he could no long hold onto the rigging. Despite the hardships the *Speedwell* rounded the Horn but was wrecked later at the Juan Fernandez Islands after taking one or two prizes. Shelvocke continued his voyage in one of these, the *Sacra Familia,* and claimed to have found gold in California during his subsequent wanderings.

Her consort, the *Success,* took the route through Magellan's Strait which involved much anchoring when the wind or the tide were contrary. It was at one such anchorage in May, close to mid-winter, probably in the vicinity of Port Gallant west of Cape Froward, that they were visited by natives in a small canoe. A point which impressed the English sailors, who found the weather extremely cold, was that the natives were wearing next to nothing but maintained a small fire in the canoe. The natives were offered brandy, which they refused, but traded mussels and ducks in exchange for bread and knives. Throughout the month the *Success* was in the strait she had no difficulties with the natives who learned that they could visit the ship without fear and seamen left ashore for a night or two were well cared for in return. The *Success* completed a circumnavigation although she lost a good proportion of her crew to sickness and scurvy both in the strait and later in the Pacific.

The Dutch reappeared after a gap of eighty years in 1721 with an expedition of three ships, the *Den Arend, Thienhoven,* and *De Africaansche Galley,* led by Jacob Roggeveen for the Dutch West India Company, which had the monopoly of Dutch trade on both sides of the Atlantic and the east coast of the Pacific. The objective of this expedition was not to attack Spanish colonies, however, and Roggeveen's instructions were to find and explore Terra Australis, which Cook and Dampier had described, in case it extended close to America and could thus be claimed as within the Dutch West India Company's charter. On their way out to Cape Horn the small fleet was attacked by four pirate vessels who mistook them for heavily laden merchantmen. The Dutch drove them off but with heavy casualties.

---

[1] In the Le Maire Strait the mate of the *Speedwell* shot a sooty albatross. The incident is recorded in Shelvocke's *A Voyage Around the World,* which was published in 1726 and is said to have inspired Coleridge with the idea for 'The Rime of the Ancient Mariner'.

Discipline had always been particularly severe in Dutch ships and this fleet was no exception. Whilst slowly crossing the Doldrums, one of the crew, driven frantic by thirst, broached a barrel in the hold which turned out to contain brandy. Thoroughly drunk he staggered to the galley and attacked the cook with a knife. He was then overpowered by fellow crew members, but not before he had tried to slash his own stomach. His punishment goes beyond the normal needs of discipline even for those days and can only be described as sadistic. The fleet closed up to witness him being keelhauled three times. The practice of keelhauling is originally attributed to the Dutch but was in use with other nations between the fifteenth and eighteenth centuries. A line was taken from the main yardarm, around and beneath the hull of the ship and back to the opposite yardarm. The victim was tied to this line, hoisted to the yardarm and let go. After falling heavily into the water he was then dragged beneath the bottom of the vessel and up to the yardarm the other side. A cannon was often fired as the victim passed beneath the keel. This punishment was repeated when the victim had had time to recover his breath. The severity of the punishment depended upon how clean the bottom of the vessel was and how slowly he was hauled round. On a vessel just out of the dockyard where the bottom was cleaned, the worst the victim would experience (provided he could hold his breath long enough) was a few bruises and grazes. But where the vessel had been at sea a long time and the bottom was covered with weed and barnacles which tore away the flesh, keelhauling was often a death sentence. A broken bloody wreck, the former drunk was brought back on board and allowed to recover partially before being given 300 lashes with his hand pinned to the mast with a knife. His barely recognisable human form was chained to the deck as an example to the rest of the crew until an uninhabited island could be found on which to maroon him, but not surprisingly, after such awful injuries, he died within a few days.

The fleet separated whilst rounding Cape Horn in January; the flagship was forced to 62½° south where they spotted enormous icebergs which they correctly reasoned could not have formed in the sea and must emanate from a high continent further south. Roggeveen's expedition is famous for the island they sighted on Easter Day 1722 and named, after the Spanish and Portuguese custom, Easter Island. The visit ashore led to a misunderstanding with the natives, a large number of whom were killed, including a white priest whose presence has never been explained. They failed to locate Terra Australis but, after hassles with the rival Dutch East India Company in Batavia, finally made their way home.

The war of Jenkins' Ear between Britain and Spain, the latter supported by France, broke out in 1739 and resulted in one of the most famous of the eighteenth-century roundings of Cape Horn, that of Commodore Anson and his small fleet. Relations between Britain and Spain had always been very touchy and Captain Robert Jenkins claimed that in 1731, whilst commanding the sloop *Rebecca* in West Indian waters, he had been boarded by the Spanish *guardacostas* who had rifled the cargo and cut off one of his ears. Seven years passed before this case achieved prominence in Britain, but at a time of rising tension between the two countries, he was called to the bar of the House of Parliament to explain the incident. His story roused public indignation and it was a splendid pretext for declaring war. As a part of the operations against Spain, a fleet was dispatched to harry their possessions in the Pacific Ocean and if possible, as a bonus, capture the annual treasure galleon.

George Anson was allotted a fleet of eight ships for the task, none of them in particularly good condition. Sailors were in such short supply that the numbers were complemented by pensioners from Greenwich Hospital and a last-minute draft of 210 marine recruits. The Spanish, hearing of the assignment, launched a superior squadron under Don José Pizarro, whose instructions were to intercept, capture or kill.

The fleets narrowly missed each other at Madeira and then sailed on, the British to St Catherine's in Brazil, the Spanish to the River Plate.

The Spanish were the first to reach the region of the Cape, passing east of Staten Island and sailing well to the south before attempting to make headway to the west. On the first night the *Guipuzcoa, Hermiona,* and *Esperanza* were detached from their admiral, and a week later the *Guipuzcoa* lost sight of the other two. A strong north-westerly storm struck the scattered ships which, low on food (a rat fetched $4 amongst the starving seamen) and with the men dying of scurvy, had to struggle to stay afloat. The contest proved too great and they all retreated with the exception of the *Hermiona* who was never seen again. The *Asia, Esperanza,* and *San Estevan* were reunited at the River Plate but the *Guipuzcoa*, after losing all her masts, ran on to the coast of Brazil and became a total wreck. Pizarro repaired the *Asia* and set out again, but he was dismasted off the Horn and limped back to the Plate under jury rig. He then marched the remnants of his crew across country to Chile and only the *Esperanza* eventually managed to round the Horn, but six months later.

Anson was delayed on his way south when the *Tryal* lost her mainmast, and was towed by the *Gloucester* to Port St Julian where a replacement was fitted. He sailed through the Le Maire Strait on 7th March, just avoiding some of Pizarro's ships, which, according to their logs, were retreating and had come north through the strait on the 6th. Anson's fleet ran into foul weather immediately and by next morning the wind and current had pushed them more than twenty miles to the east of Staten Island. Furthermore it showed no signs of abating.

We had scarecely reached the southern extremity of the Streights of Le Maire, when our flattering hopes were instantly lost in the apprehensions of immediate destruction: For before the sternmost ships of our squadron were clear of the Streights, the serenity of the sky was suddenly changed, and gave us all the pressages of an impending storm; and immediately the wind shifted to the southward and blew in such violent squalls, that we were obliged to hand our topsails and reef our main-sail: The tide too, which had hitherto favoured us, now turned against us, and drove us to the eastward with prodigious rapidity, so that we were in great anxiety for the *Wager* and the *Anna Pink*, the two sternmost vessels, fearing that they would be dashed to pieces against the shore of Statenland; nor were our apprehensions without foundation, for it was with the utmost difficulty that they escaped. And now the whole squadron, instead of persuing their intended course to the S.W. were driven to the eastward by the united force of the storm and the currents; so that the next morning we found ourselves near seven leagues to the eastward, together with the force and constancy of the westerly winds, soon taught us to consider the doubling of Cape Horn as an enterprize, that might prove too mighty for our efforts.

By 23rd March, when the *Severn* and the *Pearl* had become separated, the navigator's calculations showed that the fleet should have been 300 miles west of the Cape when land was sighted unexpectedly. The ships immediately went about to gain searoom. A full month later the ships were still in latitude 60° south although trying to make westing and the crews were exhausted by the constant battle with the elements and the effort to keep the ships afloat and intact. Another storm divided them again, and the *Centurion* soldiered on alone to the first rendezvous at Nuestra Señora de Socorro on 8th May, but having lost over 200 of her crew to scurvy. Anson sailed up and down the coast hoping for his consorts to appear, but on 22nd May he was hit by one of the notorious Cape Horn greybeards, a huge wave with breaking seas at its crest, which struck the ship so hard that her ballast shifted and the masts were nearly knocked out of her. Concluding it was too dangerous to remain in the vicinity any longer, Anson set a course for the

Juan Fernandez Islands, the second meeting point.

Anson arrived at Juan Fernandez on 10th June, and was almost at once joined by the *Tryal* which had missed him at the first rendezvous and was coping with only five fit men. The *Gloucester* came into sight on 21st June with only her courses and main topsail set. Fog cut off visibility, and the ship was not seen again until the 26th, when two of *Centurion*'s boats were launched with provisions and water. They failed to return and the *Gloucester* disappeared once more. Eventually she came into the bay and was united with her consorts on 16th July. Of her original complement of 300 only eighty were alive. The last vessel, the chartered merchant pink *Anna*, arrived on 16th August. The *Anna*'s small crew of sixteen were in good shape as she had sheltered in a small bay near the peninsula of Tres Montes for two months and this place is known to this day as Anna Pink Bay.

Of the rest of Anson's fleet, the *Pearl* and *Severn* turned round and reached Brazil, the *Wager* rounded the Horn and tried to reach the first objective for the expedition, the town of Baldivia, but went ashore in latitude 47° south. Here discipline collapsed and part of the crew abandoned the officers, stole the longboat, and turned up in Brazil five months later. Of the officers, three including the captain and Lieutenant Byron, grandfather of the poet, returned to England in 1746.

Anson, with his crews curtailed from 961 to 335, purchased the *Anna* from her master for £300. She was then broken up and her crew distributed amongst the rest of the fleet. After raiding the Spanish coast, Anson burned all his ships, apart from the *Centurion* and the *Gloucester,* although the latter was abandoned after bad weather close to the Ladrones Islands. By now reduced to only seventy-one men, he nevertheless captured the Spanish Manilla Galleon, the *Nuestra Señora de Cabadonga* with a cargo worth over £400,000 and returned triumphant to England.

5

The Scientists

Although a number of successful circumnavigations had been completed, at the beginning of the eighteenth century the Pacific was hardly explored. So attention now turned to this vast and mysterious ocean with an area equivalent to the world's entire land mass. Many geographers believed that the large continent *Terra Australis Incognita* must lie somewhere in the Southern Hemisphere to balance the land in the Northern Hemisphere as otherwise the earth would topple over. Australia was sighted as early as 1606, and the Dutchman Tasman sailed along the southern coast in 1642, demonstrating it was not connected to another continent to the south, so the myth of a greater land mass continued. Interest in the subject had declined in Spain and the Netherlands during the seventeenth century; these powers were past their peak and it was the British and the French who were dominant and in worldwide competition. If another continent existed each wanted to be the first to claim it. At the same time romantic descriptions of the Polynesian way of life retailed by sailors returning from the Pacific gave the impression of friendly, happy people living in paradise. These stories were especially popular in Britain and France where an intrigued public supported further exploration. Even the collapse of the infamous South Sea Company in England in 1720, a company formed in 1711 to trade with South America and the Pacific Islands, failed to diminish a scientific quest for a greater knowledge of the world. Of the two routes to the Pacific, the one via Cape Horn was much the speediest.

Although much of the world was by now charted, the charts were not reliable as there was no definitive method for reckoning longitude at sea. The mathematical formula for calculating longitude was produced by a Flemish astronomer, Gemma Frisius, as early as 1530, but the solution depends upon precise timekeeping. The principle is that if the exact time at Greenwich is known, then each 15° of longitude east or west of the meridian through Greenwich will be one hour different. Thus if the time of noon, when the Sun is on the observer's meridian, is 2 p.m. by a clock holding Greenwich time, then the observer is in longitude 30° west. Great accuracy is necessary to avoid errors and many attempts to produce chronometers using pendulums failed owing to a ship's motion or changes in temperature. In 1714 the British Parliament established the Board of Longitude and offered the then enormous sum of £20,000 to anyone inventing a chronometer accurate enough to allow the fixing of a ship's longitude to within thirty miles after a six-week voyage (the average duration of a voyage to the West Indies). In effect this meant the error must be within three seconds a day at sea, a far greater degree of precision than could be accomplished by contemporary clocks ashore. However, John Harrison, a Yorkshire carpenter, produced four chronometers between 1728 and 1760, the first of which was carried by Anson on his circumnavigation. The fourth was copied, and the copy taken by Captain Cook on his second Pacific voyage of exploration. This chronometer more than fulfilled the requirements for the rewards when tested between 1762 and 1764 and had an error of only fifteen seconds in 156 days. Once an economic means of manufacturing copies was developed the problem of longitude was solved for general navigation. Almost inevitably Harrison only received half the reward initially and was not paid in full until 1773.

Alongside the progress in timekeeping went an improvement in methods of measuring the Sun's altitude. The backstaff was the main instrument employed from 1600 onwards, although the cross-staff remained in use. In 1731 John Hadley produced a reflecting quadrant, in fact an octant, which allowed more exact altitudes to be taken. The sextant was the logical next step and appeared in 1757. This was a modification of Hadley's octant, invented by Captain John Campbell of the Royal Navy and is the model for today's basic instrument. From the bridge of a ship and in capable hands, the modern sextant can give readings at least to within half a minute of arc, or about half a mile, but will obviously be less reliable when the ship is rolling or pitching as the observer has great difficulty keeping the reflection of the body on the horizon. From the navigation point of view, however, an error as little as two miles was a huge advance and was sufficient to enable vessels to make landfalls within sight of a desired location, providing of course they had a capable navigator.

The first expedition dispatched with the sole purpose of recharting existing landmarks and seeking Terra Australis Incognita was led by Captain John Byron, (grandfather of the poet) who was one of the survivors from Anson's expedition. His nickname of 'Foulweather Jack' stemmed from his reputation for attracting terrible weather and bad luck. He sailed from Plymouth in 1764 with two ships, the *Dolphin*, a twenty-four gun sloop of 511 tons and the *Tamar* carrying sixteen guns. As an experiment the *Dolphin* had been sheathed with copper for the voyage as the Admiralty was searching for ways to discourage weed and barnacles from growing on wooden hulls and reducing their speed. They thought copper sheets might also provide a barrier against marine borers like the teredo worm.

One of the expedition's prime objectives was to chart Magellan's Strait, a task far more challenging than anticipated since no one appreciated just how many channels and islands made up the Tierra del Fuego archipelago. Byron quickly realised he could not complete the job if he was to undertake the expedition's other objectives, but at least he made a start. He returned to Port Desire where a supply ship, the *Florida*, was waiting to revictual the ships, and then set off to explore the Falkland Islands.

Byron reported teeming marine life in the Falklands, especially whales. One drew alongside and rubbed itself on the copper sheathing; later a large bull, perhaps angered by the ship's apparent flirtation with one of his harem, charged into the ship, giving it a severe jolt, but probably doing himself more harm as the water clouded with blood. After replenishing the ship again, Byron returned to the strait and continued the survey of the narrow channels and islands, noting the currents and making tidal observations. His industry is reflected by the name Byron still being attached to a Caleta, Laguna, two Islas, and a Punta. There is also an Isla Dolphin, a Mouat Isla, named after the commander of the *Tamar*, and a Tamar Isla, Cabo, Peninsula and Puerto. After seven weeks of this work, he cleared the strait to the west and completed a circumnavigation but he failed to locate Terra Australis Incognita. The expedition was remarkable for the seamanlike way in which it was conducted and because only six men were lost from each ship, but it failed to satisfy the information-hungry scientists at home. As a result the *Dolphin* was speedily re-fitted and prepared for another voyage.

In the meantime, in 1765 one of Byron's subordinates, Captain MacBride, established a small settlement at Port Egmont on Saunders Island, off West Falkland, and claimed the island for Britain. He was unaware that one year before the Frenchman de Bougainville had settled Arcadians from Nova

Scotia on the East Falklands at a place he called Port Louis on Berkeley Sound. There may have been an earlier French settlement used as a base by St Malo fishermen, but in any event de Bougainville claimed the islands for France and named them Les Iles Malouines. Neither of these settlements lasted for very long as the Spanish, to whom the islands were known as Las Islas Malvinas (a corruption of the French title) as always fearful of threats to their dominance of South America, purchased the French colony from de Bougainville for $150,000 in 1766 and renamed it Soledad. The Spanish forcibly removed the British settlement in 1770, but it was restored in 1771 after the two nations nearly went to war over the matter. In 1774 however, the British temporarily abandoned the islands although they maintained their claim to sovereignty and the Spanish settlement was withdrawn in 1811.

The commander for the *Dolphin*'s second voyage was Captain Samuel Wallis, and he sailed in August 1766 in company with the *Swallow*, commanded by Captain Carteret. The two ships were separated owing to very bad weather shortly after passing through Magellan's Strait, but independently proceeded on their voyages. Wallis discovered Tahiti amongst other islands, and Cartaret went further south but failed to see any signs of Terra Australis although he searched through 60° of longitude in the area where the continent was believed to lie. On sailing north he came across islands in the Polynesian and Melanesian archipelagos, and surveyed part of the Philippine islands. When Wallis reached home and reported how the ships were separated, Carteret and the *Swallow* were given up for lost, but happily they returned after a voyage two days short of three years. The voyages of Wallis and Carteret, both using the Cape Horn route, were highly praised by the scientific establishment in Britain and acted as forerunners to Captain Cook's subsequent three voyages to the Pacific.

The French, under Louis XVI, had noted Byron's voyage with interest. As part of the agreement with Spain, de Bougainville was again dispatched in 1766 to hand over the small Falklands colony to the Spanish, and then continued on an exploratory voyage which took him around the world.

Louis Antoine de Bougainville was a soldier and scientist of distinction. At the age of twenty-five he published a treatise on integral calculus, the following year he became a member of the Royal Society in London whilst serving as a secretary in the embassy and he was also under the command of Montcalm in Quebec and during the Seven Years War. For the new enterprise, the French government equipped him with a frigate, *La Boudeuse* and a supply ship, *L'Etoile*. Like Byron, de Bougainville spent time surveying before sailing into the Pacific Ocean in January 1768 and his passage through the Magellan Strait is commemorated at Bahía Bougainville, on the

Brunswick Peninsula at Paso del Hambre. This expedition can claim a record in that it inadvertently contained the first woman to circumnavigate the world. The botanist on *L'Etoile* had a twenty-seven year old servant called Baré who underwent the same rigours as all the crew, including forays ashore, and only when the ships reached Tahiti, and the more observant natives insisted on giving Baré the respect due to a woman, was her sex discovered. She completed the voyage, but rather better housed than before!

When the speedy *La Boudeuse* was homeward bound through the Atlantic, she overhauled a small weatherbeaten sloop which was identified as the *Swallow*. De Bougainville had found a message left by the British on Ascension Island, a form of post-box common then, and had his vessel hove to so he could hail Captain Carteret by name. Carteret, who had no news of the *Dolphin* since the consort had been separated at the Horn nearly two years previously, must have been delighted to learn that according to information the French had received in Cape Town, she was already safely in England. It is pleasing to note that although the countries were rivals, explorers showed considerable mutual concern and respect. Shortly afterwards when the two nations were at war again, specific instructions were issued to French warships to allow Captain Cook free passage if he was encountered. De Bougainville returned to France, survived the Revolution and died in 1811. He is perhaps best commemorated by the flowering shrub, bougainvillea, but his name also features on maps as the largest of the Solomon Islands.

Before de Bougainville arrived in France another French frigate, *Le Prince*, sailed to Cape Horn, but when in the vicinity, a fire broke out in the hold. In a desperate effort to extinguish the blaze, even the precious water casks were broached, but to no avail. One boat was lowered and rowed clear of the ship but the others were burned on their booms. As men threw themselves into the sea, the loaded ship's cannons went off because of the heat and killed some of the survivors in the water. Then the fire reached the magazines and the ship blew up. Only ten men out of over 300 escaped in a small yawl, and led by the first lieutenant, managed to sail 600 miles to Pernambuco in Brazil where the Portuguese Navy gave them shelter until a passage home could be arranged.

The voyages of Byron, Wallis, Carteret and de Bougainville partially filled in the gaps in Europe's knowledge of the Pacific Ocean, but there were still vast uncharted areas and the belief in Terra Australis continued to attract government attention. The main objective of the next scientific rounding of the Horn was to observe the transit of Venus and the Sun on 3rd June 1769, and for this purpose the Royal Society sponsored a Royal

Navy expedition. After completing the observations the expedition was to sail in search of the southern continent, a task made more urgent, from the British government's point of view, by de Bougainville's activities. A robust collier was chosen for the project, and renamed the *Endeavour*. She was a vessel of 366 tons carrying ten guns and a crew of eighty-four including a number of scientists, amongst whom were Joseph Banks and Daniel Solander.

The command of the expedition was originally intended for Alexander Dalrymple, one of the leading proponents of the theory of the Great Southern Continent and who subsequently became the first Hydrographer of the Navy. Dalrymple was a civilian, however, and his appointment was unacceptable to the Royal Navy whose poor opinion of scientists as expedition leaders went back to Edmund Halley in 1698. Instead they selected one of their own surveyors, James Cook. Cook had started life in the Merchant Marine and, having attained the rank of mate, decided the life lacked the challenge he desired and volunteered for the Royal Navy as an able seaman. He rose quickly and within two years, at the age of twenty-nine, was serving as master of the *Pembroke* during the successful attack on Quebec. In naval ships the master was responsible for navigation and pilotage, the equivalent of a modern navigation officer, but he did not hold a commission. Cook's excellent work during the Quebec campaign was rewarded by the command of the schooner *Grenville* for five years. During this time he surveyed the coast of Newfoundland, which brought him to the notice of the Royal Society. From the Society's point of view he was an acceptable alternative to Dalrymple and was granted a commission by the Royal Navy and given the rank of lieutenant.

Cook's task was to show that a viable route around the world via Cape Horn existed through the ocean subsequently named the Southern Ocean, but better known to mariners as the Roaring Forties. The *Endeavour* entered the Strait of Le Maire on 14th January 1769, six months out from London, and like so many before her, immediately ran into strong westerlies which, with the adverse tide, caused her to pitch so much that the whole bowsprit was frequently under water. Since a vessel's bowsprit pointed upwards at an angle of at least 25°, the pitching must have been memorable! After suffering for three days she sought shelter in the Bay of Good Success to take aboard wood and water. The scientists went ashore and were met by natives of the Haush tribe with whom friendly relations were established; so much so that the party was allowed to roam inland and spend a night ashore in complete safety, although two servants died of the cold. Departing on 22nd January, the *Endeavour* hugged the coast despite the adverse weather and was off the Horn on the 26th. Three days were passed sailing off and on

Cape Horn in order to confirm the exact longitude of such an important point. The wind then drove the ship away to the south, as far as 60° 10' south where, during a calm, the skiff was lowered and Joseph Banks took a gun and shot some birds whilst being rowed round the ship. The *Endeavour* was thirty-three days in all doubling the Cape, which is taken to mean from 50° south on the east to 50º south on the west; considering the time spent exploring, this was quite respectable. But Cook was a very fine seaman and had no hesitation about setting the stunsails off the Horn when conditions allowed. His account of the passage round the Horn is so matter of fact that he could have been sailing round the North Foreland on the Kentish coast!

They arrived at Tahiti on 10th April with not one case of scurvy, mainly thanks to Cook's attention to the ship's cleanliness and his men's diet. It was during this period that lime juice was beginning to be recognised by the British for its anti-scorbutic properties. This has subsequently led to the American sobriquet 'Limey' to describe British seamen – something that no British sailor need to feel ashamed of. Having completed the observations of the Venus transit, Cook headed south to 40° latitude to search for Terra Australis Incognita. At this latitude he found a large southerly swell which indicated no land, so he altered course to the west and sailed in that direction until making a landfall in New Zealand, previously discovered by Abel Janszoon Tasman in 1642 and thought to be a peninsula of a large southern continent. Cook's circumnavigation of the islands proved this was not the case. After this quick exploration of New Zealand his intention had been to make a run to Cape Horn along the 40th parallel, but as it was late in the year he turned westwards and came upon an extensive coastline. Cook surveyed the whole of Australia's eastern seaboard, but as far as he was concerned Terra Australis Incognita was still to be discovered before completing his voyage via the Cape of Good Hope. Although Cook lacked an accurate chronometer, he plotted the longitude of many islands with great accuracy by lunar observations (this entailed measuring the angular distance of the moon from a known star).

Four years after his initial visit, Cook, by now promoted to the rank of commander, was back in the region of Cape Horn with a 562-ton collier purchased by the Admiralty in 1770 and named HMS *Resolution*. She was accompanied by another converted collier, renamed *Adventure*, commanded by Tobias Furneaux. They sailed in 1772 and in January 1773 were the first vessels to cross the Antarctic circle. While examining the Indian Ocean south of 60° southern latitude, the ships were parted, but rendezvoused by prior arrangement in the Cook Strait in New Zealand during May. The following November they were split up again and Furneaux sailed for home via Cape Horn. He arrived a year earlier than Cook, making the *Adventure* the first ship to circumnavigate the world from west to east. Meanwhile, Cook, who was investigating the Pacific section of Antarctica, spent Christmas Day 1773 at 70° south, but later reached 71° 10' south in what is now the Ross Sea, a proximity to the South Pole that was not exceeded for over fifty years. After this adventure there was no reason for not heading homewards, but since he had supplies for a further year and his ship and men were in a good state, he passed 1774 continuing his exploration and surveys in the Pacific. In October he set off for Cape Horn taking a course in latitude about 55° south and demonstrated that if the southern continent existed, it must be even further south. Despite no sighting of land, Cook was convinced by the size of the icebergs that there was land towards the South Pole.

With favourable winds Cook sailed along the south-western coast of Tierra del Fuego, naming Cape Desolation and Cape Gloucester on Charles Island in the Grafton group (which had been mentioned by Drake's Portuguese pilot) as well as York Minster on Isla Waterman. When the wind came round to the south-east, they sailed into what is now known as Cook Bay and charted Christmas Sound. Christmas Day was celebrated in Cook Bay and they dined on geese shot by shore parties and met the Alakaluf Indians of whom Cook, who had many contacts with new Indians in his travels stated:

> Of all the nations I have seen, these people seem to be the most wretched.
> They are doomed to live in one of the most inhospitable climates in the
> world without having sagacity enough to provide themselves with such
> conveniences as may render life in some measure, more comfortable.

The significance of these remarks in view of the changes made during the next century, and particularly by Darwin, is that Cook, who had encountered cannibals in his Pacific voyages, did not hint that the Alakaluf were cannibals.

They left Cook Bay on 28th December 1774, sailed to the Bay of Good Success and then explored Staten Island. They discovered a useful anchorage, which was named New Year's Harbour, and commented on the vast numbers of seals, sealions and gulls. After clearing the waters of the Horn, they touched at South Georgia which Cook christened and claimed for Britain, before continuing towards Cape Town along latitude 55° south, still seeking to discover the elusive land mass of Terra Australis Incognita. He did find the South Sandwich Islands, although bad weather prevented him from ensuring they were only islands, but was unable to locate Cape Circumcision, which the French believed might be a northern point of the mysterious southern continent. (Cape Circumcision was probably Bouvet Island which the *Resolution* rounded at the beginning of her voyage.) The expedition was a triumph and Cook was rewarded by promotion to the rank of Post Captain and the fellowship of the Royal Society.

Cook's final voyage was intended to discover the western end of the North-West Passage. On his way northwards through the Pacific he came across the Hawaiian Islands, and being unaware that the Spanish had discovered them in 1555, he christened them the Sandwich Islands. His voyage proved that Siberia was not part of North America but he was unable to make much progress through the passage. Returning south again he called once more at the Sandwich Islands where he was tragically murdered by the natives.

His voyages dispelled once and for all the rumours of a huge undiscovered continent in the southern seas as far as 55° south, but more than that, he set a very high standard for accuracy and observation which influenced all subsequent explorations. Perhaps the greatest tributes to Cook come from his colleagues; the Russian Bellingshausen described him as 'That great explorer', and the Frenchman Jean François de Galaup, Comte de La Pérouse, said of him, 'No one will ever again equal that immortal navigator.'

La Pérouse led a French expedition to the Pacific via Cape Horn in 1785 to maintain the search for the western entrance to the North-West Passage and two vessels, the *Boussole* and the *Astrolabe*, passed Cape Horn in August that year. Bad weather drove them away from Alaska, but they visited Japan and China, then went south and called in at the fledgeling English settlement in Botany Bay. On 7th February 1788 he departed and was never heard from again. In 1826 Captain Dillon came across the wreckage of two ships, thought to be La Pérouse's flotilla, on the reefs of Vanikoro Island, north of the New Hebrides. Of passing interest is that a young artillery officer, Napoleon Bonaparte, applied to join La Pérouse's expedition, but was turned down. Had he been selected, European history might have been dramatically altered.

The most famous mutiny in maritime history owes its origins as much as anything to Cape Horn because HMS *Bounty* failed to double it. Bligh was an experienced seaman, good enough to be the *Resolution*'s master on Cook's last voyage, a post which required exceptional qualifications. The *Bounty* was another ex-merchantman of 215 tons with a crew of forty-five and was commissioned to transport breadfruit from Tahiti to the West Indies to provide a staple for slaves employed in the sugar plantations. The expedition sailed two days before Christmas 1787 and reached the waters of the Horn in mid-March, a very fast passage. They rounded the Horn, but were then driven back to the east by exceptionally strong gales. For a month the gallant little ship battered against the westerlies but without making progress and eventually Bligh, with some crew injured and the remainder exhausted, was forced to turn before the winds and took the passage south of the Cape of Good Hope and Australia to Tahiti. Cape Horn was therefore an essential ingredient in the ensuing drama because had Bligh been able to sail into the Pacific when he first rounded the cape, possibly the mutiny would never have occurred. The story of the mutiny itself is too often recounted to bear repetition, but Bligh, having completed an epic voyage with eighteen loyal crew in an open boat from near the Tonga Islands to Timor, a distance of 3,600 miles, was promoted, commanded ships in the battles of Camperdown and Copenhagen and was then appointed governor of New South Wales. Whilst in this post he quarrelled with his deputy, was arrested and sent home, but subsequently rose to the rank of Vice-Admiral.

One of the fastest 'doublings of Cape Horn' – the passage around the cape from 50° latitude on one side to the same latitude on the other, was made by Captain Etienne Marchand in 1790. This French officer called into Helena on a homeward voyage from Bengal and met an English Captain Mortlock who was returning from the Pacific. Fired by the Englishman's description of the trading opportunities in the Pacific, Marchand prevailed upon the authorities in Marseilles in an attempt to exploit the possibilities, and the *Solide* was rapidly fitted out for the venture. She was well staffed as amongst her fifty crew were five lieutenants, two surgeons, a boatswain, two masters, two carpenters, three waiters, a cook, and a baker! The Horn was rounded in April, late in the year, but often a season when easterly winds prevail. He travelled through the Pacific, called at China, and was back in Toulon twenty months later with the crew in good health. It was a remarkably swift and competently organised circumnavigation, and further French expeditions might have followed had not the revolutionary war interfered. As a result of these hostilities the next French expedition via Cape Horn, undertaken by the *Bordelais*, had to wait until 1816.

Dumont d'Urville, a French naval officer and one of the founders of the Paris Geographical Society, was dispatched in 1822 with the objectives of extending scientific knowledge and searching for traces of La Pérouse. Dissatisfied with the results of this three-year voyage, he sailed again almost at once for a further three years. On each occasion he circumnavigated the world. Subsequently he explored Antarctica to the east and west of Cape Horn, and penetrated sufficiently far south to discover land which was named Terre Adélie after his wife.

Cape Horn was now established as the obvious, although often difficult, route between the Atlantic and the Pacific, and this led to a reappraisal of traditional world sailing routes. The Russian, Admiral Adam Ivan Krusenstern, who served in the Royal Navy for four years until 1797, proposed to the Tsar Alexander I that access from western Russia to China and their growing settlement at Kamchatka in eastern Russia would be speedier via Cape Horn. Two ships, the *Nadezhda* and the *Neva*, purchased in England, were commissioned and departed from Kronstadt in 1803. During the next three years they rounded the Horn, explored extensively in the northern Pacific and achieved the first Russian circumnavigation.

Further Russian Pacific exploration ensued. The most notable of all the Russian explorers was Thaddeus Fabian von Bellingshausen who served with Krusenstern in 1802–6. In 1819 he commanded an expedition whose purpose was to enlarge on Cook's work in the south. He had two vessels, the *Mirny* and the *Vostok*, and during the course of an impressive voyage surveyed the South Sandwich and South Shetland Islands and must have come within sight of Dronning Maud Land although he never claimed to sight Antarctica itself. His name is commemorated in the Bellingshausen Sea, and the voyage, although not widely publicised at the time, led to his country's continuing interest in the region.

Until the end of the Napoleonic Wars in 1815, nations had jealously guarded the secrets of their hydrographic charts. However, the end of the wars saw the Royal Navy as the unchallenged maritime superpower, and confident of their strength, the Admiralty took the unprecedented step of making British charts and copies of captured charts universally available. To accumulate data on the oceans, expeditions were dispatched to the four corners of the world to produce accurate surveys of little-known or partially surveyed areas. The bulk of this work was of outstanding quality, especially when one considers the equipment and ships which were employed, and the Admiralty Sailing Directions, published to accompany the charts, are still a byword for clear and concise descriptive writing.

There is considerable doubt over who first sighted Antarctica but, between 1815 and 1830, its approximate shape was established. The English Sealing Company of Samuel Enderby and Sons were active in the area and encouraged by their masters to explore and gather information. The Enderby brig *William*'s Captain William Smith, was blown south of Cape Horn in 1819 and sighted land about 62° 42' south, and later landed on the South Shetland Islands. The following year, in company with another Enderby ship captained by Edward Bransfield, he observed and named Trinity Land which was almost certainly the tip of Graham Island. (This title is missing from some American charts, where it is called Palmer Peninsula after an American sealer captain, Nathaniel Palmer, who found land at this point a few months later.) Other Enderby captains included James Weddell, a former Royal Navy master, who between 1822 and 1824 charted the South Orkney Islands and penetrated to latitude 74° 15' south into the Weddell Sea. Additional discoveries were probably made, but the little sealing vessels were amazingly fragile for the waters in which they plied their trade, and seven at least never returned from the South Shetlands area in 1820–22. In 1831 John Biscoe was ordered to seek new sealing grounds in the brig *Tula* and cutter *Lively*. Although he believed Antarctica consisted solely of an immense expanse of floating ice, he is credited with the first sighting of land, which he named Enderby Land. It was Biscoe who gave Graham Land its modern title after the First Sea Lord of the day. Whilst these English and American sealers were operating mainly in the cause of commerce, basic exploration was advanced in the next decades by Balleny, Kemp, Wilkes, Ross and others. By 1840 all the islands in the Southern Ocean were identified and any imagined barriers to sailing-ship routes south of Cape Horn could safely be ignored. The round-the-world route was opened.

Although generally the focus of attention moved south, there was unfinished work in the channels of Tierra del Fuego itself and a systematic exploration and survey of the archipelago was organised by the British Admiralty in 1826, the outcome of which was possibly the most famous of all the scientific expeditions to Cape Horn. Two vessels, the *Adventure* and the *Beagle*, were employed and the *Beagle* has gained justifiable acclaim as the ship which carried the young naturalist Charles Darwin around the world – a journey which inspired his 'theory of the origin of species'. The ship made two visits to Tierra del Fuego, and her work in the archipelago supplied the mariner with charts which at last showed the mysterious channels and rocks which were such a hazard in the past.

The *Adventure* was a converted transport of 330 tons, and was one of the early ships commissioned specifically for surveying, in which role she had been engaged since 1817. For the voyage to Cape Horn she was commanded by Captain Philip King. The *Beagle* was built at Woolwich in 1820 as a brig-rigged four-gun sloop of 235 tons, but in 1825 transferred to the surveying service and sailed under the command of Captain Pringle Stokes. The ships separated once they reached the strait in order to cover a greater area. An idea of the problems experienced, particularly among the fierce williwaws in the western part of the strait, can be gathered from the following entry in Captain Stokes' diary:

January 31st, 1827. The hands were turned out at daylight to up anchor; but the heavy squalls off the high land of the harbour rendered it too hazardous until a temporary lull enabled us to make sail and re-commence beating against a dead foul wind, much rain, hard squalls, and a turbulent cross sea.

About seven in the evening a squall burst upon the ship with fury far surpassing all that preceded it, had not sail been shortened in time, not a stick would have been left standing, or she must have capsized. As it was the squall hove the *Beagle* so much over on her broadside, that the boat hanging at the starboard quarter was washed away. I stood to the north shore, to look for an anchorage under the lee of a cape, about three leagues to the north-west of Cape Tamar. On closing it, the weather set in so thick that at times we could scarcely see two ships' lengths ahead.

On this occasion they ran back to Port Tamar, losing the ground gained during the day, went aground on an uncharted rock ledge at the entrance to the port, but luckily the ship came free and found a snug anchorage inside. Altogether not the sort of day that any shipmaster would enjoy and Captain Stokes must have been relieved to anchor securely for the night, even though all the hard sailing would have to be repeated. The wind was unfavourable for the ship to depart the next day, so Stokes launched one of the boats and continued working until the ship could be extricated to join him in Puerto Misericordia (known to the English as Port Mercy). Going aground was a danger for any ship in uncharted waters, but particularly so for a survey vessel as by the nature of her profession, she was frequently close inshore. The surveying routine was broken only in the winter months when the ships retreated north to an anchorage such as Chiloé where progress was compared and the hard-pressed crews allowed a well-deserved respite.

At the end of the second year, as the *Beagle* sailed into Chiloé, the men aboard *Adventure* noticed the familiar figure of Captain Stokes was missing from his usual position on the quarterdeck. Worn out by the work, and no doubt depressed by the gloom of the surroundings, he had taken his life and had been succeeded by his First Lieutenant, Skyring. However, the commander-in-chief of the station refused to confirm this appointment and promoted his own Flag Lieutenant Fitzroy to command the ship. Robert Fitzroy, who was only twenty-three years old, had joined the Navy at the age of fourteen, and whilst it is fair to say that he was well connected, even powerful relations could not have arranged so early an advancement unless he had shown considerable ability.

The survey carried on, Fitzroy took the *Beagle* southward to chart the western side of the archipelago and anchored inside the islands using whalers to ferry small parties with theodolites and sextants. Christmas 1829 was celebrated whilst straining at the cable in a gale near Landfall Island with one party stranded ashore and it was only after seven days, during which they were attacked by the natives, that they were able to get back on board. Another group was less fortunate as their boat was stolen whilst they were working on an island and they returned to the ship in a basket constructed of reeds and caulked with clay – hence the island's name of Basket Island. A search was mounted for the boat, and although oars and other bits came to light, the boat itself just vanished. It was during the course of the search, and whilst taking hostages in the hope they could be exchanged, that a young twenty-six-year-old native man was brought on board and named York Minster. Later when the *Beagle* set sail for England, he was joined by an eight-year-old girl called Fuegia Basket, a fourteen-year-old boy, Jemmy Buttons, and a twenty-year-old man, Boat Memory.

Fitzroy's worthy intentions in taking these Fuegians to Britain were to provide an education and subsequently repatriate them so they could help their countrymen and women by example. Boat Memory died of smallpox shortly after arrival, a bad omen for the Fuegians, but the others were a great attraction and even met King William IV. Rumours that the Fuegians were probably cannibals naturally aroused intense interest, although Lucas Bridges, who lived in the region all his life, states they had an abhorrence of eating human flesh. Bridges believed the rumour was due to the natives either misunderstanding the question, or saying what they imagined would please their interrogators.

After her first voyage, the *Beagle* underwent a complete refit, during which Fitzroy had the deck raised a foot to improve the accommodation and her performance as a seaboat. She sailed again for Tierra del Fuego on 27th December 1831 with the three surviving Fuegians and Charles Darwin. Missionary zeal was then at its height in Britain and Fitzroy was prevailed upon to take a missionary with him who, it was hoped, and with the Fuegians acting as interpreters, could persuade others to accept Christianity. They arrived at Tierra del Fuego on Christmas Eve, but Fitzroy was in a hurry, and put quickly to sea again. It would have been more prudent to have found a sheltered anchorage as the weather drove them south and on their return they narrowly missed stranding on the Diego Ramirez Islands. The heavy weather persisted, and on 13th January, when sailing under reefed trysails and fore-staysails, they saw three enormous seas approaching.

At ten there was so continued and heavy a rush of wind that even the diminutive trysails oppressed the vessel too much, and they were further reduced. Soon after one, the sea had risen to great height, and I was anxiously watching the successive waves, when three huge rollers approached whose size and steepness told me at once that our seaboat, good as she was, would be sorely tried. Having steerage way, the vessel met and rose over the first unharmed, but her way was checked; the second deadened her way completely, throwing her off the wind; and the third great sea, taking her abeam, turned us so far over that all the lee bulwark, from cat-head to the stern davit, was two or three feet underwater. For a moment our position was critical; but like a cask she rolled back up again, though with some feet of water over the whole deck. Had another sea then struck her, the little ship might have been numbered among the many of her class that have disappeared.

Fitzroy was lucky, he only lost the quarter boat, but a French whaler, the *Magellan*, was driven ashore in Berkeley Sound in the same gale.

The *Beagle* eventually anchored in Goree Roads, on the south-east corner of Isla Navarino close to the channel which now bears her name. A party was launched in the ships boats to land the missionary and the three Fuegians in Jemmy Buttons' tribal area near Ponsonby Sound. Tents were erected and the young missionary was abandoned ashore with stores and the Fuegians whilst Fitzroy sailed into the Beagle Channel and surveyed for ten days. In this short time the camp was overrun by natives, and the missionary's life threatened. The Fuegians, accustomed to a harsh life in an extreme climate, saw brotherly love as a sign of weakness, and reacted as any strong animal will to one who is vulnerable. The three Fuegians quickly reverted to their former way of life, perhaps to divert any threat from themselves. Sadly, Fitzroy collected the failed missionary and the remnants of his stores and sailed away. When he came back a year later, only Jemmy Buttons remained, and although he seemed pleased to see his erstwhile shipmates, he declined to accompany them because he wished to stay with his own people.

Meanwhile in order to speed up work, Fitzroy purchased another ship out of his own pocket, and renamed her *Adventure*. She was an American sealer of 170 tons costing £1,300, and after recruiting additional crewmen, Fitzroy departed from Montevideo with both ships. After wintering again in Montevideo he returned to the Horn via the Falkland Islands which he described as an ideal site for a penal colony. In the meantime Charles Darwin was exploring and collecting samples from the interior of Argentina and just avoided being caught up in General Rosas's revolution. The following autumn the ships went north to Valparaiso and arrived on 22nd July 1834, which gave Darwin the opportunity to explore in the Andes. At this point Fitzroy received notice from the Admiralty that they were not prepared to buy the *Adventure*, pay her running costs or be responsible for the expense incurred in hiring the extra seamen. As a result Fitzroy fell into a fit of depression at the prospect of coping in Tierra del Fuego with just one ship, because although a great deal had been accomplished, there was still much unfinished business. He and the men were tired after a year and a half spent in the desolate channels and some may even have considered desertion unless matters improved. The crisis was resolved by Lieutenant Wickham, Fitzroy's second-in-command, who pointed out that the instructions did not insist on a completed survey, but only that Fitzroy spend as much time as he could spare. The *Adventure* was sold for £1,400 which showed a modest profit, and the *Beagle* went southward again to being a survey of the Chilean coast. Near Cape Tres Montes she was driven into a small bay by bad weather and rescued five men who had deserted from an American whaler during the previous year. Interestingly these men, who had lived off the land, were in better physical shape than the seamen who crewed the *Beagle*.

This was the end of Fitzroy's work around Cape Horn. His surveys, together with those of Stokes, provide the basis of modern charts and are updated by the Chilean Navy. Indeed when a recent survey indicated a discrepancy with the earlier work, it was realised that Stokes and Fitzroy were the more accurate. The *Beagle* headed slowly northwards and it was fortunate she was at sea when the great earthquake of 20th February 1835 destroyed many of the coastal towns, and deposited ships high up the shore. The ship finished her voyage around the world and achieved immortality, not only through her soon-to-be illustrious scientist, but also from the charts and wealth of names she gave to large areas of the Tierra del Fuego archipelago.

6

Whaling and Trading

For 250 years after Magellan sailed into the Pacific, Spain had the monopoly of trade on the Pacific coast of America apart from the occasional raid by pirates or military expeditions. The hub of operations was the town of Panama which had defended communications across the isthmus to Nombre de Dios and later Porto Bello on the east coast. The produce from all over central America was collected here and escorted by a strong fleet of warships back to Spain. Once a year all the profit from the Philippines arrived on the Manilla Galleon, to be added to the haul. These fabled treasure fleets were vital to the Spanish economy and a tempting challenge to her enemies.

Since there was no foreign power established in the Pacific Ocean it was safer for the Spanish to bring this treasure across the Pacific rather than risk an encounter with French, English or Dutch vessels on the Cape of Good Hope route. In Panama the Manilla Galleon's treasure was combined with goods gathered from Valparaiso to California. Even the Río Plata region in modern Argentina was connected to this coastal route by long mule trains traversing the Andes to Peru.

The west coast was scattered with settlements populated by Spaniards, Indians and the inevitable half-castes, all controlled by governors, soldiers and the dreaded Inquisition, which in most cases acted as an extension of the state. The difficulties of rounding Cape Horn, the only route then free of Spanish control, effectively kept foreign trade away from the whole west coast. On the Atlantic seaboard, however, it was impossible to prevent foreigners from trading illicitly with a population starved of European goods.

The first foreign attempt to crack the trade monopoly on the Pacific coast was made in 1699 by the Frenchman Gouin de Beauchesne with two vessels. After an unpleasant passage round the Horn they arrived at Valparaiso to be greeted by gunfire. A *modus operandi* was soon arranged, however, whereby the officials put up a show of resistance but allowed the local merchants to trade. The sale of merchandise imported directly from France was no doubt as welcome to the soldiers and officials as it was to the traders. The voyage was a success, and plans were under way for a second adventure in 1700 when Philip V of Spain issued instructions forbidding further activities. Nevertheless nine years later another fleet commanded by Chabert took the same course, but sailed on to China before returning via Peru and Chile. It is rumoured this fleet arrived home at Morbihan carrying over thirty million francs' worth of gold earned during the voyage.

Commerce was expanding in Europe, and as the monopolies granted by various governments to favoured companies effectively restricted trade with India to all but the chosen few, we have seen how there were always adventurers prepared to look to the Spanish colonies to evade their own national monopolies, despite the risks involved. The attitude of Spanish officialdom varied considerably from port to port and there was no way of telling what reception awaited a ship until it had actually anchored. A governor prepared to turn a blind eye to a foreign ship on one voyage might die or be replaced before it returned a second time, and the new governor might enforce the rules more strictly. Confiscation and prison could easily await the unwary.

Although records are scanty, ships undoubtedly continued to pass around the Horn to trade clandestinely with the merchants of Chile and Peru during the seventeenth and eighteenth centuries. But apart from this, and scientific and military expeditions, there was little incentive to sail through the waters of the Horn; Australia was not colonised until the end of the eighteenth century and trade with India and China mainly used the Cape of Good Hope route.

The first legitimate traders to use the Horn for access to the Pacific were probably from newly populated North America, and at the outset their intentions were not to seek trade with the Spanish territories. Until the late eighteenth century the regular route from North America to the Orient was via the Cape of Good Hope, and the American ship the *Empress of China*, registered in New York, entered this trade in 1784. Four years later two ships, the *Columbia,* captained by John Kendrick, and the *Lady Washington* captained by Robert Gray, started a new trade when they entered the Pacific by way of Cape Horn to purchase furs at Nootka Sound on Vancouver Island. Having obtained a cargo, the *Columbia* sailed to China where she traded the furs for tea, and then returned to New York via the Cape of Good Hope. Other ships followed after the success of this voyage.

Another trade that brought vessels to Cape Horn was whaling which the British started to pursue in the southern Pacific in 1787. The main targets were the sperm, right and bowhead or Greenland whale. Larger whales such as the blue were too big for the contemporary equipment, namely a hand harpoon launched from a 27-foot open boat. Four years later seven New England whalers followed suit and an early American vessel, the *Rebecca*, reported encountering thirty-nine whalers off the Chilean coast in 1792, twenty-one from Britain, eight from Nantucket and nine from Dunkirk, although thirty-three of these had American masters. Initially the ships hunted along the Chilean coast between latitudes 8° and 30° south. Since at that time it was essential to land the blubber and render it to oil in vats ashore, some arrangement must have been made with the authorities to allow this activity. But the introduction on board of huge cauldrons encased in brick, known as tryworks, enabled the ships to hunt further afield over the Pacific. Periodic shore visits were limited to replenishing provisions and fresh water.

Whaling was a dangerous occupation. The whales were approached cautiously as they lay on the surface and when the ship's boat was within range the harpooner stood up and thrust a harpoon into the creature which usually sounded, or dived, sometimes to great depths. The English whale line attached to the harpoon was 120 fathoms or 720 feet long and, owing to the speed of the whale's descent, it was necessary to pour cooling water over the lead where the rope passed over the gunwale. The whale could remain submerged for up to half an hour but when it resurfaced for air the slack on the line was taken up and additional harpoons were launched until the creature was dead. The whale often thrashed around and if its huge tail caught the boat it could be smashed to matchwood, frequently killing or injuring the crew. The carcasses were towed alongside the ship where all the blubber was removed together with the valuable whalebone. The corsetry industry created a demand for the baleen plates through which plankton is strained, because of their strength and flexibility. Once stripped the carcass was normally cast adrift as there were no means of storing any other useful parts. In the very early days before the blubber was boiled in a temporary camp ashore or on board, it was cut into small chunks which were pressed through the bungholes into barrels, a tedious, greasy and smelly process called 'making-off'.

The standard vessel employed for whaling was of a medium size, the dimensions being dictated by the number of whale boats they carried. In the early days this was three, but it later increased to four, and subsequently six, all about twenty-seven feet long and crewed by five men. From an initial tonnage of about 250, the ships grew to a maximum of 450 tons from the 1830s onwards. They were normally of oak construction and particularly solid, but their basic design differed little from contemporary heavy merchantmen; indeed many were straight conversions. Fortunately one of these vessels survives. The *Charles W. Morgan*, which gave eighty years of service, is moored at the Mystic Maritime Museum in Connecticut, and the conditions of life in this hard, foul-smelling occupation are well displayed. Although the accommodation seems relatively spacious, especially when compared with the crowded quarters aboard a warship such as HMS *Victory*, it can hardly be termed luxurious as a home for the whalerman on voyages of up to three years.

In the war of 1812 the American whaling fleet on the Chilean coast suffered badly at the hands of the British whalers who were armed and issued with letters of marque which permitted them to prey on American ships. To prevent these depredations the forty-six-gun frigate USS *Essex*, commanded by Captain David Porter, was sent around the Horn and into the whaling grounds with instructions to attack the British vessels. She captured over twelve ships, including one she named *Essex Junior*, which was armed and equipped as a warship. The *Essex* and her consort were eventually blockaded for six weeks in Valparaiso by the forty-four-gun frigate HMS *Phoebe* and twenty-eight-gun sloop HMS *Cherub*. Commander Porter tried to escape but lost his topmast in the process and surrendered after an action lasting two and a half hours. Most of the British whalers and the *Essex Junior* were recaptured, and the *Essex* was taken into the Royal Navy. However, Porter's raid rattled the British, maybe because they feared another attack, and thereafter their whaling activities in the Pacific went into decline.

There is a nice story concerning a young American midshipman, David Farragut, who was aboard the *Essex* during the battle with the *Phoebe*. Aged twelve years and smarting from his ship's defeat, he was further enraged when a British midshipman claimed his pig as a war prize. The British captain stopped the boys wrestling over it and made them box properly for the pig. Farragut was declared the victor and the pig was returned. Farragut subsequently became the US Navy's first vice-admiral and later full admiral, and is best remembered for his order 'Damn the torpedoes, full speed ahead' when forcing his way into Mobile Bay in 1861 during the American Civil War.

Unlike the British, the American whalers were soon back in business after peace in 1815, and by the middle of the nineteenth century there were over 600 of them regularly hunting in the Pacific. Throughout the century more than 2,000 operated in the area, making on average five voyages each, and this enormous enterprise continued until the outbreak of the American Civil War in 1861. Not all used the Cape Horn route to the expanding whaling grounds, which now extended into the North Pacific, but on average three sailed around Cape Horn for every one that went via the Cape of Good Hope.

American whaling interests might have recovered after the Civil War, but in 1871 the bulk of the fleet was destroyed when it was trapped in the Arctic. Other economic factors were in any case working against whaling by this time. Coal oil or kerosene was now available in quantity and at a competitive price and rising costs generally made whaling a less attractive investment in comparison with the returns from the land-based industries. So the numbers of ships remaining decreased rapidly and by the beginning of the twentieth century there were only twelve whalers left on the American Registry. The traditional trade staggered on for two more decades, and the final expedition sailed from New Bedford in 1922. Uncharacteristically the Americans did not join in the last and greatest slaughter of these magnificent mammals.

What appeared to be diminishing trade had a revival at the beginning of the twentieth century when the Scotsman W. S. Bruce reported whales in profusion around South Georgia. Bruce was unable to raise the finance for a whaling enterprise based there, but in 1904, Captain Carl Larson, who had captained the *Antarctica*, the expedition ship of Otto Nordenskjöld in 1901–3, and after whom the Larson Ice Shelf is named, formed the Compañía Argentina de Pesca and set up a shore processing station at Grytviken Bay. The business boomed and other stations were set up. In 1912 the largest whale ever caught, a blue whale 112 feet in length and weighing close to 100 tons, was landed at Grytviken. Whaling continued here until 1965 when only 239 whales were landed, compared with 7,825 in 1925–6 for example, and the hunting became uneconomic. The industry, based on South Georgia, South Africa and the South American stations had destroyed itself by becoming so efficient that it had reduced many whales species, including the magnificent blues, to near-extinction. Public opinion in most countries has now turned against the trade and it is to be hoped that the numbers will be allowed to build up again without human interference.

Another mammal, the fur seal, was assumed to have become extinct about 1907 through being overhunted, but by the 1930s occasional sightings were being made. The species has recovered dramatically and in 1990s there were thought to be more than one and a half million around South Georgia. The elephant seal escaped the massacre as it was not as valuable as the fur seal, although an adult male could provide a large amount of blubber. Oil taken from seals never rose above ten percent of that obtained from whales and as they could not support an industry on their own, their hunting ceased once whaling became uneconomic.

Whaling ships made up the bulk of commercial traffic passing Cape Horn until the development of the round-the-world route from Europe to Australasia and the removal of Spanish restrictions on trade in their American colonies. The eventual opening up of the western coast of South America to outside trade was caused by events far away in Europe. In 1808 when Napoleon invaded Spain he removed the existing government and all the Spanish colonies were thrown onto their own resources. In 1810 Chile took its first step towards independence and opened its ports to general trade. This independence lasted until 1814 when the royalists regained control. However, having tasted a modicum of freedom, the Chileans quickly tired of the repressions reintroduced by the royalists, and in 1817 an Argentinian, General José de San Martin, led an army over the Andes from Mendoza, defeated the royalists and established Bernardo O'Higgins as supreme ruler of the country. Much of the equipment and many of the ships and men who helped fight these wars of independence came from Europe and North America via Cape Horn. One of the best known was Thomas Cochrane, 10th Earl of Dundonald, who after an illustrious career, had been driven from the Royal Navy in 1814 on a stockmarket fraud charge. In 1817 he took command of the rebellious Chilean naval forces and his capture of the Spanish 40-gun frigate *Esmeralda* in Callao harbour in 1820 was a major influence in confirming independence for Chile. The desire for freedom is infectious and the same year José de San Martin led a Chilean army into Peru and removed the Spanish viceroy. Peruvian independence was declared in 1821. The whole western coast of South America was now open to trade.

Although South America was the source of gold which helped to keep the Spanish Empire solvent, it was a less valuable metal which initially prompted the stimulus for trade with the rest of the world. Copper ore had been mined by the Indians on the western slopes of the Andes in Chile and Peru from early times, and Spanish workings commenced in 1601. The ore was originally brought to the coast on the backs of llamas. Early in the nineteenth century some ship owners, mainly Welsh, built tough little barques especially to carry the ore to Europe. Ore was a heavy cargo and placed great strains on the vessels, which were given deep keelsons to act as shifting boards to prevent the cargo slipping from one side to the other in bad weather. Few of the barques exceeded 500 tons and most were smaller. The outward cargo was usually high quality Welsh coal as although Chile has enormous coal reserves, they are not of good quality. The round trip was renowned for its hardships, but paradoxically the seamen prided themselves on serving aboard ships in this trade as it was considered to provide the finest training in seamanship going.

Guano followed copper ore as the next important export to Europe. Guano is rich in phosphates and ammonia and was recognised as a valuable fertiliser. This commodity, basically seabirds' dung, is present in huge deposits offshore on the Chincha and other islands where the Humbolt current carries plankton northwards from the Antarctic. This provides a rich source of food for fish which in turn support a vast seabird population which has nested without fear of human molestation for hundreds of years. Off Pisco alone the islands are thought to sustain over five million birds, mainly gannets, and it is estimated their consumption exceeds 1,000 tons of fish a day. So large was the bird population that the depth of deposits varied from fifty to 200 feet. For many years it was Peru's prime export. Initially the deposits were dug by labourers recruited from amongst the indigenous peoples, but later the islands were used as escape-proof prisons and the inmates had to perform this unpleasant task. The guano dug on the islands was put into bags and then loaded into lighters which ran a ferry service to large ships at anchor. Clouds of yellow dust covered everything in the vicinity, whilst the smell of ammonia pervaded even the most inaccessible corners of the ships. Sometimes the loading could take as long as three months during which ships remained rolling at anchor. After three months covered in guano dust even Cape Horn must have seemed attractive to the seamen!

In 1830 another valuable cargo was discovered and the export of nitrate ore (better known as saltpetre) commenced from the small fishing village of Iquique in the Tarapaca province of Peru. The trade grew steadily as Europe's demand for nitrates increased for, amongst other uses, the manufacture of explosives. Tarapaca is almost waterless but contains enormous deposits of nitrate of soda which were easily mined from the desert plateau between the Andes and the sea at an altitude of 3,000 feet. By the end of the 1870s the trade was sufficiently vital to become the major cause of a war between Chile and Peru and resulted in the province being ceded to Chile in 1883. As with other heavy cargoes the ore was transported to the coast by pack mules and donkeys, but later a number of light railways were constructed between the diggings and the nearest bay where a ship could ride at her anchors. Caleta Buena, Tocopilla, Taltal, Arica, Iquique, Pisagua and

Antofagosta developed into quite large communities as loading ports for
vessels in the Cape Horn trade.

Initially the small Welsh brigs and barques were sufficient for the
developing trade in nitrates, but as demand grew, larger vessels were brought
onto the run, culminating with the giants of the German Flying P Line,
which dominated the bays and roadsteads packed with sailing vessels. The
ore was loaded in large bags and stowed by expert stevedores who could
drop a bag perfectly into place in the ship's hold to create a pyramid. Once
in place the bags frequently coalesced with their neighbours and had to be
broken out with crowbars at the end of a long voyage. A nitrate cargo was
welcome in one respect as evaporation from the ore killed any rats or mice
lurking in the ship, but it was unfortunately equally dangerous to the
numerous ship's cats! However, the greatest danger from the cargo was
from fire, and once alight it could only be extinguished by water that had
nitrate soaked in it. Barrels of this water were always kept handy when the
cargo was stowed and when possible they were kept on deck whilst under
way. Nevertheless, like coal, nitrate ore was responsible for the loss of
many good vessels by fire.

The *Criccieth Castle* suffered the fate of many sailing ships loaded with
coal when spontaneous combustion took place off the Horn in 1907. The
ship turned round and headed for Montevideo where the fire was extinguished
and the cargo restowed. Possibly this fire weakened the vessel as three
voyages later, when homeward bound from Peru with a cargo of nitrates,
she encountered a heavy gale, which turned out to be the forerunner of three
weeks' solid bad weather. The ship was lying hove-to when a particularly
heavy sea struck under the counter and broke the rudder stock. The rudder,
now loose, banged back and forth with terrific force and eventually sprung
the plating at the stern post, causing leaking so severe that even if the pumps
could have been manned, it is doubtful if they would have kept pace with
the inrushing water. Attempts to jettison cargo to lighten the ship were
abandoned when it was realised that there was by then more water than
cargo in the hold, and the decision was made to abandon ship. The ship's
side was cushioned with sails to prevent the lifeboats being crushed as they
were lowered, and two boats containing the entire crew and the captain's
wife and four-year-old son got away. Course was set for the Falklands,
about 180 miles away, but another severe gale blew up, sinking one of the
boats commanded by the mate. The next day a four-masted barque sailed
past within a mile but did not see the surviving boat or its occupants. It
continued towards the Falklands, slowly losing crew as they died of cold,
and eventually beached near Cape Pembroke where the lighthouse keepers

carried the survivors ashore. They had been in the boat, with one keg of water and no food, in gales and freezing conditions for a week. The captain's family survived and his wife even gave birth to a baby girl two months after they landed.

The Welsh, having been amongst the earliest to trade to the west coast of South America, operated on the nitrate trade long after most British sailing-ship owners sold their fleets. Their route changed, though, and the ships began to make round-the-world voyages with general cargo from Europe to Australia and thence with coal from Newcastle, New South Wales, to the south-western American coast and finally home with nitrates.

When the nitrate ships had safely rounded the Horn on the outward passage with a cargo of manufactured goods or coal, or arrived from Australia with coal, their worries were not necessarily over. The route northwards along the Chilean coast is aided by the wind and current and not particularly difficult unless the wind drops. In a calm, though, the current could push a vessel to leeward, or northward, of her destination. Then a long tack has to be made out into the Pacific followed by a sweep to the south before the coast can be approached again, sometimes adding as much as a month to the passage time. The seabed rises steeply all along the coasts of Chile and Peru, apart from the bays which formed the principal anchorages. In places where the coasts are particularly steep ships might drift ashore in calm weather and run aground to be pounded to pieces by the swell before their anchors could grip. Longer anchor chains were not an option as the chain cable's weight would put enormous strain on the anchoring equipment. In any case, as few of the vessels had steam-powered windlasses, the crew's muscle power would have been insufficient to raise the anchors.

If navigating the coast was tricky, the ships were often no safer when at anchor in port. Earthquakes were a feature of the area and the attendant tidal waves swept anchorages and left many ships high and dry hundreds of yards from the water. The *Beagle* witnessed such a wave at Talcahuano in 1835, which appeared to originate from a submarine volcanic eruption close to the port. The wave left a schooner in the midst of the town's ruins, threw one ship ashore, back out to sea, ashore and back again. Two ships anchored in thirty-six feet of water were whirled round each other so their anchor chains were wrapped three times, and both reported being aground for a while as the water level fell. Land in the area rose three or four feet but, as was often the case, slowly subsided over the next few months.

Iquique was racked by an earthquake in 1866, and completely destroyed in 1877 when a tidal wave finished the destruction left by another earthquake and fire. Arica underwent similar crisis in 1868, 1877 and 1906. During the disaster of 1868 the first movement of water occurred half an hour after the earthquake and was comparatively gentle. The lower part of the town was submerged and ships in the bay grounded. Then a much larger wave appeared some sixty feet high and breaking at its crest. This swept all before it, depositing the *Chanarcillo* of Liverpool ashore 500 yards beyond the normal high-water mark, the Peruvian frigate *Americana* 300 yards inland, and destroying three other vessels with all hands. At Huanillos in 1877, the *Avonmore* was capsized by the tremendous seas generated by a series of shocks. A tidal wave hurtled many of the survivors shorewards and then out to sea again. Not surprisingly the majority were drowned, including the captain's wife and two sons, whose bodies were packed in a box of guano and sent to England for burial. Valparaiso sustained a number of earthquakes and one of the worst, rumoured to have reached ten on the Richter scale, occurred in 1906 when the earth trembled so much that it was impossible to stand. The twenty-seven ships at anchor felt the tremors and all hands were called to stand by for the anticipated tidal wave. No wave materialised on this occasion, but the seamen standing by saw the town's lights suddenly extinguished, and in the following eerie silence, the crash of collapsing buildings coupled with the cries of terrified inhabitants clearly came across the water before fire consumed the ruins. Although these were exceptional, lesser tremors were common, and most ships relied upon paying out all the cable and praying the anchors would hold as the ship was lifted bodily by a wall of water. Failure to release the brake on the anchor cable could lead to hawse pipes being pulled out and the cable slicing through the hull and jamming. This was almost worse than dragging the anchors, as if the anchors held but the cable was not fully paid out, the ship was unable to rise to the wave, which would sweep the decks, as happened to the *Independence* in Pabellón de Pica in 1877.

Although the earthquakes gave some warning of a tidal wave's approach, it was usually insufficient for a sailing ship to prepare and move out to sea. The other menace to shipping, the Norther, was at least slightly more predictable and if sailing ships could not beat out to sea, there was time for steamers to get pressure on the boilers and gain an offing from the coast. The damage caused by these winds, which sometimes reached hurricane strength, was considerable, especially in the crowded anchorages of the nitrate ports. If the anchors held, many of the ships inevitably crashed into each other, causing damage to spars, masts and hulls, and if the anchors failed the ships were driven ashore. The *Foyledale* was discharging lumber in Valparaiso when a Norther arrived and despite having anchors out ahead and astern they had insufficient holding power and the ship went ashore.

The crew, together with the captain's wife and daughter, climbed the mizzen rigging for safety but many, including the two ladies, were lost during the night. Part of the cargo broke adrift and created a bridge across the seventy yards separating the ship from the shore, and four nimble seamen managed to run across, but an apprentice who followed slipped and was drowned. At daybreak a breeches-buoy was rigged, and the remaining crew were rescued. A greater tragedy was created by the sinking of the steamer *Arequipa*, which was raising steam to clear the port when one of the huge metal mooring buoys crashed into the stern and damaged the propeller. The ship lay sideways to the seas, and water poured into the stokehold until it extinguished the boiler fires. Eighty of the 100 persons aboard were drowned, amongst whom was the captain's wife. The ladies paid a high price to accompany their husbands as sea.

The expansion of Chilean and Peruvian trade was not the only source of increased traffic around the Horn. In addition to this and the Chinese trade, vessels began calling at the Pacific islands following whalers' accounts of potential cargoes. Hawaii received various visitors after Cook in 1778, but it was not until 1795 that King Kamehameha I consolidated control over most of the islands and established a firm rule. When traders showed a keen interest in sandalwood, he encouraged barter for this commodity. Ships from the eastern United States sailing to China stopped at the islands to take on the timber which they sold very profitably at their destination. So attractive was the trade that by 1825 the sandalwood forests were all but exhausted. King Kamehameha's reign ended in 1819 after he had thwarted Russian attempts to colonise his kingdom in 1815–16 and eliminated Spanish pirates two years later. In 1820 shortly after his death the first New England missionaries arrived, the islanders adopted Christianity, learned to read and write, and were able to support two newspapers by 1834. The first press on the Pacific coast of America was imported into Oregon in 1839 but it had been exported from Hawaii. This settled country became a source of reliable trade and when the sandalwood ran out it was replaced by sugar. The islands were ideally placed in mid-Pacific to act as a port for repairs and relaxation for crews and, on average, more than one a day arrived there throughout the middle of the nineteenth century.

Although American commercial shipping had been busy in the Pacific for some time the United States Navy did not assert its presence, after the loss of *Essex*, until 1819 when the USS *Macedonian* sailed round Cape Horn to protect American interests and provide security for foreign merchants. This ship was a war prize and taken into the navy in 1812. Under Captain Downes, who had been a lieutenant aboard the *Essex*, she rounded the Horn with her topmasts struck, as was usual to reduce windage and top weight, but with her stunsail booms set. She anchored in Valparaiso 79 days out from Chesapeake Bay. Working alongside HMS *Andromache* which was maintaining a British presence in the area whilst the South American wars of independence continued, the two warships helped to free American and British ships and men from the Spanish blockade and the patriots' press-gangs. This was the foundation of a permanent American occupancy of the Pacific and evolved over the years into their Pacific Fleet. When the *Macedonian* sailed she was relieved by the USS *Constellation*. Later, when steamships entered the fleet, these used the Magellan's Strait as the route to and from their stations until shortly after 1848 when the United States annexed California. Then a naval base was established at Mare Island in San Francisco Bay and ships no longer automatically returned to the east coast at the end of their commissions. Until the opening of the Panama Canal in 1914, however, all the ships joining the fleet had to come from the east via Cape Horn or Magellan's Strait.

A trade in hides from California to the United States east coast developed quite early in the nineteenth century. We are indebted to an attack of measles for one of the finest contemporary accounts of life aboard an American merchant vessel, a hide drogher, in the 1830s. Richard Henry Dana was a student at Harvard University when he contracted the disease which affected his sight and interrupted his studies. A doctor suggested a trip to sea and Dana took the advice literally and signed on before the mast on a brig named the *Pilgrim*. The ship sailed from Boston for the coast of California via Cape Horn in August 1834.

The standard watches of the day, four hours on duty followed by four hours off, assuming there was no call for All Hands, came hard to a man from a gentle background, but he soon settled in, and learned to reef and steer with the best of the crew. The ship took a course between the Falklands and Staten Island and pressed on in the lee of Tierra del Fuego, but once she cleared land to the west a storm approached, presaging its arrival by large black clouds rolling in from the south-west. Dana describes the common experience of a heavy sea building up extremely rapidly, accompanied by heavy sleet, hail and gusty squalls, and the necessity for the crew to claw aloft to reduce sail as the ship plunged, frequently bows under, into the seas. The captain at this stage in Dana's odyssey supplied the men with a glass of grog every time they reefed the topsails, a very welcome refreshment to men whose hands were frozen from the exposed work aloft.

As was the custom when sailing from east to west, the ship remained largely on the starboard tack and beat well to the west before altering course gradually to the north. Navigators by this time were well aware of the east-running current in this area, and no seaman wished to hazard his ship by placing her close to the west coast of Tierra del Fuego where there was no sea room if a storm blew up and, if forced to heave to, she would inevitably run onto the rocks. For the sailors this hard beat to windward against the might of the Southern Ocean meant constant work aloft with sails and ropes stiff with ice, until the captain reckoned he had made enough westing to clear the coast on the opposite tack.

Almost more alarming than the constant storms were the short intervals of calm in which the ship bucked and rolled in the residual swell with the sails slatting and the crew lashing everything tight to prevent wear. The calms were frequently accompanied by thick fog which warned of the possibility of icebergs near by. There are few happenings which are more eerie than sitting in a stationary vessel surrounded by fog. The ship feels as isolated as if it were on another planet, and ears strain for the sound of a fog horn or the lapping of water on ice. There is an air of tension about the deck, sailors speak in soft tones, and everyone knows when in vicinity of the Horn that when the fog lifts it probably means yet another storm is on its way.

The *Pilgrim* was nine days from passing Staten Island until she squared her yards and headed north, a fast passage, lightened by meeting a whaler, the *New England* of Poughkeepsie, whose captain rowed over for the day to compare longitude and news, and darkened by the loss of a sailor who fell from the mast into the sea whilst heavily laden with gear. The boat was launched but the man sank from sight before they reached him. As was the custom, his belongings were auctioned immediately amongst the rest of the crew.

Dana spent a year on the Californian coast whilst the ship discharged her cargo and took aboard hides, the main product of that country. His account of the coast whilst it was a part of Mexico, is fascinating, but of even greater interest is his description of a sailor's life before the mast. Once a sailor had signed articles, he was completely at the mercy of his captain this far from civilisation, and some captains took full advantage of the situation, flogging the men at a whim, well aware that the sailor could not protest to anyone, and if he resisted this unfair treatment he would be charged with mutiny. Dana considered his captain's behaviour so barbaric that he requested an exchange of berths with a seaman from another vessel, the *Alert*, which was engaged in the same trade. The captain, who was no doubt impressed by Dana's family contacts in Boston, allowed the change and so freed Dana from the tyranny on board the *Pilgrim*.

The *Alert* left San Diego on 8th May 1836, and by 1st July was down to the latitude of Cape Horn, but 40° of longitude to the west. This was midwinter in the southern hemisphere and icebergs from Antarctica were encountered in large numbers, necessitating frequent calls for all hands to wear the ship and avoid a collision. Then the wind filled in from the east, a not uncommon occurrence in winter, and for eight days they beat southwards in case the wind changed and Tierra del Fuego became a lee shore. Finally the wind veered south, and before a gale they saw land which was thought to be Cape Horn, but eventually recognised as Staten Island – the ship had no chronometer on board and so could not work out her longitude. The yards were squared to the southerly wind as they set a northerly course between the Falklands and Patagonia, and arrived back in Boston in September, but not before some of the crew were laid low with scurvy, and the *Alert* had to hail another ship for onions and potatoes, the juice of which was squeezed between the swollen gums of the sick men until the swelling subsided sufficiently for them to eat properly again. Dana returned home with his eyesight cured and wrote a classic book, *Two Years Before the Mast*, which he described as the 'voice from the forecastle.'

When Dana visited California, San Francisco was known as Yerba Buena and one of the anchorages for the collection of hides. In 1848 the whole province was ceded to the United States after its war with Mexico and only nine days before the handover James Marshall discovered gold in the Sacramento. In 1847 the town had a population of 447, ten years later it was a city of hundreds of thousands and most of these immigrants came by sea by way of Cape Horn from every country in Europe and the American eastern seaboard. People, their supplies, and ultimately a huge trade, developed as California was opened up and, until the railway was built across the United States, all cargoes came either via Cape Horn or the Isthmus of Panama.

As in California, it was the discovery of gold that led to a huge expansion of what became known as the Colonial trade from England to Australia and New Zealand via the Cape of Good Hope and home round the Horn. Immigrants had been run out to Australia for many years, frequently in appalling conditions, but most of these vessels took the Cape of Good Hope route home since it was considered easier and safer. The first gold strike was made in Australia at Clunes in March 1850, but it was eighteen months before really large deposits began to appear. The news travelled like a flash of lightning. In Melbourne and Geelong, workmen, policemen and even the professional classes, including clergymen, gave up their jobs and went inland. As in San Francisco four years before, ships arrived and immediately lost their crews and sometimes their officers as well. In 1852 the mail steamer had to be loaned seamen from a Naval brig in order to sail at all at a time when seamen were being offered the relatively huge sum of £100 to sign on for a voyage home. Such was the demand for berths out to Australia that existing vessels were taken off the Indian trade and orders and charters were hurriedly placed with the North American owners and builders for large fast clippers similar to those trading round to California. Inevitably shippers, passengers and owners looked to fast passages and this meant taking the Horn route home.

The Colonial trade quickly became as important as any other, as gold and wool began to pour back to Europe, joined by other minerals as they were discovered. Gold was found in Otago in New Zealand in 1861 but five times as many Diggers came from Australia as from Britain and in any case, shipping services had greatly increased by this time.

Ships' reputations as passenger carriers depended upon the comfort of their cabins and the ability of the captains. Fast passages were at a premium and 85 days became a good standard for an outward voyage. The homeward voyage took a little longer but 100 days via the Horn was the average. Later, as the Tea trade lost out to steamers, many of the very fast tea clippers such as the *Cutty Sark* and *Thermopylae* joined the Colonial wool trade and these times were reduced by fifteen days, helped by the competition to reach London for the January wool sales. The *Thermopylae* showed the way in 1879–80 on her first wool trip with a passage of 81 days from Sydney to London in a fleet of twenty-three ships, six days faster than any other. The *Cutty Sark* did not join the fleet until the 1883–4 season when she made a passage of 82 days, five days faster than her rival, in a fleet of thirty-three. The following year *Thermopylae* won in 79 days but in 1885–6 *Cutty Sark* achieved the extraordinary speedy run of 72 days, five ahead of *Salamis* and seven faster than *Thermopylae*. The fastest run of 71 days, was by *Cutty Sark* in 1887–8. The penalty for not making London in time for the auctions was a three-month delay, which meant warehousing the cargo in the interim and heavy costs as a result. The wool clippers, as they became known, were often loaded so that the fastest sailed last, thus evening out the odds with the slower vessels and making for a better race.

Trade to Chile and Peru was showing a steady increase and owed much to coastal shipping, which was the only practical method of communications in the days before railways and passable roads. About 1830 a young American, William Wheelwright, bought a sixty-ton schooner named the *Fourth of July* and began a packet service along the coasts of the two countries. Wheelwright had already founded and lost one mercantile business in Chile, but he was an energetic person who regarded one failure as experience and the basis of the next enterprise. His packet service proved popular, especially as land transport along the Chilean coastline was beset by physical difficulties. The service expanded, but realising that the calms and light southerly winds made a predictable service impossible, he attempted to interest local businessmen in organising a steamer company to supply a more reliable enterprise. Unable to raise the required capital locally, or in his own country, he turned to Britain for support and raised sufficient capital to order two 700-ton paddle-wheel steamers, the *Peru* and the *Chile*.

The ships left Britain separately, but rendezvoused at Rio de Janeiro and proceeded from there in company. They anchored at Port Famine, scene of Sarmiento's ill-fated settlement, and, having negotiated Magellan's Strait, headed for Talcahuano. The passage through the strait had been a calm one, but once past Cabo Pilar a storm separated the two vessels. The *Peru* reached Talcahuano seven days before the *Chile* and whilst she waited, kept her boilers going on local coal dug out of the cliffs. The two ships arrived together at Valparaiso on 16th October 1840 after an outward voyage of 52 days.

Thus was born the Pacific Steam Navigation Company, whose services were to contribute so much to the opening up of the west coast of Southern America. The first years were full of practical complications, which were largely overcome by Wheelwright's energy and the initiative shown by his senior captain, Captain Peacock. Finding coal for the steamers was an immediate worry. The best quality Welsh steam coal, exported for the new service by sailing ships via Cape Horn, proved unsuitable, and at one stage the two ships were reduced to using wood to fire the boilers. But Wheelwright, remembering the *Peru*'s outward voyage, started to mine the slightly better quality coal at Talcahuano, and soon had his supplies assured. The company grew with the local economy, and for many years provided the only serious communications along the narrow coastal belt between the Andes and the sea which makes up the greater part of Chile.

The early years were not without other incidents and the new company's agents in Lima were nearly the cause of a diplomatic row when they refused the President of Peru passage in one of the ships. As usually happened in such emergencies, Wheelwright himself took charge and rushed to Callao to save the day. Despite many such teething troubles the business prospered and the company soon extended its routes to open a passenger, mail, and high-value-freight cargo service from Panama to Europe which linked in with all the ports as far south as Coronel. All the ships were built in Britain, however, and had to travel out to the coast by way of Magellan's Strait.

The *Chile* and *Peru* were not the first steamers on the coast although they can claim to be the first intended for commerce. Admiral Cochrane had brought out the *Rising Star*, a full-rigged ship but fitted with an auxiliary engine for the fledgling Chilean Navy in 1822. A second steamer, the *Telca*, arrived under sail and her engines were fitted in Guayaquil in 1825. On the first trip to Callao she ran into fog and out of fuel and the passengers complained so loudly that the frustrated captain blew up the ship by firing a pistol into a barrel of gunpowder. Only one seaman survived the resulting explosion, a drastic method of dealing with difficult passengers!

The steamers' ability to make voyages without being delayed by the vagaries of the wind, and so provide a regular service, ensured their adoption. In 1848 the first American steamer company, the Pacific Mail Company, set up to run a service between New York and Colon in response to a subsidy from Congress, sent its first paddle steamer, the *California*, round through Magellan's Strait to launch its service. She was fortunate enough to arrive just as the great Californian gold rush started and made an immediate profit. Two sister ships, the *Oregon* and *Panama*, followed in 1849.

In the meantime the Pacific Steam Navigation Company extended its services from the Isthmus of Panama down the whole coast of western South America and passengers from Europe took a ship to the eastern side of the isthmus and then travelled by train to the west coast where the PSNC steamer awaited them. The Panama railway was opened in 1855, creating a speedy method of crossing the isthmus, and steamers began making their way round to the American west coast, usually via Magellan's Strait, to start services connecting with the whole Pacific basin. In 1856 the PSNC were one of the first companies to introduce the new compound steam engine which halved the consumption of coal for the ton/miles travelled and thus made their service more competitive and profitable. Despite these savings, the expansion of the company's fleet created a huge demand for coal which could not be supplied from local sources. One interesting solution to this was an agreement with the government of Peru to charter twenty sailing ships a year to carry guano to Europe and on the return voyage, of course, the ships came loaded with good-quality Welsh steaming coal.

The expansion of the coast trade was not achieved without paying a high price. Many of the Pacific Steam Company's ships were wrecked or damaged in the early years before good charts. Repairs were very difficult, but the company found a solution by building its own workshops, capable of almost rebuilding an entire ship if necessary. In 1866 at Callao an enormous floating dock was assembled with sections shipped out from Glasgow. It displaced 3,000 tons but could handle a ship of twice that tonnage, which showed considerable foresight since the company did not build a ship of over 6,000 tons until 1899.

So far all trade to the west coast was either by sailing ship around the Horn or by steamer to Panama and then steamer again down the coast. In 1866, the Pacific Steam Navigation Company had a dispute over rates with the owners of the Panama railway who they believed were taking a disproportionate amount of profit for the journey and they threatened to start a direct steamer service from Britain through the Strait of Magellan to Valparaiso if the share of proceeds was not distributed more equably. This threat was ignored by the Panama Railway Company and so new ships were ordered and a direct service commenced in 1868.

The company had been carrying mails since 1845 and had a number of government contracts which guaranteed payment if the terms of an agreed service were reached. Hitherto the mails had either gone via the Panama route or overland from Montevideo and Buenos Aires, but with the opening of the direct monthly service from Europe to Valparaiso in 1869 an alternative route became possible and the company applied to the Post Office in Britain and offered to take mail and newspapers straight to the south-west coast. Their application was successful and the service was inaugurated by the *Patagonia* the same year. The contract called for a monthly sailing in each direction with calls at Rio de Janeiro, Montevideo and Valparaiso. The contract time for the voyage from Liverpool to Valparaiso was set at thirty-nine days, less than half that required by a sailing ship. The advantage of holding a mail contract lay not just in the prestige but also in the attractive financial inducements that went with it. The PSNC were doubly fortunate since they not only obtained the mail contract for Valparaiso, for which there was no competition, but also the Rio de Janeiro and Montevideo contracts because they could give a faster service to those ports en route to the south-west. The direct service was now extremely profitable, an indication as to how much trade had grown between the south-west coast of America and Europe in a period of just over thirty years.

Naturally, covetous eyes were cast towards this thriving business and attempts were made by other companies to enter into competition. Ismay, Imrie & Company advertised the steamer *Republic* for Valparaiso in 1872 and the Pacific Steam Navigation Company responded immediately by announcing that their latest steamer, the *Tacora,* would sail at the same time. Great interest was aroused by the race but unfortunately the *Tacora* was wrecked near Montevideo. Ismay, Imrie & Company won that race, but they failed to gain a foothold on a coast where the Pacific Steam Navigation Company were too well established. The PSNC was now the largest operator of steamships in the world and their fleet was greater in gross tonnage than the entire navy of the United States of America.

As the steamer service became safer and speedier passengers and expensive cargoes to and from Southern American transferred to them, leaving the bulk cargoes such as coal, guano and nitrates to the sailing ships. The Californian trade was similarly affected. The opening of the trans-continental railway across the United States supplied an even quicker passenger service than the Panama route, but the expense and lack of capacity on this service ensured that wheat, lumber and coal continued to be handled by Cape Horners for several decades.

Although the steamship route from Europe to the west side of South America went via the Magellan Strait and so was protected from the greybeards which sweep around the Horn, the strait was still extremely hazardous. The PSNC's *Santiago,* of 1,631 tons was wrecked in the strait in 1869 and the *Cordillera* in 1884. In 1889 the *Cotopaxi,* of 4,022 tons, was rammed by the German steamer *Olympia.* Captain Hayes of the *Cotopaxi* ordered full steam ahead and steered the ship for a nearby beach where she grounded just as the boilers were extinguished. The crew and passengers turned to and shifted cargo from the ship's fore part to the after end until the damaged area was above water and then, using boiler plate which was being carried as cargo, the ship's engineers managed to make a patch. Having raised steam, the *Cotopaxi* got under way again and took the Messier Channel after passing Cape Pilar. Here she proved there is no justice in this world as she struck an uncharted rock while making 13 knots and sank within ten minutes. Although the losses amongst the steamers never rose to the level of the sailing ships, the Magellan Strait continued to take a toll and the Pacific Steam's vessel *Lima* was lost there as late as 1910.

The increase in trade to South America caused changes to the traditional pattern. By 1850 Spain had lost her premier position as Chile's main trading partner and was replaced by England, France and Germany, with Valparaiso as the main port on the South American west coast. Copper ore, guano and silver were the chief exports but nitrates were growing in importance. Output was only 8,000 tons in 1830, but accounted for sixty per cent of all exports by 1885 and production exceeded two million tons by 1910, enough to give full cargoes for 1,000 sailing vessels a year. Sailing around the Horn for a cargo of nitrates from western South America, or WSA as it was known, was to be one of the most common routes for sailing ships and one that survived right through to the end of the age of sail.

7

The Clipper Ships

In most people's imagination, the great era of sail around Cape Horn was dominated by the graceful, hard-driven clipper ships. They are rightly seen as man's most beautiful creation in sail, but wrongly as the dominant or most efficient of sailing merchant ships. The age of the clippers lasted only a short period: in the United States for ten years between 1845 and 1855, and in Britain a little longer from 1845 to 1870. Comparatively few were built but because of the public interest and the records they set, many of which still stand for sailing vessels, they, more than any other type of vessel, are seen as the archetypal Cape Horner.

Cape Horners from the early nineteenth century until the introduction of the clipper ship, whether built in North America or Britain, were remarkably alike owing to the common tonnage rules which prevailed and were used for calculating port registration charges. The revised British tonnage rules of 1773 were followed by very similar rules in the United States. The formula for calculating the tonnage of a ship was:

$$\frac{(L - 3/5B) \times B \times \frac{1}{2}B}{94}$$

Where L = Length of keel from fore side of stem to aft side of sternpost
   B = maximum beam.

These rules, which penalised beam, resulted in bluff-bowed, full-bodied, dumpy-looking craft, with relatively narrow beams but great depth of holds. The rules lasted until 1836 when the tonnage calculation was changed to the basis of 100 cubic feet of cargo-carrying space equalling one ton, the system still in use today for cargo vessels. Another factor which encouraged square cross-sections was that dry docks were rare and many ports were tidal. As a result vessels were designed to dry out between tides and were constructed with flat floors and a box-shaped midship section to allow them to sit upright. Hulls were of wood, largely fastened with wooden trenails. To prevent water from entering between the hull planks, tarred teased rope called oakum was hammered into the gaps and then covered with pitch. The ships 'worked' at sea, the term to describe the movement of the planks in relation to each other, so water was always seeping in somewhere, giving the carpenter a full-time job attending to the caulking, and the crew regular employment at the pumps.

Although some merchant vessels were fully rigged ships, such as the East Indiamen, the most common type of trading vessels were the brig and barque (the barquentine did not make an appearance until after 1830) and few exceeded 500 tons' displacement. There was little call for larger ships except on the East Indies run where cargo was collected and stored by the company until a full load was available. Elsewhere the amount of cargo was limited by the relatively low production in the hinterlands compared to modern times and the difficulties of transportation to the ports.

Masts were supported by numerous heavy natural rope shrouds (iron wire was not economic at this stage) and the sails were loose woven flax which was inherently baggy. The ships were poor sailers, requiring a strong wind to make good progress, and were extremely inefficient to windward. In fact their performance was only marginally better than the ships of two centuries before. For a passage from east to west around the Horn, they could not expect to make good any course better than 90° to the wind, and they relied on the trade winds, or if they were travelling in the opposite direction, changes in wind direction caused by a succession of fronts, to enable them slowly to tack their way ahead. Obviously they chose the tack which was closest to the desired course except when in the vicinity of land, where lee shores were avoided at all costs. This is why many ships sailing from India to Europe went to latitude 45° south, nearly 600 miles south of the Cape of Good Hope, when rounding that point, in order to make westing but with searoom.

There had been little inducement for the British to improve their ships until after the prolonged Napoleonic Wars. To counter French privateers the Royal Navy operated a convoy system throughout the war whilst English ships were within enemy waters and this meant that every ship in any particular convoy had to keep to the speed of the slowest. Although at the same time the Americans had needed faster ships to evade the British blockade, by the end of the 1812–1815 war the United States merchant fleet was decimated and when peace with Britain returned replacement tonnage was built largely on the old lines. The United States recovered slowly from her war with Britain, but gradually acquired a fleet which came close to rivalling that of her recent antagonist.

So the merchant ships which were the foundation of trade around the Horn were heavy, indifferent sailers, and required a large crew to maintain the rigging and sails and man the pumps to keep them afloat. Unlike modern steel vessels, they were organic structures, and could not be left unattended even if their crews were paid off and they were awaiting a cargo. Timber was becoming short in Britain but the availability of huge quantities of timber in North America gave rise to a large shipbuilding industry there and much of Canada's production was for British owners. (It reached a third of total ships built and half the tonnage in 1840.)

After 1815 with the introduction of industrialisation and the recovery of world trade, the requirement for larger ships became logical. Larger vessels made economic sense as the number of crew to man a ship of 600 tons was less than double that of a 300-tonner. Larger vessels were usually longer and there is an empirical formula that says longer vessels will always sail faster than shorter ones, everything else being equal, and more mileage per annum meant more freight could be earned.

In 1836 the British tonnage laws were amended so that they no longer favoured long narrow deep vessels, but it was some time before the effect of the change was noticeable. The United States tonnage laws were not altered until 1864, but the urge for speed, especially on the North Atlantic and Californian trades, produced a new ship which, if not as economic from the tonnage dues point of view, more than compensated for this in speed and carrying capacity.

The impetus for faster vessels originates from the requirement for speedier passages for valuable cargoes such as tea from China where a large premium could be earned for the first cargo to arrive home. Passengers eager to reach the gold fields where fortunes could be made overnight were also prepared to pay a premium for a quick passage. The fastest ships were the new clippers employed on the tea run and many of these were quickly transferred to the Californian trade around the Horn where more freight could be earned. Their immediate popularity and profitability encouraged shipowners and builders to produce similar vessels, all built for speed rather than cargo-carrying capacity. They became known as clippers because the title had become synonymous with speed.

The term clipper was originally applied to the fast schooners from Maryland and Virginia which were called Baltimore Clippers. They developed during the war of 1812 where speed was again at a premium to avoid the British cruisers and they were used subsequently for the slave trade between Africa and the United States. The hulls were longer, with less freeboard than conventional vessels, the stem was sharply raked and they had overhanging counter sterns, all of which reduced the wetted surface of the hull (or the amount of actual hull in the water for a given deck area) and thus reduced resistance. Square rig was a long time coming to the class and the first of these vessels to adopt it was the *Ann McKim* of 494 tons built in 1833 although it is claimed she owed her origins to contemporary French Naval ships which were constructed on the principle of a long, lean hull with three tall raking masts and were then considered the fastest sailing vessels afloat.

Like most developments in naval architecture the clipper evolved rather than suddenly appeared on the scene in its ideal form. The first true clipper ship is usually recognised as the *Rainbow*, built in New York in 1845 for the China trade, to the design of John W. Griffiths. The particular features of her design were the long straight keel, slightly raked stern-post with a counter and transom stern, moderately sharp, convex bow entry and full-rigged ship rig. Her dimensions were 160' 9" between perpendiculars, 31' 8" beam, and 19' 5" depth and she displaced 1,043 tons. Her design provoked a certain amount of comment, not all of it complimentary, but she soon gained an enviable reputation for fast passages to confound her critics. Unfortunately she went missing with all hands in 1848, but by then her main features had already been copied by other builders. Her owners were so pleased with her that they had another, slightly larger vessel built to Griffiths' design, the *Sea Witch*. This vessel still holds the record of 77 days for a sailing ship between Hong Kong and New York, and on one occasion averaged 263½ miles a day for ten days.

The fast and profitable passages of these ships on the China run, as well as the *Oriental* and *Samuel Russell* which were built along similar lines but to another designer's plans, encouraged more owners to copy them. By 1850 most of the famous shipbuilders on the North American east coast were turning out clippers in response to the demand of the Californian trade.

Of all the designers and builders of clippers Donald McKay is perhaps best known. His *Flying Cloud, Staghound, Sovereign of the Seas, Great*

Republic, Lightning, James Baines, Champion of the Seas and *Donald McKay*, (the last four were British Black Ball Line ships and used for the Liverpool – Melbourne run) were all masterpieces. Until recently, the records for a sailing ship from New York to the Equator and New York to Cape Horn were held by the *Great Republic*, 15 days 19 hours in 1856 for the former and 45 days 17 hours in 1856–7 for the latter. *Flying Cloud* held the record from Cape Horn to San Francisco of 39 days set in 1854, and New York to San Francisco of 89 days the same year. These records stood until 1989.

Flying Cloud's dimensions demonstrate how ships' sizes increased in response to the demands of the Cape Horn route to California. She displaced 2,376 tons, carried 25,000 square feet of sail, an overall length of 225 feet, (waterline 209½ feet), a beam of 40' 8" and a draft of 20'.

The *Great Republic* caused a sensation even before she was launched. Donald McKay built her on spec with the intention she should be the largest, fastest and finest sailing ship afloat. She was launched on 4th October 1853 in Boston and the day was declared a public holiday in honour of the occasion. Her rig was unusual and enormous for the time. She was given a four-masted barque rig, called a shipentine in the United States. Her mainmast was 228 feet high, and the mainyard 120 feet long and 28 inches in diameter. Her total sail area was 15,653 square yards (140,877 square feet). She had four decks with eight feet between them and her registered American tonnage was 4,555 tons, nearly twice that of *Flying Cloud*. The planned complement was 100 men and thirty boys.

History has been kind to the memory of *Great Republic*, but in reality she had a very checkered career and no one will ever know how she might have performed as Donald McKay designed her. After completion, she was sailed to New York to load for Liverpool, but when ready to sail on Boxing Day 1853 she was set afire by sparks from a neighbouring bakery. Although she was burnt to the water's edge, it was decided to rebuild her but minus one deck, which reduced the tonnage to 3,356 tons, and with 17 feet cut from the lower masts and 20 feet from the main spar. Her first voyage was to Europe, where she was too deep draughted to enter any of the docks in Liverpool or London. Her next voyage was under a French charter to transport supplies to the Crimea and it was not until December 1856 that she joined the Cape Horn trade to California, but with her jigger mast removed to give her a ship rig. Despite this she took only 92 days on her first voyage, averaging over 19½ knots in a broad reach for a number of hours. No cargo of sufficient size presented itself in San Francisco, so she sailed to Callao to load 4,500 tons of guano for London. However, even ships of the

Great Republic's size were mere playthings to the Cape Horn greybeards and south of the Horn a sea fell aboard with such force that it stove in the deck and broke four deck beams. Sea water reached the guano cargo and the ship's provisions were so tainted that she had to call into Port Stanley for replacements.

Two further voyages were made on the Cape Horn run, then the ship was chartered to the Union Government as a transport in the Civil War. There was a problem concerning her ownership since the majority of the shares were owned by Southerners, but this was resolved when A. A. Low and Brother bought them out. After being put aground on two occasions whilst engaged in war work, the ship was released and returned briefly to the Cape Horn trade for one trip, during which she narrowly missed being intercepted by the Confederate ship *Alabama*, before being laid up for two years and then sold. Her new owners from Nova Scotia sold her for £3,500 to the Merchants' Trading Company of Liverpool in 1868, and she ran on various trades until 1872 when close to Bermuda, she developed a leak and was abandoned with twelve feet of water in the hold.

Unfortunately in the rush to build the American clippers not all were well constructed. With the hard driving that was a feature of the era, many were soon strained so badly that extensive repairs were necessary. Although some of the clippers lasted over thirty years, for the majority their economic life was short or they became victims of the American Civil War. Two famous ships which wore well were the *Young America* and the *David Crockett*, both launched in 1853, probably the apogee of American clipper building when over 100 such ships were launched. The *Young America* is reported to have cost $140,000, but measured only 1,439 tons, so she was expensive to build, but perhaps the price reflects the quality of her construction. She earned $86,000 freight on her maiden voyage to San Francisco, and was recognised throughout her life as a good earner. Apart from the jibboom being broken on her third voyage around the Cape in 1856, the worst damage she sustained was in 1868 when a Pampero wind caught her aback near the River Plate and removed most of the upper masts. Captain Cummings had the choice of sailing into Montevideo for repairs or carrying on for California, and he chose the latter. This decision was all the more courageous since the cargo of railway lines was believed to have shifted and the ship was half full of water. For a week the crew worked to rig jury sails before the ship pressed on, finally arriving eleven weeks after her partial dismasting. The damage had no permanent effect on the ship's speed, because two years later she set the current record for a passage between San Francisco and New York of 83 days. Her end came in 1886 when, under the Austrian flag and renamed the *Miroslav*, she was posted missing on a voyage from Delaware to Fiume. The *David Crockett*, of 1,547 tons, did make her debut in the Cape Horn trade and stayed there until 1857. That year she had two weeks' beating round that famous point against westerly gales, during which her maindeck was swept bare. She lasted until 1899, but for her final ten years served ignominiously as a coal barge in Philadelphia.

The end of clipper building in America came as a result of two factors in 1855. Firstly the gold rush was coming to an end, but the opening of the railway across the Isthmus of Panama attracted away both the passenger and high premium cargoes. The principal cargoes left for the Cape Horners became bulk grain from California and nitrate ore from Chile and Peru. Since neither of these paid a premium for a fast passage the clippers were replaced by a more efficient cargo-carrying vessel with a fuller hull form which carried a greater cargo for its length.

On the other side of the Atlantic, the first sharp-ended vessel was the schooner *Scottish Maid*, built by Alexander Hall & Co. of Aberdeen, but it was the loss of the East India Company's China trade monopoly that led to the first extreme British clipper in 1850, called the *Stornoway*. She was smaller than her American counterparts, as were most subsequent British clippers, but by no means less speedy. As a generalisation it might be said that the large American clippers would usually produce a better day's run before the strong winds of the Roaring Forties; the British clippers tended to compensate by having a much better light-weather performance. Since the clippers of the two nations seldom met to race there are few direct comparisons but analysis of the voyage times indicates very even performances.

Both varieties of clipper, the small British and the large American, were originally developed independently for the tea trade, but whereas the Americans stopped building the out-and-out clipper after 1855, the British persevered until shortly after the opening of the Suez Canal in 1869. The famous *Thermopylae*, for example, perhaps the fastest clipper ever, was only 991 tons and made her debut in 1868. She sailed around Cape Horn when the tea trade was abandoned to steam and was then engaged on the Australian wool run to Britain, setting the existing record of 59 days from London to Melbourne.

Although the clipper was an extreme type, many of their design and construction features were incorporated into and influenced the general cargo carriers. Greater lengths, finer entries and sterns, broader beams, and shallower holds became the norm. Wire was adopted for rigging as improvements in its manufacture made it economic and masts and spars were usually iron. Sails were improved with the use of more tightly woven flax or cotton which gave a better shape and enabled ships to sail closer to the wind. The latter had very obvious benefits wherever the vessel was required to beat, as when doubling the Horn from east to west.

All these features allowed builders to create larger vessels with more efficient rigs and thus kept the sailing ship competitive against the improving steamers at a time of rapidly expanding world trade. British sailing-ship tonnage grew from 3,400,000 tons in 1850 to 4,200,000 tons in 1860. United States sailing-ship tonnage rose from 2,900,000 to 4,400,000 during the same years. Other countries showed similar expansion, but mainly in wooden sailing ships: Norway's from 300,000 to 560,000, France's from 675,000 to 930,000, and the Canadian fleet, largely based in Nova Scotia, rose to a million tons. The only sizeable steamship fleet was under British registration, and that went from 170,000 to 450,000 tons, but was mainly employed on mail and ferry runs. At this time steamships relied on sail whenever practical as the engines were inefficient and needed huge quantities of coal, much of which was stockpiled by sailing ships at coaling stations placed at strategic points all over the world. In 1860 the bulk of the world's trade was still carried in 25,600 sailing ships. Nevertheless by this time steamers were encroaching on the more profitable routes and taking over most of the local trade along the coastline of southern America.

Competition from the United States merchant marine disappeared during the Civil War. Much of her shipping was destroyed or transferred to foreign flags and when the war finished the need to replace this tonnage using iron or steel, then highly expensive in the United States, meant that east coast shipyards were no longer competitive. The replacement problem was aggravated by a self-defeating law designed to protect the local shipbuilding industry which forbade the purchase by United States citizens of cheaper foreign vessels. As always, this protectionism may have kept the shipyards in business but the quantity of orders fell as American owners found they could not pay uncompetitive prices. The vacuum created by the inevitable American withdrawal was largely filled by the British.

There was another economic plus for the British. The United States was a rapidly expanding country with an enormous flood of immigrants coming in from Europe. The needs of these people were met by imports whilst the economy recovered from war, but there was a shortage of export cargoes for their ships. The British, on the other hand, were the world's leading suppliers of high-quality steam coal, and there was an increasing demand for this commodity everywhere, not just to service steamships, but for many industrial purposes. As a result British sailing ships always had an outward

cargo and they returned home with bulk cargoes – wheat from Australia
and California, wood from Australia, copper, nitrates and guano from Chile
and Peru – and could therefore trade profitably on nearly all routes.

Nevertheless the Americans were not driven completely from the seas
and their designers still had one or two tricks up their sleeves. As the Civil
War came to a close in the mid 1860s, they produced a new type of ship for
the Californian grain trade. With the coming of the Trans-American railway
even the Panama route had ceased to be able to compete but there was an
expanding amount of trade that could not all be carried on the railway.
What was now needed was a large and powerful cargo carrier with a good
turn of speed that was capable of weathering Cape Horn with an economical
crew. This led to the introduction of the 'Down Easter'. Although this type
resembled the clippers in outline, they were not so sharp in the ends and had
little dead-rise, which made them fuller bottomed to enable larger cargoes
to be carried. The name came from the Down East states of New England,
particularly Maine and the provinces of eastern Canada where this type
were principally built using the vast resources of local timber.

The *Glory of the Seas* has been described as the last of the American
clippers although she might well be called the first of the Down Easters.
She was the last merchant ship to be built by Donald McKay in 1869. Like
all contemporary American ships she was constructed of oak, her planking
six inches thick, and her frames 11 inches square. She had three decks, each
of eight feet, and a carrying capacity of 4,000 tons, not much less than the
Great Republic of sixteen years earlier. Ship rigged, and, typical of American
vessels, she crossed a skysail over the single topgallant, her sail area
amounted to 72,000 square feet. Like other McKay ships she was built on
spec and her first voyage was under the builder's ownership after which,
when she had proved herself, she was sold. The outward passage from New
York to San Francisco took 120 days and then she took 112 days from there
to Liverpool. Her best time from New York to San Francisco was 95 days,
only six slower than the record, and from San Francisco to Liverpool 103
days, not as good as some of the clipper ships, but certainly not slow.

The *Glory of the Seas* was still afloat in 1910, forty-one years after she
was launched, when a steamer ran into her. But so tough and well built was
the old ship that it was the steamer which was dry docked for repairs. From
1913 she was employed as a cannery ship and her end came in 1923 when
she was burned for the copper used in her construction, despite an effort by
ship lovers to save her.

One of the strangest vessels ever to sail the Cape Horn route was the
Three Brothers (formerly the *Vanderbilt*) and purchased by the Howes

Brothers at a government auction in 1873. She had initially been designed for Commodore Vanderbilt in 1857 as a paddle-wheel steamer for his Atlantic run, and was considered to be the fastest steamer afloat for a while, setting a new record of 9 days 8 hours from New York to the Needles. She was presented to the US Navy in 1862 and saw service as a warship armed with fourteen guns. She narrowly missed meeting the *Alabama* off Capetown in 1863, and escorted the monitor *Monadnock* round Cape Horn to San Francisco in 1866 where she was laid up. The Howes brothers removed the machinery and gave her a ship rig which, with a registered tonnage of 2,932 tons, made her one of the largest sailing ship in the world. She left San Francisco loaded with a cargo of 5,000 tons' weight of grain and after an uneventful passage round the Horn reached Le Havre in 111½ days. For the rest of her life she ran on the grain trade before being sold as a coal hulk in Gibraltar in 1885.

The latter part of the nineteenth century was the sailing ship's hey-day, during which it is often reckoned to have reached the pinnacle of perfection. The opening of the Suez Canal in 1869 forced sail away from many of the traditional routes as steamers travelled more quickly and reliably from Europe to India and the Far East via the canal than sail could by way of the Cape of Good Hope or Cape Horn. Only where the canal gave no advantage could sail remain competitive and as the last decades of the nineteenth century passed sailing vessels became more efficient and more economic, with the introduction of larger vessels and cut-down rigs. Large topsails, for example, required many hands, but if the sail was divided into two, an upper and lower topsail, fewer men were needed to handle an individual sail. Topsails and even topgallants were divided, although not on American ships, which were easily distinguishable by the deep topgallants until the demise of sailing ships. Sails that provided slight speed benefits for a great deal of work, such as stunsails, also almost completely disappeared to reduce the crew's workload. Naturally no one actually suggested that the men's lives be any easier, but shipowners benefited by reducing manpower and therefore their costs.

Most sailing ships of this era never expected to handle all sails simultaneously and it was supposed that sail would be increased or decreased by the men moving from one sail to the next. The only danger came when a sudden squall hit the ship and it was impossible to remove all the sails in a hurry. On these occasions many sails could be blown out, or, if they were new and held, the ship might end up on her beam-ends with the risk of the cargo or ballast shifting dangerously which could lead to the vessel being abandoned.

Iron, which was introduced for strengthening purposes in some seventeenth-century Indiamen, came increasingly to be employed as a construction material particularly by the British. First there were composite ships, with iron frames, beams, knees, stem and sternposts, and later the whole structure was built in this material. More efficient iron, and later steel wire, enabled rigs to be increased and double topsails and topgallants were introduced to provide greater overall sail areas which could still be handled by men. Sailing ships might carry five or more square sails per mast instead of the three which had been common half a century before. The newer iron ships differed considerably from the earlier wood and composite vessels. They were longer and narrower for the equivalent tonnage, with less freeboard, but with a raised forecastle and poop instead of the flush deck so common in the tea clippers. Steel followed iron as a building material, the first steel ship being the *Altcar* from Liverpool in 1864, although it was not common in sailing ships until the 1880s. Although steel was more malleable iron appears to have been superior for hull construction, or the iron ships of the 1870s were better built, since many of the iron ships of that period far outlasted the later steel vessels. The British iron- and steel-built ships, designed and produced by such famous yards as Harland and Wolf, Barclay Curle, Russell's and Steel's, were every bit as fine as the Down Easters although they tended to be slightly smaller, and lacked the hard-driven reputation.

The first American iron sailing vessel did not appear until 1883 when the *Tillie E. Starbuck* was launched for Mr W. H. Starbuck, at Chester, Pennsylvania. She was 270 feet overall, with a 42-foot beam and a deadweight capacity of 3,750 tons. She was rigged as a ship, with double topsails, single topgallant, and three standing skysail yards. Although slower than most of her wooden contemporaries, she served regularly on the East West United States run until 1907 when she was lost off Cape Horn on a voyage from New York to Honolulu and the crew, with one exception, were rescued by the British vessel *Cambuskenneth*. Her owners were obviously satisfied as they ordered another during the same year, the *T. F. Oakes*. This vessel gained a name for slow passages and once took 195 days between New York and Cape Horn. On another voyage from Hong Kong to New York in 1896 she was blown off course by a typhoon and the captain decided to sail via Cape Horn instead of the Cape of Good Hope. Cape Horn was reached after 168 days, but at this point only the captain, his wife and the two mates were left on their feet, the rest of the crew being down with scurvy. Food was obtained from a passing vessel and the ship staggered on with the captain's wife steering whilst the three men handled the sails.

Eventually when the situation had become even more desperate, the British tanker *Kasbek* sighted her, took her in tow and lent some crew to assist them. She dropped anchor off the Quarantine Station in New York on the 259th day out.

A typical large cargo carrier of the latter part of the century was the *Nord*, built on Clydeside for the French company A. D. Bordes in 1889. A four-masted steel barque, 335 feet in length with a beam of 46 feet and depth of hold of 25½ feet, she was capable of loading 5,000 tons of cargo. There was no midship house but she had a 40-foot-long poop and 37 feet of raised forecastle. The bulwarks were 4½ feet high and the hatch coamings 3 feet. Double-bottom tanks could hold 800 tons of water and the hold was divided by bulkheads into three of which the midship one could take 1,100 tons of water ballast, thus enabling the vessel to avoid the costs of loading and discharging ballast every time she needed to sail without cargo. Two water tube boilers supplied steam to the windlass and four deck winches, greatly reducing the sailors' work. She was equipped with six boats, four of which could be rigged for sailing. All the masts, yards and the bowsprit were of steel and she carried a spare topmast, 45 feet long and 1½ feet in diameter. She had dedicated sail lockers near the break of the poop which were accessed through a special hatch. All in all a very fine workmanlike vessel.

The Americans, who had been slow to adopt iron, were even slower to turn to steel and their first sailing vessel built of this material was not launched until 1894, when Messrs A. Sewell & Co launched the *Dirigo*. Although constructed in Bath, Maine, she was designed in England and all the plates and frames were manufactured in Motherwell and shipped across the Atlantic for assembly. She was in fact a typical example of British ships from that period. Capable of carrying 4,500 tons of cargo and able to stand without ballast, she had a number of successful voyages around the Horn until sunk by a German submarine in 1917.

The temptation to increase mast heights and thus the sail area, once the stronger iron masts, spars and rigging were introduced, was irresistible to many builders and owners. New sails such as skysails were added above the royals and the *James Baines* set a moonsail or moonraker above that. All these additions increased the weight and strain of the rig aloft and a spate of dismastings in the mid 1870s resulted. In 1878 the *Frank Curling*, on her maiden voyage from New York to San Francisco, capsized off the Horn. It was believed the captain held onto too much sail in order to make a fast passage and the cargo shifted and the ship turned over. The introduction of lighter and stronger steel in place of iron restored the balance.

There was a great boom in shipbuilding at the beginning of the 1880s but it lasted only until 1885. In the United States hardly any Down Easters were built between 1886 and 1889 and prices in Britain fell so much that a good vessel could be acquired for about £14 per ton in 1885, whereas the *Cutty Sark* had cost £21 per ton to build in 1869. American shipowners were suffering from competition with foreign vessels, particularly the British, and now with a glut of ships searching for too few cargoes they began to withdraw from business. In 1885 over fifty vessels were laid up in San Francisco for months. The trade had become uneconomic, particularly for Americans who were forced to accept about eighteen per cent less freight money, probably owing to a poorer outturn of cargo due to inevitable leaking in wooden hulls. As a result many American owners transferred their tonnage to the expanding coastal trade at home, which had become more profitable because it was barred to foreign shipping and there was less competition.

At the outset the large ships and barques competed effectively on the American coastal trade, but it was quickly realised that schooners, some of which reached well over 1,000 tons, were more economical on routes where headwinds might be expected at least on half the voyages. Shipyards were soon turning out this type of vessel. The manning scale of a schooner was usually taken to be two men to a mast, whereas a square-rigger's crew became based on one man per 100 gross registered tons. The schooners, with their better windward ability, were better suited to running back and forth along a coast than a square rigged vessel, but they never really made an impression on the deep sea trades as their rig was not nearly so efficient down wind. Many of the American Down Easters were saved from scrap or sale to foreign flag only by a general improvement in world trade at the beginning of the 1890s, and in particular the new American export of kerosene oil, known as case oil, for which there was a universal demand. This cargo, being stowed in sealed metal containers, was less susceptible to damage from water leaking into the holds, which was common in American wooden-built vessels, and so there was a better outturn of cargo and more freight to be earned. Case oil to Japan and the Far East from New York and other east coast ports became a common cargo for all sailing ships as they could make the voyage almost as quickly as a steamer if they used the Cape Horn route.

Trade improved earlier for the British and another boom in British sailing-ship building began in 1888 but it was to be the last. The popular British vessel was not dissimilar to the Down Easter. Shipbuilders extended the full mid-sections and cut down on the fine long entries and runs which were a feature of the clipper ships. This created a slower vessel but a superior cargo carrier. During the five years the boom lasted shipyards such as Russell & Co. were producing between twenty and thirty ships a year. It was said the ships from this period, designed to compete with utility steam tramps, were built by the mile and cut off by the fathom, but some examples were handsome in appearance and were perfectly good sailers. It was the sailing ships built during this boom that were to form the last of the sailing Cape Horners.

Steamships, which reached a rough parity in costs per mile by 1865, did not emerge as a more economic method of transporting cargo until the introduction of the triple-expansion engine, the first of which was fitted in the *Aberdeen* in 1881. The expansion properties of steam were known for some time, but the inability to construct boilers capable of supplying steam at sufficient pressure was only solved by the slow improvements in steel manufacture in the middle of the century. When steel for this purpose became available in the 1870s the compound engine was introduced in which the steam, having passed through one cylinder, was evacuated into another larger one where it continued to provide power. In the triple expansion engines of the *Aberdeen*, steam initially at 125 pounds per square inch, went through three progressively larger cylinders, providing more horsepower for the same amount of heat supplied to the boilers. Within five years boiler pressures were improved to 200 pounds per square inch and a steam vessel could average 9 knots using only half an ounce of coal for every ton of displacement per mile steamed. Since sailing ships' average speed was 5 knots, and the courses far longer due to the vagaries of the wind, they were now doomed to extinction.

8

The Cape Horn Breed

The French four-masted barque *Loire,* three weeks past the Falklands, was still battling to make any progress against strong westerly gales. A slight shift in the wind direction gave the captain an opportunity to make westing and all hands were called to set more sail but by nightfall the wind had increased again and the decision was taken to reduce sail once more. The sails had just been hauled up when a particularly heavy sea swept over the main deck. The crew grabbed for anything to avoid being swept overside but one unlucky man was not quick enough and his shipmates watched horrified as the wave carried him away. Rushing aft, the mate came across the bosun who was holding a lifebelt. 'Shall I throw it?' he asked. The mate paused. Knowing the situation the ship was in, it would be at least an hour before they could get back. It was the captain who told him not to bother, as it would only prolong the agony of the man they could see waving beseechingly a ship's-length away. To heave to and lower a boat would have been a long and highly dangerous procedure, with the new certainty of the boat and her crew being lost, not to mention the risks to the barque herself if she tried to come round in those seas. 'There is nothing we can do,' said the captain, and the mate and bosun knew he was right. The safety of the vessel and the remainder of her crew had to take priority and the unfortunate seaman became yet another casualty in the endless battle with the Horn.

The captain's remark may seem callous to modern eyes but in the circumstances it was realistic. The smallest boat on board would have been lashed down on its skids, its purpose to save the crew if the ship foundered

or the captain ordered them to abandon. To launch it would have taken a
minimum of half an hour in ideal circumstances but on a vessel swept by
waves the task would have taken longer and run the risk of injuring or
killing men just to get it over the ship's side. Then it had to be boarded and
kept clear of the ship because one heavy roll would have sent it cannoning
into the side and smashed it to pieces. The captain was acknowledging the
realities of the situation.

The seamen of the early Cape Horners were largely volunteers, particularly
in the merchant ships, only in the Navy were men pressed. Here was no
place for the man who considered himself above his fellows. A man was
and is judged at sea by his competence, not by birth or race, particularly
among the merchant Cape Horners which made up by far the largest
proportion of the vessels rounding Cape Stiff. Officers and petty officers
were respected and usually obeyed without question, but this respect had to
be earned. The men would far more willingly sail with a tough captain who
was competent than with an easy-going one whose lack of authority might
risk their lives.

Teamwork is the operative word aboard any sailing vessel and never
more so than in the large square riggers which carried no more seamen than
the crew of a modern 80-foot maxi yacht. The enormous loads, although
reduced by tackles, required the crew to haul as one if they were to have any
effect. Probably the first lesson that any seaman had to learn was how to
throw his weight in time with ten or more men, and to help the men keep
time, songs, known as shanties, were sung with the work. There were three
basic types of shanty: the capstan shanty for a steady operation like walking
round the capstan pushing on a bar; the halliard shanty for long and heavy
pulls such as hoisting a yard aloft; and the rowing or forecastle shanty.
Each crew would elect a shantyman, not necessarily the best singer, but one
who knew the words and how to direct the rhythm. As an operation was
started the shanty man would sing out a verse and the men would follow
with the refrain, emphasis being put on certain words when they would
throw their weight onto the rope. Modern shantymen give little impression
of a real shanty bellowed out on a heaving deck with a howling wind for
accompaniment. Many shanties became universal. Such favourites as the
capstan shanty 'Rio Grande' can be found in English as well as German.
Words sometimes crossed the language barrier with different meaning. The
French used *mes bouées* – my buoys, having heard the English sing 'my
boys'. Even stranger was ' Oh cheerily men', which became *Oh Celimène,*
while *Saloabobèche* is a corruption of 'son of a bitch'.

Ships usually managed to sail with full crews at the start of their voyages

from Europe or the north-east United States and returned with the same
men, less those who had died during the voyage. It was the discovery of
gold in California and Australia that changed all this. During the gold rush
years whole crews abandoned their ships and obtaining men for vessels
homeward bound became a real problem for captains. Ships that had arrived
with full crews were held up for weeks or months as there were no
replacement seamen available.

At the height of the gold rush San Francisco became a repository of
deserted vessels of every description. A contemporary account in the French
paper, the *National*, sets the scene:

> Few harbours can present so remarkable a scene. Three to four hundred
> ships are moored here and the flags of every country in the world are
> fluttering from the forest of masts. There are weird-looking Chinese
> junks bobbing in the water next to three-masted Russian vessels and
> American warships. But what is striking about them all is their silent
> and deserted appearance. A more powerful force than discipline has
> drawn away the crew. The yellow fever, as the Americans call it, has
> infected everyone; the gold of Sacramento has drawn all to it like an
> irresistible magnet.

Even after the initial rush of prospectors, there were many who were happy
to forget the hardships of the forecastle for the apparent delights and better
prospects beckoning in California. In some instances desertion was a self-
inflicted problem as, if the stay in port was likely to be protracted, captains
were liable to mistreat the men to encourage desertion and save on wages.
Men usually signed a contract, known as the Ship's Articles of Agreement,
for a round voyage and if they deserted they forfeited all their pay earned to
date so there was every incentive to remain with their ship. On one occasion
a Scandinavian crew refused to desert even though they were worked to the
limit to encourage this. However they changed their minds one night after
the second mate ordered them aloft to the main truck and made them crow
like rooks whilst he took loose shots in their direction with a revolver.

As a consequence of the shortage of prime seamen for ships leaving port,
captains resorted to the crimps to supply crew. Crimping was not restricted
to San Francisco; it occurred all around the Pacific Basin and Shanghai
gave its name to the expression which meant the same thing. But San
Francisco was by far the worst port for this practice. Some characters like
Three-Finger Daly and Shanghai Brown achieved universal notoriety and
earned their money by obtaining crews at so much a head. In some ports the

rate was set at $10, but if a captain had a particularly bad reputation, the price rose dramatically. The methods of acquiring men included drugged liquor and mugging. Either way, the result was the same. The sailor awoke in the forecastle of a ship already under way through the heads of San Francisco Bay. On one occasion when a particularly infamous ship, the *St Paul*, lay at anchor awaiting a crew, the most hardened seamen made themselves scarce, and the San Francisco crimps captured and doped a Baptist minister to complete the numbers. A hundred and one days later the ship arrived at Liverpool where he was signed off the ship's articles but friends had to send money for his passage home. One hopes he found the experience instructive!

Sometimes crimps boarded newly arrived ships and attempted to persuade the sailors to desert with financial inducements. A sailor on an unhappy ship, who perhaps had little money due after stoppages for clothing and tobacco, both of which were the captain's monopoly, might well be tempted to desert. At least he could enjoy a few days ashore with money in his pocket, whereas if he stayed with the ship he was unlikely to be granted shore leave. The *Joseph B. Thomas* arrived in San Francisco Bay from Liverpool and anchored close to the *John McDonald*, which was awaiting a crew to sail with a cargo of grain. The moment the anchor was down the crimps appeared aboard the *Joseph B. Thomas* and whilst plying the men with liquor, offered all sorts of jobs ashore. By nightfall only the mates and two hands were left aboard. The following day the captain's wife of the *Thomas* visited the captain's wife of the *McDonald* and arrived as most of her husband's crew were being bundled aboard unconscious or drugged. The bulk of the crew were Scandinavians, but two Canadians who had stronger heads than the others objected, and in front of the two captains' wives had their faces punched to pulp with knuckle dusters. In the long term such treatment was self-defeating, though, as after a voyage of three months or more around the Horn the seamen were exhausted and their bodies needed time to recover. Weakened by hard work and lack of proper vitamins, those seamen who were shanghaied aboard another ship soon after arrival were susceptible to scurvy or other diseases. Perhaps the final insult was that the crimps' fees were deducted from the sailors' wages. A seaman aboard the *Commodore T. H. Allen*, who arrived in New York in 1889, complained about being shanghaied in San Francisco but was beaten by the mates. When he asked for his pay, he was informed that nothing was due as everything had gone to the crimps and one of the mates had to lend him 50 cents for a ferry from the docks. Despite the efforts made to capture trained seamen, the bulk of the men supplied by the crimps were of poor quality, with little seagoing experience and no understanding of the discipline required to survive the immense forces of nature unleashed around Cape Horn. A ship crewed with untrained landsmen like this could hardly expect to achieve a fast and safe passage.

Few captains would risk sailing without a full forecastle especially as crews were cut down to a minimum, and the crimps took full advantage of the situation. Occasionally there was an exception such as Captain Batchelor of the 2,825 gross ton *Cedarbank*. He had lost half his crew of eighteen in Hong Kong, but was fortunate in having eight apprentices in the half-deck, so with these and his nine remaining ABs, he sailed to Portland in Oregon, where the crimps met the ship and started offering the crew whisky and telling them tales of the money to be made ashore. At the same time they told the captain that the price of a seaman was going to be £60 per head. Captain Batchelor's response was to drop an anvil through the nearest crimp's boat, but when two of his seamen were arrested on a trumped-up charge, the captain lost his temper, went for one of the crimps again and was arrested for attempted murder and assault.

The trial was a farce. The sheriff who had arrested Captain Batchelor was the crimp's brother and although the charge of attempted murder was dropped, the captain was given a month's imprisonment. After serving his term he returned to the ship and found that in his absence one man had been lost, but the mate had managed to capture another to replace him. The ship was now loaded and ready to sail, but as she was being towed out to sea, the sheriff and crimp chased after in a launch ordering the captain to return to port as he had too few men on board for his ship to be managed safely and demanding that two of the seamen be handed over as they had warrants for their arrest on a charge of stealing. As none of the men had been allowed ashore by the mate for their own protection, this was yet another trumped-up charge. The captain's answer was to say he would wait for them once he had crossed the bar, but needless to say, once the tug was cast off, he cracked on sail and headed for Queenstown, County Cork, round the Horn with a depleted crew of five ABs and eight apprentices. Not many captains were so resourceful or successful in evading the clutches of the crimps but this is hardly surprising when the crimps could rely upon corrupt officials to support their trade.

Shanghai Brown was eventually hoist by his own petard in 1896 when he was shanghaied himself by the apprentices of the British vessel *Springburn* and forced to sail before the mast on a winter voyage around the Horn. History does not relate if this taste of his own medicine persuaded Brown to give up his trade, but the *Springburn*'s apprentices earned themselves undying fame amongst deep-water men.

The only way to avoid the clutches of the crimps was to remain aboard during the entire stay in port, an almost inhuman requirement for young men who had been cooped up for more than three months. Some captains refused shore leave in order to avoid losing their men. On French ships shore leave was forbidden unless accompanied by an officer, and then only to visit the agents. Under an edict passed in 1793 French ships were not allowed to carry more foreigners than twenty-five per cent of their crew. French seamen were, in any case, considered to be a part of their naval reserve and most had served at least two years in the Navy. The result was greater discipline and a greater national character than found in most ships. The unwary French seamen might be shanghaied, but he was a rarity.

The odious practice of crimping continued in the land of liberty until 1906 when pressure from foreign governments and the growing scandal forced the United States authorities to act and thereafter the crimps were brought under some semblance of control.

Ships which made fast passages were naturally more attractive to shippers and the pressure was on captains and mates to drive ships and crews relentlessly. Trying to sail a ship with the crew the crimps provided put great strain on the officers and they would not have been human if their tempers did not become frayed. Some did their best to instruct the men, others just shouted or resorted to violence. A Yankee mate was synonymous with bullying and brutality and many boasted of the skulls they cracked with iron belaying pins. They needed to be tough to control the crews they shipped which, apart from being dredged from the waterfront might well be a hodgepodge of nationalities. Discipline had to be enforced and the Yankee mate considered himself unworthy of the job unless the crew were cowed and obedient. Captains were usually similar characters since they obtained their positions by proving they were good mates. It was customary for them to address the crew before a voyage, and this is a typical example.

I'm master of this ship and I want to start square with you. We've got a long voyage before us and there's plenty of work to be done. I want you to understand I'm great on discipline, and you can have hell or heaven onboard, just as you please. All you've got to attend to is to do your duty and obey orders; that's what you shipped for, and that's what you're paid for. If you do your duty it will be all right; and if you don't it will be all wrong.

The first man that disobeys my orders I'll put daylight through him

– quick, and here's the little joker I'll do it with [exhibits a revolver].
If any of you men try to make trouble aboard this ship I'll make it hot
for you. I'll make mince-meat of some of you quicker'n hell's scorch
a feather.

Such men had small regard for life, and there was scant law in practice to
protect the seamen. Whatever the truth of a situation, it was accepted that
the average seaman was a drifter and waster and few courts would take the
word of even a number of them against that of the captain. But despite their
ferocity towards the crew, many Yankee captains and mates were first-rate
seamen and it was these men who drove the clippers to achieve fast passages
and became the legends of the Cape Horn route.

There is no accurate count of the number of vessels that disappeared
around the Horn. Drake's pinnace is the first recorded loss, but her end was
witnessed, many others just disappeared leaving no survivors to carry the
tale home. During the hey-day of the sailing ship the radio had not yet been
invented and even in the later years few square riggers were equipped with
them. Vessels sailed for a specified destination, and unless they reported to
another vessel during their voyage, that was often the last heard until a
message arrived, usually a few months late, to say that they had arrived. It
was only when survivors struggled to safety or were rescued by another
vessel that the outside world learned of some of the accidents that befell
vessels in the vicinity of the Horn.

Ships that were abandoned by the crew were usually left without their
hatch covers so that they would founder quickly and not become a menace
to others. The survivors were then faced with a difficult voyage in a small
open boat and the currents off the Horn would quickly drive them eastwards
in the one area of the Southern Ocean where vessels seldom ventured. Ships
were quick to alter course to the north once they had rounded the Horn and
the outward route to Australia did not enter the Southern Ocean until the
longitude of Tristan da Cunha Island. Between the Horn and Tristan da
Cunha the only visitors were sealers, whalers and, later, research vessels.
The only hope for a boat that had drifted east was to try and make South
Georgia because if they missed that they would certainly starve, assuming
they kept their boat afloat. Ernest Shackleton's epic voyage from Antarctica
to South Georgia in 1916, after his vessel had been crushed by the ice, was
an exceptionally fine piece of seamanship but unfortunately not frequently
emulated. The strength of the Southern Ocean current can be judged by the
drift of the *Blue Jacket*'s figurehead. She was abandoned on fire off the
Falklands in March 1869, and her figurehead, which was unmistakable

although slightly charred, washed ashore on Rottnest Island off Fremantle in Western Australia in December 1871.

In the particularly hard season in 1905 of 130 ships that sailed from Europe from May to July, sixty-two British, thirty-four French, twenty-seven German, four Italian, two Norwegian, one Russian and one Dane, four were wrecked and twenty-two put into ports of distress after damage off the Horn. By the end of July, fifty-two had reached their destinations but fifty-five were still unaccounted for. Some of the wrecked ships were originally posted as missing, but eventually evidence emerged as to their fate. The figurehead of the *Loch Vennachar* was washed ashore on Kangaroo Island in South Australia and a solitary survivor of the Tasmanian ship *Brier Holme* found his way to Hobart to report the loss of his ship.

The *Garsdale* was one of the wrecks. Registered in Liverpool and of 1,755 tons she had sailed from South Shields on 22nd June 1905. Her main backstay began to render when the ship was off the Horn in a strong westerly gale and high seas. The captain tried to wear ship to reduce the moment on the masts but the mainmast went overside in the process. Wearing, which meant going round onto the other tack by circling downwind, would have put strain on the after side of the mast, exactly what a backstay is meant to hold. The weakened backstay broke the moment the weight came on it. And yet the captain would have had little choice. To have continued heading to windward meant pounding into the seas which would have soon broken the stay anyway so he had to gamble on it holding until he could sail the ship into sheltered waters. In breaking, the mainmast also brought down part of the mizzen and foremasts. Shortly thereafter the foremast also broke, taking the forward lifeboats as it went, but the ship was not taking water and the crew of twenty-nine kept working to try and save her. After two days and no respite in the weather conditions, the Frenchman *Bérangère,* which was in the vicinity, was hailed and asked to take the crew off. The *Garsdale*'s boat was smashed as it was lowered and the crew were forced to jump into the raging seas and be picked up by the Frenchman's boat. Nineteen of the crew were rescued in this way. It is not known what was the *Garsdale*'s eventual fate but she probably drifted to the east until she foundered.

The crew of the *Alcyon* were not so fortunate. Homeward bound from the Chincha Islands in Peru with a cargo of guano she was off the Diego Ramirez Islands when hurricane-force winds took the masts out of her. The ship began to sink and as the islands were only four miles to leeward the crew took to two boats and headed in their direction. One boat was swept past the islands by the wind and current and never seen again. The other, in attempting to land on the leeward side of the island, was thrown onto a rock, overturned and washed out to sea. Only three men managed to get ashore and find shelter in a crevice, and one of these had suffered such severe head injuries that he soon died. The two survivors fed themselves on the raw flesh of an albatross and drank melted snow for six days until an observant lookout on a Norwegian ship saw a vest attached to an oar being waved and dispatched a boat to collect them. The two men eventually arrived home at Le Havre several months later to find, not surprisingly, that they had been given up for dead.

The *Bidston Hill*, a four-masted ship, was also lost that year in May when the master tried to sail through the Le Maire Strait but this time it was the lack of wind that caused the disaster. Having cleared the strait the ship was tacked, but it appears that this manoeuvre was made too early. Instead of clearing Staten Island, she was inexorably being drawn closer and closer to the cliffs until she was too close to be saved. One boat was got away but the other was probably crushed and its crew killed by spars falling from the mast once the ship hit the cliff.

Attention has focused on 1905 because it was a particularly bad year but losses in other years were only slightly fewer. The *Falklandbank* sailed from Port Talbot with coal for Valparaiso in 1907 but was never seen again. She was thought to have foundered off Cape Horn. The *Toxteth* foundered off Cape Horn the same year. In 1911 the *Gulf Stream*, commanded by Captain David Nicoll, disappeared on a voyage from Glasgow to Vancouver. She was posted as missing in February 1912 and thought to have perished off the Horn. A House of Lords paper, presented by Lord Muskerry, noted that between 1904 and 1908, twenty-six of the large British sailing ships, totalling 31,490 tons, had been posted missing taking with them fifty-nine apprentices and 312 able seamen, sixty-seven of which were British.

To obtain some idea of the hardships faced by the crew of a clipper ship as she beat round the Horn, one has only to read the account of Felix Riesenberg, who, as a young man, sailed aboard the *A. J. Fuller,* captained by Charles M. Nichols in 1898.

We were standing down to Cape Horn. For a week past it had been getting colder and colder. The sea, seldom quiet in those latitudes, kept the ship lively; frequent shifts of wind, always strong, made constant work at the braces, between our spells at the bilge pump, for water was working into her with the regularity of fate. Seldom did the pumps suck until six bells. Only when the working of gear kept us from pumping would the watch go by without that back-breaking labour.

Our watch, the port, had turned in below for the eight to midnight. The sky was covered – black – one of those nights when nothing can be seen except the light thrown upward by the breaking sea. A strong, full topsail breeze from south-southwest held us on a taut bowline, edging towards the reaches of Cape Horn. To windward stretched the plains of Patagonia; we were south of the River Plate, off Port Deseado, or possibly San Julián. The forecastle was damp, cold. A few pipes glowed, but only for a brief half hour when the last man of the watch was huddled in his blankets, knees braced against the bunk boards, extracting the last moment of rest out of his watch below. The forecastle lamp, set into a hole in the fore and aft bulkhead – to give light to both sides – dim and smoking, lit the narrow, steaming, breathing room. Shadows of swaying oilskins moved across the bunks like spectres. Half an hour passed, or it may have been more.

BANG, BANG, BANG. The sleepy men awakened.

Impatient thumping on the forecastle door by a hard fist. 'All hands on deck! Out! Every Mothers sons of a bitch! Out you go!'

'God damn it! What's liftin now? Why did I ever leave the Dutchman?' The men were struggling into damp oilskins.

'Here you, bear a hand. The Mate's up. Jesus! Better move. Out you go. Damn it! Oh Hell! Close that door you slob. We're swamped!'

'On deck, every lousy soldier!'

The wide form of the mate stood at the forecastle door, dripping wet; his voice was like the roar of a bull. Eight forms catapulted past him into the surge of a heavy sea thundering over the break of the forecastle deck, sending the gang aft like chips on a stream. A tumbling mass of black cloud rolled overhead; wind sang in the slanting rigging. Forks of lightning bared the scene. Sails and gear aloft were thrashing, thundering, their noise lost in the storm.

Hang on! Oh! God! My mouth was full of salt water. Black, cold seas – solid ocean was lifting us, sweeping the gang along the lee side of the house, into the waist. Running ropes streamed across the deck. The water was filling our oilskins, our boots, wetting our shirts up under our armpits. The slippery deck rose, and she ascended to windward, hitting us, knocking us down. Another flash, followed by a close reverberating thunder, deadened our hearing. The white fire has for an instant lit a picture of indescribable confusion and speed. A light glimmering at the poop. Captain Nichols was up, clinging to the mizzen rigging.

The mate held on to windward of the mainmast. A short, thick man, a Nova Scotia sailor, roared down the waist, 'Aloft – secure tops'ls!'

Above us the heavy canvas was straining at the gear. As if striving to get away from the scene, to leave the drowning deck, soaked cold and aching from the blows, half a dozen of us went into the black pandemonium of the night, flattened against the rigging, hauling ourselves upward. Below, another huge sea had washed the deck, white with swirling, yeasty phosphorescence; above sounded the sharp cry of cold, stiff cotton canvas, freed from restraint. Higher up we heard the curses of men lighting the topsail; the starboard watch attempted mastery of the sail.

'Hell!' Hail began to pelt against the rigging. The whip of the storm bore down on the ship with vindictive force and nothing could be heard over the howl of the wind.

Six of us gained the yard, edged out on the icy footropes, clung to the wildly swaying spar, joining four half frozen figures; puny gnats tossed by black, stiff, billowing canvas. A flash revealed drawn faces, ragged oilskins. Tommy and Axel were near me. Ten of us hugged the yard, our fingers on the iron jackstay, grasping the loosened sea gaskets. Able seamen passed these instinctively about the sail, caught turns, and hove in. A land-lubber, the greatest of athletes, assuming such a one to have been foolish enough to ship deep water, would have been useless. Sailors I thought – God, what men!

'Hell' a gasket parted. The belly of the sail was loose.

Cold bodies were forgotten. Fingernails were broken off and bleeding; no one knew: We smothered the bulge of sail. 'Now together!' The new turns held. A man a foot away was shouting, voicing grisly oaths. Axel with ribald words, throwing his great strength into the fight, his blond hair streaming in the night for his so'wster had gone, seemed like a god in some titanic joust with a giant bat. The screaming of the wind and the cut of sleet were our thunderous applause; the mighty tossing of the ship, exaggerated because of our height, gave grandeur to our victory. We had saved the topsail!

We were at the yardarms to finish the job – five men to lee, on the sharply slanting spar. The brace had slacked, and the heavy, jerking yard swung low with each scend of the ship. We went over in a mightier blast. The yardarm pointed down. While seething water rose up almost to the flemish horse; it boiled with pale light, fascinating, singing, beckoning, a soft inviting bed of bubbling foam. How easy, I thought, to drop into that celestial stew of a billion stars, seething below me; there at least was rest.

Slowly our men worked back into the slings of the yard. On deck they had tautened the lee brace. We were climbing down the futtocks. A deafening crack shattered the night, banging into our ears, a more terrific howl of wind cut through the wire rigging as a mounting squall of spume drove over the top. The lower topsail, heaviest of storm canvas, had vanished. Shreds of the whipping sail scourged us as we worked downwards to the hard reality on deck.

Light was lifting to the east. The storm had settled to a dead monotony of punishment. Three thousand tons of wood, laden with cargo, a black, white-decked hull lifting mighty built up masts, stayed by steel, was creaking and complaining, as if lashed on the eternal grating of the sea.

Never before had men, mere bodies and brains, driven by the shouting curses of their masters, attempted so much at sea. There was a mere handful of us. Never before or since had so much been thrust on a single man.

We lost our watch below, and at eight bells in the morning, back in the forecastle about a steaming can of deep-water coffee, old Smith remarked, 'That was quite a capfull of wind, me lad.'

'Yeh, but wait till we get to the Horn.'

By midnight the ship was hove to on the starboard tack, clear of the coast and to south of the Ramirez, below Cape Horn. Hurricane squalls began to roar across the ocean. We were under storm canvas, a goosewinged lower main topsail, a fore storm staysail and reefed main trysail. The oil tank forward was dripping into the sea; two oil bags were slung from the weather fore and main channels. All the preventer gear was taut, the rolling tackles bowsed for full due. Every precaution known to sailors was taken onboard the Fuller, from relieving tackles on the helm to extra lashings on the head spars. The deafening screech of the blasts was fiendish. After a while I began to wonder how much harder it could blow without blowing us apart.

As sharp cross seas washed her fore and aft, all hands – for the forecastle was by then afloat – huddled near the mizzen rigging. 'It's like heaven now; we're all officers, livin' aft or dyin'.' The irrepressible Jimmy, wedged under the lee of the cabin trunk, looked at this great storm without fear. The galley was washed out; the foreward cabin deck was afloat. Four men braced themselves about the spokes of the double wheel. All loose gear went streaming to leeward, into the sea through the open scuppers or over the bulwark . . .

Morning broke in dim blurs of tattered blue above a scene of wildest grandeur. With the sun, which we did not see, the storm began to abate. Twenty feet of our lee bulwark had gone in the wake of the main hatch, and there the tarpaulins were flapping. The crew, frozen but with that congenial discomfort of salt water, watched lanky old Chips, the faithful, skimming along the deck with his sounding rod sheltered under his long oil coat. He braced himself above the main fife-rail, having jumped above a sea, and plumbed the bilge. Here was a note of order. The mate, coming to life like a walrus, roused the half dead crew, leading us against the gale, to haul aboard the gear and to set some sail – for not a rag of canvas was on her, merely empty bolt ropes and frayed bits of cotton whipping to leeward.

The work was backbreaking. Since many of the ships were hurriedly built, they leaked and the drudgery of spending the Dog watches at the pumps was a common feature and remained so until iron and steel replaced wood as the material for hull construction. On one clipper it is recorded that when turning to the crew on a Sunday morning, the mate sent a ship's boy to his cabin to collect a sign which read 'Sunday'. 'Look at that,' said the mate, 'because that's all your going to see of Sunday,' and he put them to work, although it was normally a day free except for watchkeeping.

Few accounts of cruelty during this era have survived since few bothered to complain officially and there was little law and order in the San Francisco of the period. Later in the late 1880s, a register of seamen's complaints called the Red Record was established and from this we learn that even thirty years after the trade began, brutality was still common aboard American ships and complaints still had little effect. For example on the *Reuce* off the Horn in 1891 the mates lashed a seaman to the mizzen stay and left him there suspended by arms tied behind his back for over an hour. In the same year the carpenter of the *I. F. Chapman* was handcuffed by the hands and feet to the spanker boom and when a sympathetic helmsman released him he soon joined the carpenter. When the men reported the incident at the voyage's end in San Francisco, the investigating commissioner judged that the punishment was not very cruel! From personal experience of being triced up (by seven senior apprentices when I was a first-tripper), the worst part is the slow tearing of the skin around one's wrists and ankles, which is slowly removed by the rope and leaves a scalped area of raw flesh.

Tricing was comparatively tame compared with the horrors devised by some of the 'Bucko' mates. On the *Edward O'Brien II* in 1890, the mate knocked down the second mate and then stamped on his face, hit a seaman over the head with an iron belaying pin and kicked the unconscious man in the head and ribs; hit another sailor with a capstan bar and kicked him unconscious; lastly punched the boatswain for failing to hear an order. The mate was charged but bailed, and one can imagine he quickly made himself scarce from the waterfront where a vengeful crew were searching for him. The only real opportunity for the seamen to settle grievances was after the ship had arrived in port and paid off and they could lie in wait for the bullying mate on dry land where there was little chance of the police catching them.

Two years later the *Edward O'Brien II* reappeared in the Red Record when the mate decided to make things lively. The crew complained, and the mate vowed to subdue them before Cape Horn was reached and the second mate offered to fight any three men from the forecastle. One seaman accepted the challenge, but the second mate grabbed a belaying pin and, aided by the cook, steward and carpenter, attacked the crew and knocked down three men and then placed them into irons. One of the men was dragged into the cabin and repeatedly kicked until the second mate was exhausted. When the captain protested at the treatment, he was ignored. The desperate seamen swore they would spend all their wages in having the mates punished but these prudently disappeared when the ship arrived at San Francisco.

An even more serious allegation was made against Captain H. A. Williams of the four-masted barque *Frederick Billings*, the first vessel with this rig to be built in the United States since the *Great Republic* nearly thirty years before. In 1892 she had a very hard passage round the Horn during which six seamen were washed overboard. It was claimed the captain pushed one seaman, who was clinging to the mizzen chains, into the sea with a boathook. In any case he made no attempt to recover any of the men, although the weather may have made this impossible. This complaint was dismissed as trivial by the commissioner in San Francisco!

Owners did not want to know about crewing problems or the welfare of the men whose efforts created the wealth which enabled them to live in fine houses, become respected members of the community, and attend church on Sundays pretending to be good Christians. Their concern was profit. However, the existence of the Red Record slowly produced a move to check the worst excesses, though if the commissioner was unsympathetic, the seamen had little chance of a fair hearing. As the 1890s progressed matters did improve and this was best illustrated by the award of $3,600 to the *Reuce*'s crew for poor treatment, but how many men were incapacitated or murdered at sea on Cape Horners prior to the Red Record will never be disclosed.

Bullying was not an American monopoly, but it was harder for British and French captains to obtain crews from amongst their own countries' pools of largely professional seamen if they had a bad reputation. A French captain from Nantes became known as Oiseau Noir for his behaviour, but he got his come-uppance from one mate, Alphonse Rio. The vessel had loaded in the Plate and a fire was started by the crew in order to finish the voyage there and then. She was saved by the exertions of the mate who was knocked down by the captain during the course of a row. When the vessel sailed the crew mutinied but were starved back to work. The captain then demanded the mate's logbook and having read it told the mate to re-write it excluding the passages which reflected badly on him. The mate refused and another fight developed but this time the mate won. The mate ended his career as the Minister for the French Merchant Marine.

In the early part of the twentieth century, when British shipowners were desperately trying to save money, they stopped employing British seamen on account of the higher wages they were demanding. Some resorted to employing Scandinavians and Germans who were usually reliable, but many vessels were forced to sail with a rag-tag of crew, some of whom had never been to sea before and were not even fit enough to climb aloft along the spars. Small wonder that captains reduced their rigs, preferring to sail more slowly rather than take risks with a crew who could not take in sail quickly in an emergency. Such crews were almost inevitably undisciplined and if given shore leave would return on board in a drunken state seeking to sort out their real or imaginary grievances against the officers. Late in 1914 the *Glenholm* had almost completed unloading her cargo of Welsh coal in Valparaiso when the crew returned aboard, some very drunk. The trouble-makers came aft shouting for the mate, saying that they wanted to settle with him. The mate went on deck to see what the noise was about and was attacked with belaying pins. The other mates and the captain went to his assistance, ordering the apprentice to hoist the Police Flag. Knowing that the police would soon arrive, the trouble-makers climbed up into the rigging but were subsequently arrested and the three ringleaders were sent to prison for three months. A Valparaiso prison, for friendless, penniless, mutinous seamen whose consuls would not want to know them, was probably one of the most unpleasant places to be on earth.

A more serious case of mutiny occurred on the *Manga Reva*, which, as the *Pyrenees*, had been stranded on Manga Reva as recounted by Jack London in his *South Seas Tales*. After being rebuilt in 1904 she sailed with various cargoes around the Horn and was on a voyage from New York to San Francisco in 1913 when the crew got seriously out of hand. The captain had taken ill for a number of days, but had struggled on deck to take the longitude one morning when some of the seamen ran aft brandishing revolvers. The mate, who was forward at the time, ran aft but was overpowered and handcuffed by the mutineers at gunpoint. The captain was also put in irons along with the second mate. The mutineers now found themselves in a situation they had not anticipated since they had expected one of the mates to join them. None of them could navigate and they proved indifferent sailors without supervision. They were eventually forced to ask the captain to navigate them to Bermuda, but he refused, only agreeing to take them to Delaware. On arrival the ship went aground and the mutineers were taken away and subsequently given sentences of up to three and a half years. The *Manga Reva* continued to trade until 1917 when she was reported as missing on a voyage from London to Hampton Roads and it is believed that she was sunk by a German submarine as none of the crew were ever heard of again.

There is a fine line between what may be termed a mutiny and taking over command because the captain appears incapable, and the courts had a record of ruling in favour of the master if there was any doubt. Captain Fromke of the famous German Laeisz Line had a reputation for fast passages and he drove both vessels and crew hard with a higher record than most for men lost overboard. In 1912, whilst close to the Horn in the *Pommern*, he refused to respond to the request from the mate to reduce sail and almost drove the barque under in a storm. Eventually half a watch was washed overboard with no chance of their being saved in the prevailing conditions and the mate could bear it no longer. He locked the captain in his cabin and took over. At the subsequent Board of Enquiry the mate was reprimanded for not reducing sail earlier, although had the captain retained any shreds of sanity it is easy to imagine that the mate would have been imprisoned for mutiny. Fortunately the Laeisz Company took a different view of the circumstances. The mate kept his command and, having been interned in Chile during the war, was given command of the *Passat* when Laeisz bought her back in the post-war years.

Few women sailed aboard the Cape Horners. The total lack of privacy did not provide a suitable environment for mixing the sexes. Most sailors hated having women on board anyway, as it forced them to watch their language and behaviour. Nevertheless women were carried as passengers. Although they lived in better conditions than the men in the forecastle they still suffered as much from the cramped and confined situation, indeed it must have been more frightening to be confined below listening to the crash of waves breaking aboard and hearing the cries of the captain or his mates without really knowing what was going on. Occasionally a captain might take his wife with him and these ladies had to be a tough breed. Captain Learmont's wife gave birth to their third child as her husband nursed his vessel through the English Channel in a gale, others were not above exhorting a crew to better efforts or nursing injured hands. Mrs Patten, whose husband commanded the American clipper *Neptune's Car*, took over command off the Horn when her husband went blind. The mate had previously been placed under arrest for incompetence and insubordination and the second mate could not navigate, so Mrs Patten, who was only twenty-four years old, took command and successfully took the ship from the Horn to San Francisco in 52 days.

Shipowners took full advantage of the demand for Cape Horn trained officers by increasing the number of apprentices, which cost nothing but their food, and reducing the paid seamen even further. An apprentice's indentures, for four years, cost his family £50 which was returned when the time was completed. The same indenture form existed in 1957 when I became an apprentice, but by then the family no longer had to deposit £50 and we were paid. The salary of a first-year apprentice in 1957 was £90. Otherwise the agreement was unchanged; it barred us from frequenting ale houses or places of ill repute and we were given instructions in preparation for our Second Mates' Certificates. But at the end of the nineteenth century apprentices received no wages and precious little instruction on most ships, although this was a part of the master's duties. They might just as well have signed on as seamen since anyone could take a Second Mate's Certificate if they had four years' sea time under their belt. As it was apprentices were cheap labour, and it is unsurprising that many left the sea as soon as possible, or signed on to steamers. In Germany and France the apprentice system was unknown, all officers served their four years as an ordinary or able seaman and then went ashore to specialised schools to pass their certificates of competency. Such schools existed in Britain as well, and given the paucity of instruction given to embryo officers in British ships, they were just as necessary.

Captains of sailing ships were caught in an economic and an age trap. If they wished to transfer to steam, they would start at the bottom or perhaps as mate, with the attendant drop in pay, and only slowly work their way back into command. Small wonder they hung onto their commands at £12 a month, and many tried to boost their income by cutting corners on the food they purchased for the crew. British ships, or Limejuicers as they were called, had an unenviable reputation internationally for their poor food, whereas the Germans and French were good feeders, and it was said of the Americans that you could eat the food of two men provided you did the work of them both. Another petty method of earning a few extra pounds

was by selling the crew slops (clothing and a few essentials) at greatly
inflated prices. The crew had no choice. There were no alternative shops to
buy from, and shore leave in ports was a rare luxury. Such masters were
hardly the sort to encourage changes to a system that was well established
and which they understood. Young masters who attempted to run their ships
on more modern lines were looked upon as upstarts who would modify their
methods as they grew older – if they survived.

The captains were trapped, the officers had some choice if they were
sufficiently young, the apprentices had options on completion of their
indentures, but what drove the seamen to sign back onto a Cape Horner's
articles? Sailing a square-rigged ship which, at best, could point to within
65° of the wind, was a muscle-breaking task. Crews were small and worked
four hours on duty and then, in theory, four hours off. However, since the
whole watch on deck could handle only one sail at a time, anything more
than a routine change in the set of the sails required both watches, and there
was no chance of this being made up to them. Once the vessel was in the
vicinity of Cape Horn, especially on an east-to-west passage against the
wind in winter, handling ice-covered sails, became a battle needing as much
energy and effort from a man as a battle between armies and held almost the
same likelihood of injury or death. The struggle against the winds off Cape
Horn was not over in a day. It usually lasted at least two to three weeks on
an average passage, but could take months. It was not just the work aloft
that was dangerous, halyards, sheets and braces were all led to the deck, so
that once a sail had been adjusted aloft, the men had to trim it from the deck,
often in conditions where icy seas would knock the whole watch off their
feet, giving them a good soaking if they were lucky enough not be carried
overside. And all this for barely edible food and £3 a month! They knew the
life was dangerous, even if they did not realise that they had a one in twenty
chance of being killed each voyage. The desertion rate from British ships
was enormous, frequently requiring eighty men to be signed on the articles
during a voyage just to keep the ship manned with a crew of twenty. Men
did not desert unless conditions were very poor on board or something a lot
more attractive beckoned because they forfeited all accrued wages and if
caught, could be fined or locked in irons. It was suggested by David Lloyd
George, then President of the Board of Trade, in a debate in the British
Parliament in 1906, that there were probably about 27,000 cases of desertion
from British ships every year. In Portland, Oregon, it had reached the
appalling figure of forty per cent of all British crews on ships arriving there
in 1903. Although some of these men would have been crimped, the high
figure also indicates that seamen were finding more favourable opportunities

ashore or in foreign, mainly American, ships. It is a great indictment of conditions in British merchant sailing ships.

There can be few reasons why men kept coming forward to join the Cape Horners, but they were powerful ones. The principal was pride in being considered a Cape Horner, and as such the very cream of all seamen. Others might take to the easier life aboard a steamer but it was recognised that only the best seamen went on the Cape Horn sailing ships. This gave the man extra stature amongst his peers.

A related reason was pride in a reputation for fast runs in the races between ships on the same passage. Large sums were gambled on the outcome of these races, which were followed with great enthusiasm by people ashore. Any captain with a speedy ship would happily bet on his vessel against another, and word of the wager spread in no time. In 1889 three ships loading in Honolulu, the *W.F. Babcock, St Catherine,* and the *I. F. Chapman,* agreed to race to Delaware for a purse of $1,000. The *Babcock* was the first away on 8th March, the *Chapman* sailed on the 14th, and the *St Catherine* on the 17th. All three arrived off Delaware breakwater on 16th July. The *Clan Mackenzie* was one of the faster British ships and renowned for her performance in heavy weather, once overhauling *Thermopylae*. She beat the large Down Easter *W. F. Babcock* by fourteen days on a passage from San Francisco to Europe, and by a month on the next voyage outwards. Such races kept the crews on their toes, and encouraged captains to push their vessels to the limit, even in terrible conditions on a westerly passage around the Horn. It also gave seamen something to boast about, as being a crew member on a crack Cape Horner was the pinnacle of his profession.

A third reason for sticking with this harsh way of life was more deepseated. It was the comradeship that is built up in a small team of men sharing great dangers and hardships. Whilst at sea they were totally isolated from the rest of the world. For four or five months, whilst making passage from the west coast of South America to Europe, this small group of men shared their lives and its dangers. For these men, like front line soldiers, it was difficult to explain to those at home the dependence and trust in your fellow workers that has to develop. Once freed from the risks at the end of the voyage, they found themselves in the company of landsmen who could barely comprehend their lives, and whose major concerns seemed petty when compared with the frequent battles to save a ship and crew. They felt out of place in shore society and began to yearn for the security and comradeship of men who shared their experiences. And so they signed on again. The life was harsh, poorly rewarded and dangerous, but it was the only life they could understand.

9

The Last Flourish of Commercial Sail

The merchant sailing ship was brought to the peak of perfection, one of man's loveliest creations, just as the steamer drew level in operating cost. Sail had already given way to steam on the fast mails and passenger route to the west coast of South America and in 1883 steamers began to compete on the Australia and New Zealand run around the Horn back to Britain.

The first companies to operate a regular service to New Zealand were the New Zealand Shipping Company and the Shaw Savill and Albion Companies who had all operated fleets of sailing ships until steam became efficient enough to compete. The *British King,* a four-masted steamer that set sails during the long runs through the Southern Ocean, was the first to sail on the new service, although she was beaten for the honour of being the first steamer on the route by the German *Marsala.*

No less than five more new steamers joined this service in 1884 and times between England and the Colonies began to reduce quickly, reaching 34 days by the turn of the century as faster steamers were introduced. The *British King* holds another place in history as the first steamer to carry frozen meat to London from New Zealand, a trade that was to see enormous expansion in the following decades and do much to develop the economy of the increasingly independent colony. Sail was able to compete for a while in this trade and vessels were specially adapted for the purpose. Shaw Savill had two such ships, the *Dunedin* and the *Marlborough*, in the trade until both disappeared in 1890 on voyages to Britain. The *Dunedin* sailed in

November 1889 and simply disappeared. No sign of her has ever been found since. The *Marlborough* sailed in January 1890 and was posted as missing in April. At about this time another ship reported seeing men signalling from one of the islands near Cape Horn but was unable to put a boat in to reach them on account of the poor weather. A Chilean warship was sent to search the islands but no survivors were found. In July that year the barque *Cordova* was wrecked on Tierra del Fuego, but the whole crew managed to get away and landed at Thetis Bay. They spent two weeks surviving as best they could, then decided that part of the crew should take the boat to the nearest habitation to obtain help. This boat was lost with her crew somewhere on the way towards Staten Island. The five remaining survivors, which included the captain, decided to send two men towards Good Success Bay where it was thought some whalers might be ashore boiling their blubber. They set off along the coast, passing the wreck of the barque *Godiva* which had gone ashore carrying a cargo of coal, and a small boat hauled up on the shore. This boat was marked *Marlborough of London*. Nearby they found a tent made from part of a sail and within this lay seven skeletons. Outside was a pile of mussel shells. Quite who these men were has never been discovered as it is unlikely that the bodies of survivors from either the *Marlborough* or the *Godiva* would have become skeletons so quickly. Perhaps unnerved by this unpleasant sight the two men decided to return to rejoin their companions and they were eventually picked up by the barque *Banco Mobilirio* and taken to Coquimbo after spending thirty-three days ashore. No other trace of the *Marlborough* has ever been found although the press were still reporting sightings more than twenty years later.

With a regular service, averaging even in the early years two to four weeks faster than the speediest sailing ships, steam quickly took over the passenger and subsidised mail service and their faster passages meant that they took the more valuable and better freighted cargoes on this route as well. Frozen meat continued to be a steamer cargo around the Horn right up to the opening of the Panama Canal, but the passenger traffic switched to the composite route across the Isthmus of Panama about the turn of the century.

What has been described as the 'incredible defiance of the Industrial revolution by sail during the second half of the nineteenth century' in fact continued right up until the great depression of the 1920s. The introduction of an efficient triple expansion steam engine in 1881 put the last nail in the coffin of economic sailing ship operation. Although this seems obvious to us today, it was far from being clear at the time. In the first place it took time for sufficient ships to be built to replace the enormous cargo-carrying capacity of the world's sailing fleet; and secondly, sailing ships themselves continued to become more economic, as the reduction of many ships to barques, by removing the square sails on the mizzen mast, decreased the number of crew required to man a vessel and lowered its operating costs.

Other methods of improving efficiency were still being introduced, such as Captain Jarvis's brace winches which made bracing the yards easier and safer. It is perhaps significant that this inventive Scot had to cease development work on this and many clever ideas for improving the handling of sailing ships, because he could not interest anyone in his own country. The Germans, however, were quick to see the advantages and adopted the winches with enthusiasm. Unfortunately some slip in the patenting deprived Captain Jarvis of any benefit.

Although technological innovation could improve the efficiency of the sailing ship, there was no way this kept pace with the rapid advances in the development of the steamer. In 1870, the year after the opening of the Suez Canal, sailing ships were carrying sixty-eight per cent of all cargoes but this had fallen to twenty-seven per cent by 1893. Where the sailing ship could still provide an advantage over the new passenger and tramp steamers was on the longer voyages where port congestion or slow cargo handling meant delays. The sailing ship cost very little to keep in port, just her crew's wages and the pitiful food. A steamer, costing five or six times as much to build, just could not afford lengthy delays as they had to keep on the move to pay off their investment. This left the long ocean routes, such as grain from western America to Europe, coal from Australia to South America, and the South American nitrate trade to Europe, open to sail at least until the building of the Panama Canal. Even there though, the freight rates barely covered the operating costs. In the first decade of the twentieth century the rate for nitrates from Chile and Peru to Europe fell to 15/- (75p) per ton. A 2,000-ton ship could thus earn £1,500 on her homeward voyage from a cargo she may have waited three months to load. With running costs of perhaps £200 per month, a four-month return voyage after three months' waiting and loading, showed a possible profit of £100 which was hardly a good investment. Freight rates did rise when Germany began its preparations for war and needed all the nitrate it could obtain for explosives, but even so most profit margins were ridiculously small and certainly insufficient to cover depreciation.

The reactions by shipowners to the advent of steam varied considerably. The French government introduced a subsidy for shipping because they could see the strategic advantages of a large merchant fleet and a pool of trained seamen. With this subsidy behind them the French shipowners could continue to build sailing ships and operate them at a profit. The Germans, new to the game, took a scientific look at the business and studied the weather patterns along the routes to enable their ships to make shorter and therefore more profitable voyages. They also thoroughly investigated and were quick to adopt any new idea of a technical or safety nature. For example safety nets along the bulwarks to catch men thrown across the deck by invading waves were installed on all German ships, but were rare with the British. The Germans quickly adopted the so-called Liverpool House, a central island half-way along the deck between forecastle and poop designed to break up the area of deck that could be swept by waves and additionally provide more comfortable accommodation for the crews. These, although they reduced damage on deck and made life safer for the crew, were uncommon on British ships.

The British reply to growing competition was largely one of cutting operating costs to the bone, and keeping ships running along well tried lines which avoided any new and possibly expensive ideas. There was no attempt made to follow the efficient German approach which provided well-run ships and speedy voyages and turnrounds. In some ways perhaps most British shipowners were more far sighted than their foreign rivals as however much one improved the sailing ship she could never recapture the economic lead established by steamers and cheap, abundant coal. The last proper British sailing Cape Horner was built in 1905 whereas the Germans could still consider a sailing vessel an economic proposition to build as late as 1926. Those few diehards who kept to sail hung on in the grim hope of a resurgence in the demand for cargo capacity which might occur in time of war.

The famous German Laeisz Line, better known as the Flying P Line since all their ship's names began with the letter P, is a prime example of how sail could be made to compete right up to the great depression of the 1920s. The company started with one ship, the 985-ton *Polynesia* in 1874, but twenty years later ran a large fleet of very smart vessels, all built for the Cape Horn route to Chile. Laeisz introduced continuity of employment for the crew, promotion based on ability, marine superintendents to supervise the fitting out and loading of their ships, good and trustworthy agents ashore and bonuses for quick passages and turnouts of cargo. This resulted in the officers and men having an interest in safe and speedy voyages. It also meant that on the west coast of South America, which was Laeisz's main run, their ships had full cargoes awaiting for their return voyages, and port captains were bribed to ensure that loading berths were made available when the ships arrived.

All Laeisz vessels were expected to cross the Equator when going southwards between 26° and 28° westerly longitude since an examination of ships' logs showed that this gave the fastest passage through the Doldrums. As a result of this efficient management all Laeisz vessels were expected to round the Horn three times in a year, once more that the average. Knowing that they were achieving a high standard gave pride to the crews and encouraged them to work their boats hard.

The Flying P Line also experimented with building larger vessels, on the premise that to double the cargo capacity did not mean doubling the crew or operating costs. The best-known examples are the five-masted barque *Potosi* built in 1894 and the five-masted ship, the only such ship ever built, the *Preussen*, built in 1902. These enormous vessels did not make faster passages than smaller ships, but they carried nearly twice the cargo, 6,000 tons for *Potosi* and nearly 8,000 tons for *Preussen*. Neither ship was a particular success, and both were found to be difficult to handle. However, the *Potosi* made twenty-eight round voyages to Chile from Hamburg until 1914 so she cannot have owed her owners anything. The *Preussen* drove one of her masters mad before she was wrecked just east of Dover in 1910. Her loss was due to a collision with the cross-Channel ferry *Brighton* which misjudged the sailing ship's speed and rammed the bow, removing her bowsprit and some fore upper sails, and jamming her anchors. Unable to manoeuvre, the giant ship tried to anchor off Dungeness but could not be slowed sufficiently. Tugs tried to tow her into Dover but could not control her and she drifted ashore beneath the white cliffs just to the east of the harbour. Efforts to tow her off failed and she was slowly ground to pieces. The *Potosi* survived the First World War, interned at Valparaiso (some 200 German sailing ships were interned in west coast South American ports during that war), and was given to France as a war reparation. She was subsequently sold to Argentina, renamed the *Flora* and lost due to fire and subsequent stranding in 1921 off Comodoro Rivadavia.

One other large vessel built for German owners by Russell & Co in 1891 was the *Marie Rickmers*. She had a greater gross tonnage than the *France*, of which more anon, but could not carry as much cargo by 500 tons. Of great interest in her construction was the steam auxiliary triple expansion engine, which was designed to give her a speed of 7 knots and be used to take her through the Doldrums and Horse latitudes. Her first voyage was from Barry to Singapore with coal, and from there to Saigon to load rice for Germany. She sailed with a full cargo in July 1892 and just disappeared. No trace of her was ever found.

Placing an auxiliary engine aboard a sailing ship has often seemed to be the answer to the problem of maintaining a good average speed, avoiding

long delays in the Doldrums and high towage fees in and out of port but the
reality has been surprisingly different. The cargo space lost to the engine
and its fuel, particularly in the days of coal-fired boilers, meant lost freight,
and the running costs were increased by the need to carry engineers. It was
tried in a number of vessels during the latter stages of sail but never seems
to have proved commercially successful.

The only rival to the enormous German ships were the *France* and *France
II*, the former built for the famous French shipowner Antonin Bordes. The
France was built specifically for the nitrate trade in 1890 by Henderson
and Son of Glasgow, and at the time of her launching, was, at 5,900 tons,
the largest sailing vessel in the world. She set 49,000 square feet of sail on
a five-masted barque rig. One interesting feature was large double-bottom
tanks that could hold 2,000 tons of water ballast. Like the two giant German
ships, she was found to be difficult to handle. Her enormous size led to a
collision in 1897, when the British Battleship HMS *Blenheim*, seeing the
France's anchor light forward and another lantern at her stern, assumed
she must be two fishing vessels and steered between them. Fortunately the
truth of the situation was realised at the last minute and the *France* received
only a heavy glancing blow. For some peculiar reason the British Board of
Enquiry acquitted the warship of causing the accident which did little for
Anglo-French relations at the time. The *France* made a number of fast
passages, but in 1901, when bound from Newcastle to Valparaiso with a
cargo of coal she was struck by a Pampero off the South American coast
and took a list of 45° when her cargo shifted. She staggered on for two
months before the crew were forced to abandon her. She was last sighted by
the barque *Josepha*, lying on her beam-ends with the sea sweeping over her
and she must have sunk soon afterwards.

Bordes followed her with another five-masted barque, *France II*, which,
at 8,000 tons deadweight, was the largest square-rigged sailing vessel ever
built. She was built for the ore trade from New Caledonia and launched at
Bordeaux in 1911. She set thirty-two sails in all, but was fitted with twin
screws powered by internal combustion engines, which, it was thought,
might give her a top speed under sail and power of 17 knots. As with other
vessels similarly equipped, the engines did not prove very successful in
practice and were removed. She survived the war, during which she was
considered important enough to be given an armament, although she never
had to use it. After the war she was put on various runs, and took the largest
cargo of wool bales ever loaded to that time from New Zealand in 1921.
Her next voyage was from London with a mixed cargo, and she was
proceeding to the New Hebrides to load nickel ore at Pouembout when the

wind died and she drifted ashore at Poya, some sixty miles from Nouméa. If she had still had her engines she might have been saved. Her crew abandoned her as she bumped on the reef with two of her holds flooded. It was thought that she could have been refloated with relative ease but the depressed state of the freight markets made this uneconomic and her hull was eventually sold to breakers for £2,000.

Bordes had started in shipping in a small way in 1847. After the opening of the Suez Canal and the realisation that sail would not be able to compete on runs to India and Asia in the future, to everyone's surprise Bordes started to expand rapidly by buying iron and steel vessels from the Clyde. Since no one imagined that he was prepared to risk his own fortune in what was such an obviously dying business, the rumour went around that he was the secret front man for the Jesuits and credence was given to this fantastical rumour by the name of one of his ships, the *St Vincent de Paul*. In fact only two of Bordes' ships were ever named after saints and he quickly changed the names of two second-hand vessels he bought from the *Sainte Catherine* and *Sainte Marguerite* to *Seine* and *Blanche*, perhaps because he had tired of the joke.

By 1870 the Bordes fleet consisted of fifteen ships of 16,830 metric tons. Five years later it had risen to thirty-four ships of 39,300 tons and the growth in both the numbers of ships, but in particular their size, continued right up to the outbreak of the First World War when the fleet comprised forty-six ships totalling 163,160 tons. The expansion and continued profitability of this sailing fleet, especially in the early part of the twentieth century when nearly everyone else had stopped building sailing vessels, was, to a large extent, due to the French government's bounty. This money, which was paid at the rate of 1 franc 70 centimes per ton per 1,000 miles sailed, enabled the French shipowners to continue to operate when all their competitors were being forced to sell their ships. They could build fine attractive ships, pay the money to keep them well and pay their crews a decent wage.

Small wonder that most of the unsubsidised British shipowners sold their vessels and transferred to steam. Amongst those that kept going was the Welsh firm of Robert Thomas and Company, which had started business in 1878 with a ten-year-old wooden barque. Their fleet, which had grown to thirty-six vessels by 1900, made full use of the cheap labour provided by the apprentice system, for which we must be grateful since many of these apprentices have left stirring accounts of their experiences, a small window into a world now past. This company was sometimes referred to as the Welsh Castle Line because a number of its vessels were given the suffix

Castle. The voyage of one of these, the *Penrhyn Castle*, over four years from 1900 gives a good indication of the sort of work which British Cape Horners were doing at the turn of the century.

The *Penrhyn Castle* was one of four sister ships built in 1882 with a gross tonnage of 1,400 tons. Rigged as a three-masted barque her normal complement was twenty-four comprising the master, mate and second mate, carpenter, sailmaker, steward, cook, five apprentices and twelve able seamen. She sailed outward for Cape Town with war stores for the British Army then fighting the Boers. After a lengthy stay because of port congestion she took on ballast for an empty trip to Caleta Buena for nitrates, striking her royals in order to reduce top weight. She took the eastern route, running through the Southern Ocean at about 50° south latitude and inevitably ran into foul weather although the worst damage sustained was to the barrels of salted beef and pork stowed in the hold. These broke open in a heavy roll and for the rest of the voyage the crew described their meat as having a gritty taste from having been mixed with the gravel ballast! Having loaded nitrates, and incidentally watched the *Reliance* that was loading the same cargo burned to the waterline, the ship sailed to Hamburg. Her next voyage was with a mixed cargo to Seattle. A course was taken eastwards of Staten Island on account of a falling barometer to avoid the Le Maire Strait, but nevertheless the barque had a difficult rounding of the Horn, taking 37 days and losing an apprentice overside.

At Tacoma all but two of the ABs deserted and the crimps had to supply a new crew before the vessel could sail again, this time with a cargo of tinned fruit for Durban, South Africa. Off Cape Horn, and working, as was often the case, from a dead reckoning position, rocks were suddenly spied ahead and the barque had to be brought round close hauled to avoid the Diego Ramirez Islands. Having discharged her cargo in Durban the *Penrhyn Castle* sailed in ballast to Newcastle, NSW and there loaded coal for Taltal in Chile. There was no cargo available in Taltal so the barque was ballasted again for the short run up the coast to Antofagasta where she moored in an anchorage filled with fifty other ships. Three weeks later she sailed for Dunkirk with a cargo of nitrates. This time the Horn provided a variant to the usual strong-to-storm force westerlies, and for two weeks the vessel had to beat against a 'Black Northeaster' which forced her south down amongst the icebergs. In the Atlantic off the Martin Vaz rocks near the Equator the *Penrhyn Castle* ran in with the *Gladovan* and the two ships kept together until they reached the Western Approaches. Her discharge completed, a cargo of sugar was loaded and a tow arranged round to Liverpool.

Towing between ports on the European coast was not uncommon at the

time, although it was frowned upon by owners on the west coast of South
America where captains were expected to sail into the roadstead and drop
their anchors so that the vessel lined up with the others already there to
work her cargo into lighters. Around the home coast, however, it was deemed
less expensive to take a tug than have to sign on a crew and run the risk of
a ship being delayed by beating against headwinds in confined and crowded
waters. After three months in Liverpool, the *Penrhyn Castle* sailed for
Melbourne with a general cargo, being pooped and forced to heave to for
two days in the Southern Ocean. From there she took grain to Callao during
which passage the vessel was nearly dismasted and driven ashore in a
hurricane. Finally she loaded guano at the island of Pachacamec, where the
swell, and breakdown in discipline largely caused by the captain's
drunkenness, kept her for six months. Finally in the spring of 1905 she
sailed for Antwerp. As if the vessel had not been delayed enough this time
she again ran into easterlies off the Horn, and was so delayed that she had
to call at Pernambuco for provisions to prevent the crew from starving.

   This was a fairly typical programme for a British Cape Horner at the
time, being forced to wander around the world taking cheap bulk cargoes
on long routes where steamers were not yet as competitive and which almost
inevitably involved dangerous passages in the Roaring Forties and a hard
bash around Cape Horn. On this last voyage in 1905 the *Penrhyn Castle*
was remarkably lucky as if she had left Pachacamac a few months later she
would have run into some of the worst weather recorded off that dreaded
cape which caused more than 130 square riggers bound for the Horn to be
delayed so badly that many were reported as missing. And yet in that same
year, one of these ships, the British ship *Brenda*, skippered by Captain
Learmont who had a reputation for fast passages, made Honolulu from
Hamburg in 127 days with no damage at all. This was the *Brenda*'s last
year in service as in 1906 she caught fire in Valparaiso and became a total
loss.

   Captain Learmont's recipe for rounding the Horn is instructive and just
as applicable today as it was 100 years ago:

   Cape Horn has so many moods that it was impossible to lay down any
   set plans to weather it. I had rounded it in so many different conditions
   that I knew one had to be ready to take every opportunity to obtain
   even a slight advantage. The advice given to me by my owner on my
   leaving on my first voyage as Master was good, and I never hesitated
   to make use of it as I proved it to be sound practical advice. 'Never be
   afraid to wear her'. 'Distance made good' in the vicinity of Cape Horn

was all important. Any change in the direction of the wind that stopped her making westing or northing had to be attended to, otherwise you were making easting or southing and losing ground, and the remedy was to wear ship without hesitation. It was a manoeuvre that was difficult and at times dangerous and the longer you hesitated about it the loss of ground increased. It meant turning away from the wind instead of towards the wind as when tacking; in heavy weather you could not tack a ship without taking the masts out of her, but in wearing ship the sails were full all the time; the danger lay in turning, when the sea was full on your beam and the weight of it struck the full length of the ship. Once round you had the sea on the bow but it was prudent to have the crew off the main deck before you brought her to.

Even a seaman of Captain Learmont's expertise and experience found this particular rounding exceptional as the winds remained consistently from the north and north west, so that although he had no difficulty making westing, which was usually the problem, he could not make a course to the north to get clear of the Roaring Forties.

Now that the days of professional sailors in square riggers are creeping further and further back into history, many of the tricks of handling one of these unwieldy vessels have been lost. Only the sail training ships continue the skills, but they are few in numbers and the free interchange of information, such as used to occur in the chandler's shops wherever sailing shipmen met, is inevitably rare.

Captain Learmont even picked up a helpful tip from a rival in mid-passage when commanding the *Cleomene* and racing the *Travancore* under Captain Jones from Hamburg to San Francisco. He was rowed across to the *Travancore* one day when both ships were becalmed close to each other, and the conversation inevitably drifted towards their relative performance. Captain Jones, who rarely allowed staysails to be set, pointed out that on the *Cleomene* these sails were backwinding the lee side of the squaresails. From the deck of the other vessel Captain Learmont could see the effect for himself, so on his return on board had his staysails stowed and found that his ship gained a very slight advantage over the *Travancore*.

Captain Learmont was not alone in driving his vessel off the Horn. The Bretons have always been good seamen and Captain Bourgain, commanding the French four-masted barque *Hélène*, inevitably known to her crew as *La Belle Hélène*, was bound for Iquique with coal and had been lying hove to in a gale near the Diego Ramirez Islands when her lookouts sighted the lights of three German vessels. The wind was backing and the Germans were already on the other tack being forced southwards. Captain Bourgain called his mates together and decided to risk holding onto the existing tack. It would keep the vessel no more than fifty miles from the coast of Tierra del Fuego, nothing like sufficient searoom if anything went wrong, but since the glass had steadied, better weather might be approaching and anything was better than going south. More sail was set, the crew leaping for safety into the rigging every time a large wave swept over the deck. Then the *Hélène* began to push forward, crashing into every wave and shaking water off her decks like a dog each time the bow rose. For two days she drove north of west, the seas sweeping away her boats, part of her bridge and then tearing away the hatch covers. They turned the *Hélène* into the sea and poured oil over the bow to calm the waves before reducing sail so that the hatch covers could be resecured, knowing that if they failed in this, the barque would go down. Then she was put back on course, plunging into the seas but making steady if agonisingly slow progress north and west. A day later the first sight of blue skies enabled the mates to get a sight, they were by no means safe but the glass had started to rise slightly, better weather might be on its way. The following day the wind swung southwards so the yards could be squared and the barque began to run up the coast, not fast to start with, this would have been dangerous in the residual seas, but away from Cape Horn. The *Hélène* reached her destination nearly two weeks before the first of the Germans arrived.

The use of oil by the *Hélène* was not unusual and some captains swore by it. A vegetable oil such as colza oil was recommended, and indeed was carried in ships' lifeboats as part of their normal equipment for this purpose. The oil was poured into a canvas bag filled with oakum and slitted so that the oil would feed out gradually. By allowing this bag to lie to windward, the oil slowly paid out and covered a large area around the vessel. This has the effect of smoothing out the surface of the sea, although it will not remove the swell.

Another heavy-weather ploy is to stream a warp astern and let the vessel run off down wind and waves. The American vessel *Venice* tried this in 1850 when caught by a bad blow and deeply laden so that she would not steer well. Ninety fathoms of 11-inch circumference hawser was middled, and the bight paid out from each quarter. The captain reported instant relief. I have used the same system in a small boat, but with 2-inch circumference rope. If the rope is led from right aft on each quarter, it tends to hold the stern into the seas. A small headsail will also tend to keep the bow downwind. The effect of the warp is to check the wild rushes of a small boat down the front of a wave and a headsail reduces the risk of broaching.

Amongst the many ships built in the last flourish of sailing-ship building in Britain was the *Springburn*, built by Barclay Curle. Her first captain was Howard-Rae who had a reputation for making a quick doubling of the Horn. His method was to carry everything the ship could bear whilst he drove to the south. Then, when he considered he might clear the land, he would tack and head north. He usually got away with it. In the summer of 1896 he went as far as 71° south, but still made a fast rounding. Other less aggressive captains took as long as six weeks to get round at the same time. Significantly, when Howard-Rae handed over the *Springburn* to a new captain, he was much more timid and took 48 days to double the Horn, the longest time ever taken by this ship.

Seamen always admired a courageous master who would press his ship around the Horn in adverse conditions, as this account by an apprentice aboard the *Springburn* indicates. The *Springburn* was outward bound during the winter of 1897 and lying hove to under the mizzen lower topsail weathering a Cape Horn Snorter, when the four-masted barque *Queen Margaret* came into view homeward bound.

What a magnificent sight she made. Flying six topsails, a reefed foresail, and a big main topgallant sail, she seemed as if she were daring the savage hail-laden blasts to take the sticks out of her. The amount of sail might seem small, but when one takes into consideration the extensive fury of the frequent squalls, it seemed to us to be verging on foolhardiness. Closer and closer she came, a smother of spray from her foc'sle aft to her mainmast. In a very short time she was up with us and easing off a point or two to round under our stern we read her name *Queen Margaret*, without the need for binoculars. She passed not more than forty yards from us. The thought that came uppermost in my mind was the magnificent steering witnessed. Two men were at her wheel and the one at the weather wheel grating was indeed a master helmsman.

It was thrilling to watch the mountains of water chase the ship, just falling short of pooping her, then suddenly divide and rush alongside, gaining in height and bulk until momentum was exhausted. As the sea ran past her, down would go her stern into an abyss from which one thought she would never emerge. Up to the heavens raked her jibboom, and her forefoot and keel showed clear almost aft to the foremast. It was difficult to estimate her speed, but if any ship ever topped sixteen knots the beautiful *Queen Margaret* was doing it then. Despite the shriek of the gale we could hear the thrash of her as she swept past.

The lovely *Queen Margaret* was lost off the Lizard in May 1913 when her captain took her in close to try and read a signal from the shore station. The barque struck on outlying rock, all attempts to get her off failed and she soon broke up.

Captains with a good vessel beneath their feet were not averse to showing off her paces if the opportunity arose. Captain Richard Angel, for many years master of the composite British clipper *Beltona* of 734 tons, was rounding the Horn homeward bound from Australia with a cargo of wool when he sighted another vessel ahead under reefed topsails. The *Beltona* was under her topgallant sails at the time and to show what he thought of the other captain's caution Captain Angel passed ahead and then hardened up. Wool was a light cargo, although screw pressed into a hold to provide the tightest possible stow, so if the vessel had got some ballast left in her she could be a little tender and heel well over. This is exactly what happened to the *Beltona* which heeled almost far enough to show her keel before coming round close under the stranger's stern, squaring her yards and racing ahead again having completely circled the other vessel. It was a wonderful piece of one-upmanship although few people would care to have risked such a manoeuvre in a heavy westerly gale off the Horn. It is said that the mate, once he had recovered from the experience, asked Captain Angel if they could now reduce sail and was told to set the royals and if he could not find anything else to set to ask the captain's wife for one of her petticoats!

After the appalling storms of 1905 better weather might have been expected, but another danger materialised the following year to persecute the Cape Horners. The year 1906, although less stormy, saw the return of that other peril, ice. Drake's Passage is often crowded with icebergs swept north-eastwards by the current from the Bellingshausen Sea which is bypassing Graham's Land. The mean limit for icebergs touches Staten Island and then passes north-west of the Falklands. The mean limit for pack ice lies at about 60° south, only 240 miles due south of Cape Horn, and extends in a north-easterly direction. A huge berg was observed in 1992 which drifted slowly eastwards of the Falklands and isolated icebergs have been sighted as far north as 36° south in longitude 50° west, level with the River Plate, so a good lookout is always essential for ships as they near the Horn.

How many ships have been lost as a result of hitting large icebergs will never be known. The *Carnarvon Bay*, which was in collision with a large berg in 1908 whilst in dense fog, lost her bowsprit, foreyard, and damaged her stem. Had she been travelling at speed she would probably have fractured her collision bulkhead, which all ships have just abaft the stem, and gone down very quickly. The *Guiding Star* was last seen embayed in an ice field and was never heard of again. In 1904 the French barque *Emilie Galline* sighted a large barque wedged on a berg. She was unable to read the name and saw no signs of life. Further investigation was impossible as the French ship was in a difficult situation herself.

In 1893 the *Aethelbert* drifted alongside an iceberg off the Falklands and as large lumps of ice began to fall onto the deck the crew took to the boats. Some time later their ship drifted clear and they were able to reboard her. They sailed eastwards for eighty-four miles trying to find the edge of this monstrous ice-floe, but finding that it still continued, they tacked round, and after fifteen days managed to find a clear passage to the westward. This berg must have been at least twice the size of the Isle of Wight but its sheer size would have made it stable. Small bergs, as they slowly melt below the surface of the sea, have a nasty habit of suddenly rearranging themselves to adjust to the change in their underwater shape. Few turn right over but large pieces of ice are usually released from well below the waterline and shoot to the surface. Such projectiles could easily penetrate a vessel's hull.

That same year the full-rigged ship *Cromdale* found herself in difficulty as she rounded the Horn on a homeward voyage from Australia. Her captain, trying to make his way eastwards, found himself more and more surrounded by huge bergs over 400 feet above the water and each several miles long. As the ship progressed the bergs became larger and closer together until eventually there was no way out ahead. The wind, a gale from the north-north-west, did not help, but they went about, and then a change in direction to the south-west enabled them to sail northwards and eventually find a small gap through which they were able to squeeze out into more open water. The smallest touch on one of these giant bergs would have been enough to hole the ship and, to add to the difficulties, they saw many bergs that had rolled over and were black on their surface, making them harder to see, especially at night. The *Cromdale* survived this ordeal, but in 1913 came to grief when she ran onto the Lizard in Cornwall in thick fog and soon broke up.

At least eleven vessels reported the *Cromdale*'s ice floe, and two of these, the *Wasdale* and *Stracathro* ran into a horseshoe-shaped bay of ice four miles wide at the entrance, ten miles across and twenty miles deep. Their estimate of the total length of that single berg was at least fifty miles and the *Kingfauns* which had sailed through the same area a month before reported sailing through ice for more than 400 miles.

In view of its fearsome reputation for bad weather, it is a curious fact that Cape Horn can be as treacherous in the rare calms which develop between the passage of depressions. A number of ships have drifted onto the coast when the wind died suddenly, and these include one of the early American clipper ships, the *Dreadnought,* which went ashore in the Le Maire Strait when the ship's boats failed to tow her clear in a fast-moving current. In my own experience, I have been completely becalmed for five hours only seven miles south of Cape Horn itself, the last place in the world where one expects or wishes for such an occurrence. I sat, lifting gently in the large swell, observing the clouds forming over Tierra del Fuego and watching the sea's surface anxiously for signs of a sudden squall. In fact the wind came up quite gently from the south-west and soon rose to a full gale, but by then I was moving nicely to the east. Others have been less fortunate.

Another victim of calms was the *Deccan* in 1908. She had managed to weather the Horn itself, but was too close in to Tierra del Fuego and in a calm that descended shortly afterwards she lost steerageway and began to drift towards the coast. No wind arose to give a little power to her sails, and she was swept onto the College Rocks, about four miles west of Cape Tate. At the last minute, realising the position was hopeless, the captain gave the order to take to the boats and the crew got clear just as the ship struck. Within twenty minutes they had the ocean to themselves, as their ship had been pounded to pieces by the huge swell. They rowed to Desolation Island and managed to land on a sandy beach on the southern side of the island. They had just landed when the wind started to blow strongly from the west which would have saved their vessel had it come up sooner.

For ten days the wind blew consistently, accompanied by rain, and the survivors had great difficulty in even keeping a fire going. Although they had managed to save some provisions, the captain decided to keep these for an emergency, and they lived on wild berries and shellfish. In those conditions, many of the men started to suffer from rheumatism, and resorted to the time-honoured treatment of soaking their rain-saturated clothing in sea water. A number of attempts were made to get away. The boat was launched again when the wind turned north-westerly, but it proved too strong and dangerous, and the party landed again a few miles further on. It took four attempts before the captain was able to lead a party across the 2,000-foot-high mountains that form the backbone to the island, and find a Chilean sealing cutter at anchor off the north shore which agreed to sail round, collect the rest of the *Deccan*'s crew and take them to Punta Arenas. Rumours abounded at this time concerning the skeletons of seamen to be found around the coast of this aptly named island, but the *Deccan*'s crew reported that all they had found were the remains of wrecks.

Snow, which often announces itself by the very heavy black clouds that sweep up in a heavy squall, was usually a cause of discomfort to seamen and a danger only insofar as it froze their hands and made keeping a lookout more difficult. Sometimes when the snowfall is prolonged it can settle on the surface of the sea in thick white blankets before it is absorbed. The American clipper *Golden Era* reported sailing through an ocean covered with slush from six to ten inches deep after a particularly heavy snowstorm.

Cost-cutting was put down as the cause of the loss of the *Dalgonar*, but her misfortune led to an outstanding example of the brotherhood of the sea. This full-rigged ship of 2,665 tons was built in Southampton in 1892 for Messrs Gracie, Beazley & Co at a cost of £23,361. In September 1913 she had completed the discharge of her outward cargo and loaded shingle ballast at Callao to give the ship stability for the short voyage to Taltal where she was due to load nitrates. Shingle ballast, especially when it has been dredged from the sea, lacks the clay and earth that helps to bind it, and is well known for the ease with which it can shift in a ship's hold. Strict instructions had been issued by the consulate to masters loading ballast in Callao to ensure that it was properly stowed. (They also warned captains to make sure that the quantity they ordered and paid for was actually delivered.) As was the usual custom, the *Dalgonar* erected a ballast box down the centre of the hold, made from two bulkheads of shifting boards lashed in place with chains.

On 9th October the ship was hit by a severe squall and knocked over onto her beam-ends. This would not have been so serious had her holds been full with an homogenous cargo such as wool, but inevitably the shingle ballast shifted and the ship took on a pronounced list to port. An effort was made to tack her and try to get her upright that way, but the sails were blown to shreds and then another blast heeled her over until her yard-arms were in the sea and there she stayed. In an effort to launch a lifeboat three of the crew were killed and the captain, trying to save some of his men, fell and hit his head on a davit and never recovered. The mate now took charge and ordered the masts to be cut away, but the foremast kept lifting with the swell and crashing down onto the keelson in such a manner that no one expected the ship to last for long. Dusk fell, and the crew took shelter wherever they could.

At daybreak a green light was sighted and distress rockets fired, which were answered by a blue light from another sailing ship which identified herself as the *Loire* owned by A. Bordes. She signalled 'Do you wish to abandon?' which was answered in the affirmative but the sea conditions made it impossible for a boat to be launched that day. The following day there was no improvement, except that the masts and spars had broken free, which lessened the risk of damage. That evening the *Loire* hoisted the flag signal 'EA' which means 'I will stand by you,' before standing clear for the night. At daybreak on the third day there was no sign of the *Loire*, but she reappeared at around 1000 hours to the relief of all those aboard and, as before, sailed around waiting for an opportunity to launch a boat but the conditions were still too rough. The fifth day was a repeat of the fourth, but on the sixth, although the wind was still squally, the sea had gone down and the *Loire* hove to on the weather side and launched her boat. It took two journeys in very difficult and dangerous conditions before the whole crew had been safely transferred to the French ship.

The subsequent enquiry into the loss of the vessel stated that three bulkheads should have been rigged instead of two but as often happened this appeared to be a prime case of assessors with 100 per cent hindsight who had to find some reason for the incident. A third bulkhead would have helped but nothing indicates that it would have saved the vessel.

Captain Michel Joffre showed no hesitation in fulfilling the fundamental duty of any vessel to go to the assistance of another in distress. The incident was later immortalised in a famous painting by P. Somerscales entitled simply 'I will not abandon you'. The *Dalgonar* did not sink, but stayed afloat on her beam-ends for a further six months during which time she drifted nearly 5,000 miles across the Pacific Ocean before grounding on Maupihoa Island in the Society Group. The crew should have prevented this by removing the hatchboards before they abandoned ship so that the vessel could sink and avoid becoming a danger to other shipping. It has been estimated by Commandant Rouch of the Oceanographic Museum at Monaco that between 1900 and 1907, 1,603 derelicts were sighted and a further 230 sightings were being made each year. How many vessels sank as a result of collision with a derelict will never be known since few if any sailing vessels had a radio.

By 1914 British sailing shipping had largely lost its dominance on the nitrate trade, but the Germans in particular were still sending large numbers of vessels around the Horn. Although a world slump was reducing overall numbers, British sailing ships were still to be seen on the Australian wool and wheat trade, tramping coal across the Pacific and to a lesser extent on the nitrate trade. However, the outbreak of the First World War in August 1914 gave commercial sail a last flourish for a few years. Freight rates rocketed as the need for shipping of every sort became a strategic necessity.

10

The Great War

The outbreak of war in August 1914 had an immediate effect on the Cape Horn trade. The allied British and French ships, plus neutral vessels, continued to trade as usual, bringing home the essential cargoes of nitrates and copper ore for munitions. But the German ships, some 200 of them, preferred internment in the ports of Chile and Peru to facing almost certain capture from the allied blockade in the Atlantic. Some of the German crews remained on their ships throughout the war, others made their way home by roundabout routes, and a few were recruited by visiting German warships.

In general the war gave a boost to sail because there was a desperate shortage of hulls to carry the additional cargoes of war materials, and many ships that would otherwise have been laid up or scrapped experienced a new lease of life. One enterprising skipper bought three wrecks on the grounds that he might be able to refloat one of them, but he was only saved by a hurricane from losing his entire investment. The wreck of the *Avenger* had been ashore on Ship Island in the Gulf of Mexico since 1904 and all attempts to refloat her had failed until the hurricane washed away part of the island and left enough water to get her off. She cost £15,000 to refit, but her first freight more than recouped this expense.

At the beginning of the war the largest concentration of German warships outside Europe was the Far Eastern fleet under Vice-Admiral Von Spee. Having evaded the British, Japanese and Russian fleets in Asia, the Germans made their way slowly towards Cape Horn waters, sending the cruiser *Leipzig* in advance to gather information. Rumours that German warships might be in the vicinity of the South American coast preceded the squadron, and these were fuelled by accounts of German merchant ships, with weapons hidden on board, leaving west coast ports the moment news of war was received, and fitting their guns once they were at sea. In fact very few of them carried any weaponry. But it was a time of rumour and the response of the Pacific Steam Navigation Company's ship *Orduna* was to fit herself with dummy guns made from ventilators, trestles and canvas, when she sailed from Panama to Valparaiso, hoping that her 'armament' would discourage any armed enemy merchant ship. She arrived safely at Valparaiso, not having sighted a single enemy vessel, and indeed she would have been most unlucky if she had, since their numbers had been greatly exaggerated. However the Valparaiso Port Authorities insisted that the 'guns' be dismantled immediately.

At the outbreak of the war the British had the world's largest navy, much of which was kept close to home to bottle up the German fleet, but Britain also had the largest merchant fleet and its Empire was dependent upon sea communications which had to be protected at all costs. As soon as it was seen that war was inevitable British cruisers were quickly dispatched all over the world to protect the shipping routes and search out and destroy or capture all enemy shipping. The most serious threat to Cape Horn traffic came initially from the two German cruisers *Karlsruhe* and *Dresden* which had been in the West Indies when war broke out. They disappeared and speedily made their way south down the Atlantic. That there were other German ships in the area is confirmed by the report form the cadet ship *Medway*, owned by Devitt and Moore, which had sailed from Sydney a fortnight before the war broke out, and was ordered to heave to by an unknown German steamer when off the Horn. The captain of the *Medway*'s response was to cram on all sail and show his pursuer a clean pair of heels. On her return to England, the ship lost all her cadets to the Grand Fleet, but such was the shortage of trained officers that a new contingent was quickly recruited, and the ship sailed away from the war zone. She spent the rest of the war running nitrates from Tocopilla to South Africa, always sailing eastabout, until being converted into a tanker just as the war ended.

Whilst the *Karlsruhe* did little to help the German war effort except avoid being caught, which tied up a lot of effort searching for her, the *Dresden* headed round Cape Horn to rendezvous with Von Spee. Realising that Cape Horn represented one of the choke points where the Germans might be caught if they made a break from the Pacific into the Atlantic, a British force was despatched to the area under the command of Rear-Admiral

Sir Christopher Cradock. Both sides had sympathisers in Chile and Argentina who passed on any information they could glean concerning their enemy's movements, but the first confirmation of a German presence in Cape Horn waters came from a British merchant ship, the *Ortega*, on 25th September.

The *Ortega*, a 7,970-ton passenger cargo vessel owned by the PSNC had just left Coronel on her homeward run when she realised she was being shadowed by an enemy cruiser which she identified as the *Dresden*. As she approached the Strait of Magellan the *Dresden* opened fire. The master of the *Ortega* promptly headed for an uncharted channel in the coastline as his only hope of escape, and the *Dresden* decided it was too risky to pursue him further. Having evaded destruction for the moment, the *Ortega* was faced with the danger of trying to navigate in uncharted waters with a draft of twenty-six feet. The choices facing the captain were not pleasant: head back out to sea and face the German cruiser, or carry on through the channel and face the risk of striking an uncharted rock. Perhaps conscious of the fact that he was carrying 300 French reservists returning to their own country, and anything was better than certain destruction if he turned back, Captain Kinnier chose to risk going through the channel. The *Ortega* launched one of her boats to sound ahead as she slowly steamed through the Nelson and Smythe Channels into the Magellan Strait. Each night the ship anchored, keeping a sharp lookout in case the Germans decided to attack from small boats, and radioing her situation to coast stations. The only response received was from the British consul at Punta Arenas who sent a message to London saying that the *Ortega* had been sunk with all hands! Once into the strait she headed for Punta Arenas where she met the Chilean warship *Admirante Lynch* which had been sent to search for her survivors. HMS *Glasgow* then arrived on the scene and escorted her to Rio de Janeiro.

The first confirmation of Von Spee's approach came three days later when the *Leipzig* sailed into the neutral waters of Lobos de Afuera on 28th September, where the British sailing ships *Tamar* and *Beeswing* were loading guano. Armed boarding parties were sent to the British ships to remove any Germans in their crews, but only one was found aboard the *Beeswing*. The alarm was raised and all British shipping in the area was warned of the danger from the German warships by radio or by contact if the vessels had no radio, as was the case with many of the sailing vessels. Some preferred to wait in port until the danger was past or suitable protection could be arranged, others such as the *Tamar* took their chances. The *Tamar* left Lobos de Afuera at night showing no lights, sailed to Paita to replenish stores, and then started her homeward voyage, narrowly missing becoming involved in the dramatic events that were about to unfold.

On receiving the report of the attack on the *Ortega* Cradock concentrated his ships at Punta Arenas where the British consul told him that the *Dresden* had been hiding in Orange Bay. Cradock took his squadron back out to sea and around Cape Horn to check, but found the bay empty. Running short of fuel, he sent the armed merchant cruiser *Otranto* to Punta Arenas, and sailed with the rest of his ships back to the Falkland Islands for coal.

On paper the two forces that were now closing on each other looked fairly equal. Von Spee had two armoured cruisers, the *Scharnhorst* and the *Gneisenau*, and three light cruisers, the *Dresden*, the *Nürnberg*, and the *Leipzig*. Cradock had the old battleship *Canopus*, the armoured cruisers *Good Hope* and *Monmouth*, and the light cruiser *Glasgow*, and the armed merchant cruiser *Otranto*. This apparent equality was not reflected in the ships themselves. The *Canopus* may have been a battleship with four 11-inch guns but she was from the pre-Dreadnought era and could only make 15 knots. The *Monmouth* and the *Good Hope* had been built in 1902, again before the revolution in naval construction caused by the launch of HMS *Dreadnought* in 1906, and were armed with two 9.2-inch guns and sixteen 6-inch guns, but the latter were placed low down and could not be used in a seaway. Only the *Glasgow* was modern, having been completed in 1911, and was armed with two 6-inch and ten 4-inch guns. The dissimilarity did not end there as except for the *Glasgow*, the bulk of the crews of Cradock's other ships were reservists who had joined up just before war was declared and had not yet been brought up to full efficiency. Against this Von Spee had a highly efficient squadron which had been in commission for some time and was crewed by regulars. The *Scharnhorst* and the *Gneisenau* were built in 1907 and armed with eight 8.2-inch and six 5.9-inch guns each. The three light cruisers were each armed with ten 4.1-inch guns. The British Admiralty realised rather too late that their fleet was outgunned and outclassed and radioed Cradock to restrict himself to shadowing the Germans until the arrival of the modern armoured cruiser *Defence*, which had been ordered to join him with all dispatch. However Cradock never received the message.

Von Spee's squadron rendezvoused at Easter Island on 12th October, the *Leipzig* arriving on the 14th with three colliers. They were forced to leave this anchorage two days later when the Chilean cruiser *Baquedano* objected to their presence in neutral waters. So Von Spee sailed to Más Afuera in the Juan Fernandez Islands, and, although they too were neutral, he continued to fill his coal bunkers. Obtaining coal was the German admiral's greatest problem. Germany did not have the world-wide facility of bunkering stations which had been created by the British, and their few overseas colonies were quickly captured by the allies. Von Spee had to acquire coal by raiding depots or capturing ships carrying coal cargoes. This rather haphazard system of supply explains the delays experienced by the German squadron. It would always stop and offload a captured coal cargo even if it meant delaying a major operation and this was to lead to its ultimate downfall. Vice-Admiral Von Spee's achievement in keeping his vessels supplied when all official sources were blocked was remarkable. Whilst in Más Afuera his small force was augmented by the *Prinz Eitel Friedrich*, a liner converted into an armed cruiser, which had experienced no success against allied shipping in Australian waters. Bunkering was completed on 28th October and Von Spee took his squadron towards the Chilean coast.

Cradock had sent the *Monmouth, Glasgow* and *Otranto* into the Pacific in the middle of October whilst he waited the arrival of *Canopus* with *Good Hope*. When the elderly *Canopus* arrived at the Falklands she needed five days to work on her boilers, but even when repairs were completed she could only steam at 12 knots. Rather than delay, Cradock took the *Good Hope* on ahead, leaving the old battleship to come on as best she could, guarding the fleet train made up of the essential colliers.

German wireless signals were intercepted by Cradock on 30th October, and, assuming this was from a solitary light cruiser, probably the *Dresden,* he sailed out to look for it. He had received no intelligence of the rest of the German squadron. Von Spee, in the meantime, had heard that the *Glasgow* had anchored in Coronel seeking intelligence, and sailed his squadron there to attack the British ship before she had to leave after the twenty-four hours allowed by the neutrality laws. The *Glasgow*, unaware of the approaching Germans, slipped out of Coronel on 1st November before the Germans arrived and joined Cradock. The two squadrons were now very close to each other, but each was unaware of the other's presence.

On 1st November at 1620 hours both sides sighted smoke and turned to investigate. The *Glasgow* was the first to realise the true situation, and hastened to inform the admiral. Cradock still had a choice. His ships, though older, were faster, and he could have withdrawn onto the *Canopus* before engaging. However, in the interval the Germans might have escaped, and since he did not have to sink the Germans, only damage them to the point where they would have to seek a neutral port for repairs and thus be interned, he decided to attack.

Von Spee realised who his opponents were by 1647 hours and hesitated no more than Cradock, but realising that with his inshore position his gunlayers would be blinded by the setting sun, he headed inshore until the sun had set and the British would then be silhouetted against the evening sky. The battle commenced at 1900 in a force 6 southerly wind at a range of 12,300 yards and was not long in doubt. The *Monmouth* and the *Good Hope* had their forward 9.2-inch turrets put out of action very early on and from then on, although their guns continued to fire, they scored very few hits. The *Otranto* was ordered to get herself clear and withdrew to the west at high speed. When Cradock realised that both the armoured cruisers were in a serious condition, knowing also that the *Glasgow* could do nothing against her much more powerful adversaries, he ordered her to withdraw to the south to warn the *Canopus* to save her from a similar fate. No one saw the *Good Hope* sink at about 2000 hours, but the *Monmouth* capsized at 2128 whilst trying to ram the *Nürnberg* after all her guns had been put out of action. There were no survivors from either ship.

The battle was unwittingly witnessed by the British ship *Fairport* which was homeward bound, having loaded nitrates at Tocopilla. They saw a light ahead which grew into an enormous flare on the evening of 1st November. They were not to discover the cause until they reached Falmouth on 28th February 1915, when they realised the flare must have been either HMS *Falmouth* or *Good Hope* blowing up.

Von Spee took part of his squadron to Valparaiso after the Battle of Coronel, but sailed to Más Afuera on 7th November when his twenty-four hours expired. He might well feel pleased with himself and the performance of his squadron. He had inflicted the heaviest defeat on the Royal Navy for 100 years, and smashed its reputation for invincibility. His ships had received only a few hits and did not need the services of a dockyard. On the downside, though, he had used over half his ammunition and was low on coal.

The *Leipzig* and the *Dresden* were already at Más Afuera taking coal from the French four-masted barque *Valentine* which had sailed from Port Talbot before the declaration of war. The unfortunate French captain had thought the warships were British, and when asked his cargo replied, 'First class Cardiff coal for Iquique'. He could not have provided the Germans with a more welcome present! The ship was stripped of anything useful in addition to her cargo and was waiting to be towed out to sea to be scuttled when a fire broke out on board. The danger to the Germans was that smoke from the fire might draw attention to their hiding place so the whole squadron fought the blaze. It did not save the *Valentine*, however; she was sunk in deep water off the islands a few days later. Another ship, the neutral Norwegian *Helicon*, was also brought to the anchorage and her cargo of coal removed since she was on a British charter and the German claimed that the cargo was enemy goods. She was allowed to retain enough of her cargo to give her stability, and then released. With the cargoes from these two vessels the Germans were temporarily flush with fuel.

Coaling from these sailing ships gave the Germans an unexpected problem since they were used to loading coal from steamers which do not have large spars aloft. Even in the protected anchorage the vessels rolled a little and to avoid the spars damaging the warships' upperworks the sailing ships were kept sufficiently clear with specially large fenders constructed and placed between the vessels to keep them safely apart.

Von Spee had to decide on his next more. His instructions were to break through to Germany and the High Seas Fleet would create a diversion when he got close to home to help him through the British blockade. Although he had a powerful force it could not be augmented and could not hope to compete with the allied build-up to catch him, but he had a number of choices. He could head for the recently opened Panama Canal, but he knew that a strong Allied force was gathering to his north. If he returned back across the Pacific he would probably run into Allied ships again. On the other hand, apart from the old *Canopus* and the *Glasgow* he had destroyed the only threat to a safe rounding of Cape Horn and escape out into the Atlantic. But he would need to move quickly before British reinforcements were on their way. However for some reason the German admiral did not proceed with his customary energy and only sailed from Más Afuera on 21st November 1914 to St Quentin Sound in the Gulf of Penas where he anchored to allow his ships to bunker.

Von Spee now had six warships and three colliers holding 17,000 tons of coal under his command. Before setting course back up the Atlantic to Germany he decided to use his force to strike another blow at the enemy by capturing the Falkland Islands and destroying the British radio station there, which was an important link in the Royal Navy's Atlantic communication system. There is some evidence to suggest that Germans living in Argentina were to join Von Spee and help to provide a garrison once the islands were in his hands. It also appears that the admiral had contact with German citizens in Punta Arenas, and no doubt this route was used to convey messages and pass on intentions.

The German squadron put to sea on 26th November and took the route round Cape Horn rather than risk their position being reported, which would have been inevitable if they had gone through the Strait of Magellan. The weather was not good, and a German officer reported that they rolled and pitched so much that they could not sit at a table and had to stretch safety lines across the mess rooms. On 2nd December Cape Horn was rounded, and whilst the crews were congratulating themselves on their newly earned right to place both feet on the table, two large icebergs appeared to starboard.

The next day when south-west of Staten Island, a four-masted barque was sighted beating to the west. She was the *Drummuir*, a British vessel loaded with 2,800 tons of coal and bound for San Francisco. She was stopped, boarded and taken in tow by the *Leipzig* into the lee of Picton Island in the Beagle Channel. Her cargo was transferred to the supply ships *Baden* and *Santa Isabel*. She was stripped of anything useful – even doors will help to keep boilers alight – and taken to sea and sunk. On 7th December the squadron set off to attack Port Stanley whilst just out of sight some twenty miles to their south, two British ships, the *Tamar* and *Fairport* were altering course to the north-east on their way home.

The four-day delay caused by the transfer of the *Drummuir's* coal proved fatal to the Germans. Had they steamed straight for the Falklands after rounding Cape Horn, they would only have had the old *Canopus* to contend with. However, stung by the defeat at what has become known as the Battle of Coronel, the British Admiralty had decided to take drastic measures to deal with Von Spee and two powerful modern battle cruisers from the British Grand Fleet bottling up the German fleet in the North Sea had been despatched south in great secrecy. On the evening of 6th December Vice-Admiral Sir Doveton Sturdee had arrived at Port Stanley with the battle cruisers *Invincible* and *Inflexible*, supported by the cruisers *Caernarvon, Cornwall, Kent, Bristol* and *Glasgow* and the armed merchant cruiser *Macedonia*. After their fast journey from the North Sea the warships were low on fuel and were in the process of loading coal when smoke was sighted to the south-east.

The German squadron arrived off Port Stanley shortly after daybreak on 8th December and were first noticed by the wife of a sheep farmer who passed the news to the British ships. As the Germans approached they saw large clouds of smoke coming from the harbour. This was assumed to be the coal stocks being burned to prevent them falling into enemy hands but instead it was the British force desperately raising steam. Only after 0900 hours did the gunnery officer of the *Gneisenau* sight warships in the harbour, but his captain refused to believe his report of tripod masts since he did not believe there could be any battleships there apart from the *Canopus*. At that moment only the *Kent* was ready to sail and had Von Spee attacked at once he might have given the British ships a severe mauling. Whether he even thought of it will never be known, for as the *Kent* cleared the harbour the *Gneisenau* sailed to intercept her, but at that moment received a hit on the funnel by a practice round fired by the *Canopus* and immediately turned away. The reason for a practice round being fired was that the crew of the

Canopus had been told to expect a live firing exercise that morning and in order to gain an advantage over the forward turret, the crew of the after turret had crept up during the night and loaded their guns. When the call to actions stations was made it was not possible to remove the practice shells that were already rammed home. The real shells fired by the forward gun turret fell well short of the *Gneisenau*, but the practice shell ricocheted and scored a direct hit! On such ridiculous chances the fate of battles can depend.

The Germans now assumed that another pre-Dreadnought battleship must have joined the *Canopus*, decided not to risk the attack and withdrew to the east. The British ships began to leave the harbour from 0945 when the *Glasgow* was able to join the *Kent*. The battle cruisers were able to sail soon afterwards and, knowing his superiority in speed and weight of armament, Sturdee hoisted the signal 'Chase'. By 1100 Von Spee knew that his gamble to capture the Falklands had been lost and had turned into a trap for his squadron. None of his vessels stood a chance against the superior speed and armament of the battle cruisers manned by regulars instead of reservists and it was just a question of time until the inevitable defeat took place. The first shots were fired just before 1300. Von Spee ordered his light cruisers to escape as best they could and then bravely turned towards his enemy. This time the sea was calm but the gunlayers found it difficult to observe the fall of their shot because of the smoke from the ships, and had difficulty making corrections. Nevertheless the *Scharnhorst* sank at 1617 and the *Gneisenau* just over an hour later. Von Spee died with his ship and only 190 of the two crews, which must have totalled nearly 2,000 at the beginning of the engagement, were picked up by the British warships.

The German light cruisers had turned to the south on receipt of the order to save themselves, hotly pursued by the *Cornwall*, *Kent* and *Glasgow*. The British ships slowly gained, but it was obvious that the *Dresden* was unlikely to be overhauled before dark, and so the *Glasgow*, which was the only British ship capable of catching the *Dresden*, helped the *Cornwall* deal with the *Leipzig*. The action started at 1450 and by 2030 the order was given to abandon the wrecked ship, but only seven officers and eleven men were saved. The British had sustained one death and four wounded, all from the *Glasgow*. The *Kent* in the meantime had started firing at the *Nürnberg* at 1709 and the German hauled down her colours an hour and a half later. She sank at 1926. By the time these two German cruisers had been sunk it was too late to pursue the *Dresden*, and in any case, the *Glasgow*'s speed had been reduced by a hit in her engine room. The *Dresden* escaped for the time being.

Nearer to the Falklands, HMS *Bristol* had reported more ships in sight at

1130 in the morning, and Sturdee dispatched her with the armed merchant cruiser *Macedonia* to sink what were thought to be transports bringing up an invasion force. In fact the ships were Von Spee's colliers, the *Santa Isabel, Baden,* and *Seydlitz.* Both the former ships were sunk after their crews had been safely removed but it would have been better to have taken them and their valuable cargo as prizes. Whilst the British were engaged in this operation, the faster *Seydlitz* made her escape but subsequently sought internment at San Antonio in Argentina.

With the destruction of two armoured cruisers, two light cruisers and two colliers, the Battle of Coronel had been more than amply avenged. There were still a number of German warships at large, the light cruisers *Dresden* and *Karlsruhe,* and the armed merchant cruisers *Kronprinz Wilhelm* and *Prinz Eitel Friedrich,* but they were split up, and none of them could pose the threat to Britain's supremacy at sea that Von Spee had been able to do with his squadron intact. One by one they were hunted down and put out of action.

The battle was witnessed by the *Fairport* which thought she heard thunder at 1400. Ten miles to the east the *Tamar* saw flashes and also heard thunder and took in sail as she thought a storm was approaching, although she could clearly see the *Fairport* with all sail set. The *Fairport* saw warships manoeuvring at high speed and firing their guns and initially believed she had run into a major exercise. When the crew realised they had unwittingly sailed into the middle of a major naval battle there was little they could do about it. Heavy shells fell near by, and at 1530 it looked as if the German ships were closing in on them so a large Norwegian flag was hoisted. However the Germans were far too busy avoiding the British warships and the battle gradually drew astern.

As HMS *Kent* was finishing off the *Nürnberg* another sailing ship suddenly appeared, sailing north. She has never been positively identified but is believed to be the American *William P. Frise.*

The only German survivor of the battle, the *Dresden,* went to Punta Arenas to fill her bunkers and then laid up for a while in Hewitt Bay, Tierra del Fuego. On 6th December she left this lonely anchorage after being sighted by a sealing schooner, and hid in Wughnacht Bay until 14th February. During this time she was able to take some coal from the collier *Sierra Cordoba,* but still too short to wage cruiser warfare, she sailed for Juan Fernandez, searching the sailing ship routes for a vessel carrying coal as she went. She was rewarded on 26th February 1915 when she captured the British barque *Conway Castle.* However, the ship was homeward bound, and the only coal was in the galley bunker. The *Conway Castle* was sunk and her crew taken aboard the warship. Their internment was not prolonged as a few days later a Peruvian ship was stopped and the prisoners transferred.

The *Dresden* was now in a desperate position. She did not have sufficient coals to make a long voyage, and there were at least three British cruisers searching for her in the vicinity of Cape Horn. Her fate was sealed when the British Admiralty intercepted a coded signal from a German agent in Chile confirming a rendezvous for the raider with a collier 300 miles west of Coronel on 5th March. HMS *Kent* was sent to investigate but did not arrive at the position until the 7th and the area was covered in fog. When this cleared the next day the *Dresden* was sighted twelve miles away. Although the distance was too great to be closed before nightfall the British ship gave chase. The *Dresden* made off at top speed but she had not yet rendezvoused with her collier and had insufficient coal to go further than Más Afuera where she arrived on 9th March. Knowing that escape was now impossible without more coal, Captain Lüdecke delayed by requesting that the governor send for a Chilean warship to accept his internment. It was his last chance as, if his collier arrived before a Chilean warship, he could try to escape, and could always say he had waited as long as possible. Meanwhile the *Glasgow* and the *Orama* were on their way to join the *Kent*, and the three British warships approached Cumberland Bay, where the *Dresden* lay at anchor, on the morning of 14th March.

Neither side seems to have been willing to pay too much attention to international law when it suited them. The *Dresden* was clearly in breach of the law in so far as she had remained in neutral waters for more than the stipulated twenty-four hours and had not yet allowed herself to be interned. Nevertheless she was in neutral waters. This problem did not bother the senior British captain, whose view was that whilst the *Dresden* still flew the German flag she was a threat to allied commerce and had tied up valuable warships that were needed elsewhere for more than three months. At 1850 *Glasgow* opened fire, to be joined shortly afterwards by *Kent*. Hits were scored with the first salvo, and although the *Dresden* returned the fire within three minutes she was sufficiently damaged to hoist the white flag. Whilst one of the officers from the *Dresden*, a Lieutenant Canaris who was to achieve fame as head of the Abwehr in the Second World War, was parleying with Captain Luce, who was also deflecting the protests of the Chilean Governor, there was a loud explosion from the bay. Captain Lüdecke had managed to remove his crew and detonate his forward magazine.

The only German cruiser left unaccounted for was the *Karlsruhe*, which had last been heard of steering down the American coast at about the same time the *Dresden* was making her way round to join Von Spee. In fact, although the British Admiralty did not know it, the *Karlsruhe* had blown up as she approached Barbados at the time of the Battle of Coronel. The survivors had boarded one of their tenders, the *Rio Negro*, and taken advantage of the winter to steam to Norway via Iceland. The only other German warship still at large by March 1915 was the cruiser *Königsberg*, but she was blockaded in the River Rufiji south of Dar-es-Salaam in Tanzania.

Only one other British ship was lost to Von Spee's fleet. The auxiliary cruiser *Prinz Eitel Friedrich* captured the *Kildalton* on 12th December. The *Prinz Eitel* was already towing the French barque *Jean*, which she had captured earlier with a cargo of coal. The crews of both the British and French ships were subsequently landed on Easter Island.

The war moved away from Cape Horn after the *Dresden* had been sunk, and no large German forces were ever able to break through the British blockade in the North Sea. Submarines, however, a new weapon that was to prove so effective against the blockade took a heavy toll amongst the remaining Cape Horners. The German submarine *U20*, which had sunk the passenger liner *Lusitania* without warning on 6th May 1915, was still cruising off the coast of Southern Ireland on the 21st of that month when the *Glenholm* came inward bound with a cargo of nitrates from Chile. Aboard the *Glenholm*, making her second voyage in a square rigger, was the captain's daughter Helen Campbell, who has given a tragic account of what happened.

The German submarine came close to us on the port quarter of the *Glenholm* and began to train his gun on us. The Germans did not hail or speak to my father at all as he was expecting them to do, so he then came down to the saloon to me and said: 'Come on up, Love, and show yourself.' I said I was afraid that they would take me but he assured me that they would never do that – 'He would see to that.'

I went on to the poop and looked over the rail, and down to the submarine. I was feeling very afraid and must have looked a very pathetic sight, for as soon as they saw me they put up two flags, which meant 'Abandon your ship at once.' My father said: 'Grab what you can and be quick.' I was too confused and all that I could think of was my birds, so I took the parrot from her perch and the cage with my little birds in, and while I was doing this my father was getting his papers and the officers were calling out to me to come up as quickly as possible and get into the lifeboat. They were all so very thoughtful for me.

When my father was ready, I got into the boat and we pulled away

– but as we were in the starboard boat, we had to row astern to the port side where the submarine was. The Captain of the submarine did not say a word, so my father told the crews of both boats to row as fast as they could to get away from the ship. When we reached a safe distance, the men ceased rowing and watched the dear *Glenholm* go to her doom.

Thirty-nine shots were fired into the ship, but she refused to sink, so she was torpedoed. The submarine then fired at the lifeboats before submerging, leaving the survivors to row to Bantry Bay, fortunately with no casualties. Many other square riggers fell to U-boats in a similar manner, although shelling the survivors was unusual.

The German long-range threat to Allied shipping was restricted to disguised merchant ships once their warships had been destroyed. The *Moewe,* of 4,798 tons, broke out from the North Sea in December 1915, and on her first and second voyages destroyed a total of thirty-four Allied ships, mainly in the vicinity of the Cape of Good Hope. She was by far the most successful of the disguised warships. The most unusual surface raider of the war and the one that can claim to be the last sailing warship was the barque *Seeadler*, previously *Pass of Balmaha*, captured by the submarine *U36* on her way to Scapa Flow. For the purpose of raiding Allied shipping the vessel was refitted, disguised as a Norwegian vessel and renamed the *Rena*. She left Germany with supplies for three years in December 1916 and a crew of officers and sixty-four seamen who had been given training in Norwegian sailing ship customs.

To command this unusual raider the Germans chose Count Felix von Lückner, a naval reservist who had sailed on British and other sailing ships for most of his life. He had started the war as an officer aboard the light cruiser *Emden*, but was fortunate enough to be away as crew on a captured prize when she was destroyed by HMAS *Australia*. His next ship was sunk at the Battle of Jutland but the count managed to survive, although wounded, until rescued by his own side. Luck seems to have marked his sailing career from the outset. Whilst serving as a boy on the Russian full-rigged ship *Niobe* bound for Fremantle, he had fallen overboard. A large albatross swooped down and seized his hand in its beak. With his other hand the boy grabbed the albatross's webbed foot and hung on grimly as the bird beat the air with its wings and attacked the hand with its beak. Other albatrosses hovered around, hoping to have a chance of feeding on this strange prey, but this activity enabled the ship's boat to find him quickly, which undoubtedly saved his life.

Bad weather helped the disguised *Seeadler* to escape from the North Sea, but off Iceland she was intercepted by a boarding party from the armed merchant cruiser *Avenger*. The count was prepared for just such an eventuality. A cargo of lumber was lashed on deck, making it impossible to inspect the holds, and all but a few of his men were tucked away below using hidden doors. In his cabin he even had a boy of seventeen lying on the couch disguised as his 'wife' with toothache so that his voice would not give him away. The boarding officer was completely convinced by the count's papers and appearance of the ship and failed to find her two hidden 4.1-inch guns, torpedo tubes and wireless.

The *Seeadler* made her way down the Atlantic and round the Horn into the Pacific, accounting for a total of fifteen Allied merchant ships, twelve of them sailing vessels. By the time Von Lückner had captured the four-masted barque *Pinmore*, on which he had made two voyages in 1902, he was short of some provisions and decided to man her himself and sail into Rio de Janeiro, pretending that his crew were the original Norwegian seamen. On arrival off the port he anchored and went ashore to buy stores and gather whatever information he could about the whereabouts of British cruisers which were out hunting for him. Staying only a short time to avoid the risk of his deception being discovered, he soon sailed back to rejoin the *Seeadler*. Having transferred the stores, he placed a scuttling charge aboard the *Pinmore*, which quickly sank. This was not Von Lückner's only association with Rio during his voyage. In March 1917 he sent the *Cambronne*, one of A. Bordes' square riggers into the port under the command of one of his captured captains in order to land 287 prisoners from the various ships he had captured who were rapidly depleting his stores. Before releasing the prisoners, however, he cut down the topmasts and threw all the spare sails overboard so they would not make a speedy passage and report his whereabouts to the British before he had time to get well away.

Having announced his presence Von Lückner decided that he had better move to a different part of the world, and sailed round the Horn, being forced well south by the westerlies, and into the Pacific. In a thick snow squall during the rounding, a British armed merchant cruiser was sighted and, assuming that he too must have been seen, Von Lückner set every sail he had and ran off to the east. As the snow thickened he lost sight of his pursuer and when it cleared he had the ocean to himself. In fact the British ship had not seen him. Having evaded this danger the *Seeadler* sailed on into the Pacific and managed to sink a few small schooners before sailing to Mopelia in the Society Islands where he careened alongside a coral reef. An unusual tidal wave lifted the ship onto the reef on 2nd August 1917 and since there was no way of getting her off, she had to be abandoned. The captain was eventually captured and spent the rest of the war in prison in New Zealand.

Von Lückner was a brave and resourceful seaman. Only one of his crew was killed during his interesting voyage and he always treated his captives well. He and his voyage really belong to an earlier age, but he showed the kind of daring that excites admiration and would have given him a reputation at any time. This was the last time that the waters of Cape Horn were affected by the war since no other German warships escaped the blockade of the North Sea except the U-boats and none of these had the range to get so far.

11

The Twilight of the Cape Horners

In the immediate aftermath of the First World War, freight rates held up and sailing ships were still able to find profitable cargoes. Trade was sufficiently encouraging for Gustav Eriksen, whose name is associated with the final effort to keep commercial sail operating, to spend £13,000 in 1919 on repairs to the *Grace Harwar* at Montevideo after she was severely damaged by a storm off the Horn, a sum that would buy two ships of her class within a few years.

The full-rigged ship *Grace Harwar*, of 1,749 tons, built by W. Hamilton and Co. of Port Glasgow in 1889, loaded with Australian grain for Europe, had run into a hurricane. All her sails were blown out by a particularly severe squall which drove her onto beam-ends and held her there. Her lee deck was eight feet under water which made it impossible to square the yards as the lee braces could not be eased. The seas quickly smashed the forecastle and poop doorways and water surged in, destroying everything in its path. The men knew that if they could not get at the braces, sooner or later the hatch covers were bound to go and then they would sink like a stone. With her hatches sealed, a sailing ship was rather like a submarine, water swept over the main deck and eventually found its way back into the sea through the freeing ports, special openings in the bulwarks designed for this purpose. Equipment and men on deck might be swept away but as long as the hatches remained sealed the vessel was watertight. By some means they managed to square the yards, set the main lower topsail, and heave to.

Then they started to clear the wreckage. The saloon was the first priority since this was where all the navigation equipment was kept; the forecastle could wait as apart from the fact that the crew had little enough by way of personal possessions, most of the contents had been washed overside. She looked a wreck, nothing remained of her deck equipment – even the capstan bars had gone – but when the wind eventually eased they set sail and made their way into the Atlantic. The problem was they had no charts, no sextant, nothing except a very rusty chronometer which they had managed to save. They tried to make Port Stanley but another gale drove them away so they sailed on, not knowing accurately where they were until they met an Italian steamer who managed to spare them an old sextant and a chart of the River Plate and that decided where they went for repairs.

Despite the opening of the Panama Canal in 1914, which enabled steamships, and gradually the more efficient diesel-powered vessels, to compete with even the last vaguely profitable sailing routes, a few new sailing ships were being launched. In 1920 F. Laeisz and Company, who had lost their entire fleet as war reparations, were doing their best to recover their fleet by buying each of them back as they came upon the open market. In defiance of the trends they ordered a new vessel, the four-masted barque *Priwell*.

Sail had now to compete with the increasing numbers of steamers looking for work as cargoes became scarce. This inevitably meant they had to pick up bulk commodities for delivery over long distances where time was not so important and freight rates were low. The year 1921 might be called the turning-point. Sixty-one square riggers loaded nitrates in Chile and Peru and rates for wheat from Australia were high for the early ships but deteriorated as the year passed until they barely covered costs. In all, sixty-three sailing vessels loaded Australian wheat that year, fifteen of them British, eleven Norwegian, ten from Finland and twenty-six French, but fifty-two of these never returned to Australia. Not all chose to sail home the most direct way via Cape Horn. Indeed, as word got back to the ships that most sailing vessels were laying up on completion of their discharge in Europe, many seemed to select longer routes, encouraging owners to imagine that their captains were prolonging the voyages to put off the evil day. The Cape of Good Hope route back to Europe was usually longer, although easier, as vessels could pick up the more moderate easterly trade winds if they took a course about 35° south through the Indian Ocean.

Those sailing vessels that tried to tramp found the trade uneconomic. The *Cumberland* spent two years on one voyage around the world, picking up what she could and rounding the Horn in October 1921 after a battle lasting three weeks against easterly winds. She discharged her nitrate cargo in Beira, loaded grain in Durban for home and was then sold.

There were only two obvious cargoes left where sailing ships could just cover their costs, nitrates from Chile and wheat, largely from the Spencer Gulf in Australia, both bound for Europe. These two trades involved voyages of more than 10,000 miles around the Horn and became the last resort for commercial sail and real seamen.

The Australian grain trade has become romanticised because it created the Australian grain race, but it did not start out that way since the vessels completed their loading at different times and sailed independently. Times taken on passage, although interesting, are not really comparable since vessels sailing only a week apart can encounter very different weather. Average voyage times in any year varied considerably from 139 days in 1923 to 107 in 1937, but if these average times did get better in the years between the wars it had more to do with the scrapping of the slower vessels than an improvement in sailing ability.

In 1922 freight rates collapsed to half or less the level of the beginning of the previous year. The *Lawhill*, for example, had managed to fix £6 per ton for grain in 1921, but could not achieve better than £2 the following year. Many owners decided there was no future for sail and sold their ships, or laid them up. The canal alongside the Loire called La Martinière, better known as the Cemetery, soon filled with fine Cape Horners and Brest and Falmouth had more than sixty each just lying at moorings, few of which were ever recommissioned. Apart from 1924, no French-registered vessels ever carried grain again, and only one British loaded. Apart from a small German contingent the trade was left to the Finns because they still insisted that all Merchant Marine Officers must serve their apprenticeship in sail.

As a result of the low freight rates only seven sailing vessels loaded in 1922 and the fastest passage was made by the *Milverton*, now under the Finnish flag. Her time was 90 days from Melbourne to London but she did not sail until October and so had the best weather for a passage around the Horn. Not built for speed, the *Milverton* could carry 3,500 tons of cargo and was rather typical of the type of vessel that survived, large, heavy and capacious. She was not heavily canvased and did not cross royals on any of her masts; she was built to make safe and undramatic voyages that showed a profit, not to provide pretty pictures for the front of a calendar.

The numbers were up to nine in 1923, with an additional vessel loading wool in Melbourne. As their departures were spread over seven months no sensible comparison of performance can be made but the fastest passage of 88 days was made by the *Beatrice* loaded with wool. All the Australian vessels successfully reached their destinations, but on the nitrate trade the *Peiho* went ashore in the Strait of Le Maire and became a total loss. The significance of the Australian wheat trade at this time can be gauged from the fact that in 1924, when eleven vessels loaded grain in Australia, there were still some 240 sailing vessels trading at deep sea. Thus the grain run only attracted seven per cent of the square-rig tonnage available.

In 1924 Laeisz bought the *Faith,* the former *Maréchal Suchet,* built in 1902 as one of the French bounty ships, and re-christened her the *Pellworm.* She left Nantes with the sand ballast put in when she was laid up, despite the protestations of the master who felt it was unsuitable. Closing the Horn the ballast inevitably shifted and threw the vessel onto her beam-ends. The crew had to retrim the sand but, by the time they had completed this operation, they had drifted well south of South Georgia and they refused to make the Horn passage unless the ballast was changed. This sort of accident was most unusual for a Laeisz ship and, rather than keep the vessel with such a stain on her reputation she was ordered back to Hamburg and sold.

That twenty-five vessels joined the grain run in 1925 was due more to the reduction in freight rates elsewhere than anything else. *Wilhelmine* hit ice and had to put into Talcahuano for repairs. Her grain cargo was discharged first and she ended up taking nitrates back to Europe.

Despite the decline in the numbers of sailing ships since the war and the struggle even to cover operating costs, Laeisz built a new four-masted barque for their nitrate run in 1926, the *Padua*, which turned out to be the last square-rigger built specifically for trade. She has had an interesting history and is still afloat today as the Russian Sail Training vessel the *Krusernstern*, and a regular participant in the Sail Training Association's programme. Although she has been fitted with an auxiliary engine she is a living representation of the ultimate sail-driven merchant ship. Designed to carry 4,800 tons of cargo and rigged as an economical four-masted barque, she carried 36,500 square feet of sail which gave her a good turn of speed and enabled her to average about 80 days on her outward and homeward voyages from Germany to the Chilean nitrate ports, thus still maintaining Laeisz's schedule of three voyages a year.

But if the efficient Germans could manage to keep vessels trading at a profit, the French with their higher wages, could not. The year 1926 saw the famous company of A. D. Bordes et Fils selling off all their sailing ships and a great chapter in French Cape Horners came to a close. The British deep-sea square-rigged fleet was down to four vessels by the end of that year and none of these survived in trade for long. It is claimed that the last commercial square rigger to sail under the British flag was the four-masted

2,842-ton barque *Garthpool,* owned in 1927 by Sir William Garthwaite's
Marine Navigation Company, but in fact she was registered in Montreal by
this time but flew the Red Ensign. The honour of being the last British
registered sailing square rigger goes to the *William Mitchell* and the final
square rigger to fly the Red Ensign was the little three-masted barque *Diego*
trading between Mauritius and the Cape until wrecked off the Chagos
Archipelago in 1935 after a working life of sixty-seven years.

The *Garthpool* was built in 1891 by W. D. Thompson for Barrie of
Dundee as the *Juteopolis* for the Calcutta to Dundee trade. She was sold in
1900 to the Anglo-American Oil Company (which became Esso in 1951).
In 1911 she changed hands again, being bought by George Windram and
Sons of Liverpool for £6,500 and Garthwaite bought her at the end of the
First World War. She had achieved some fast passages in her time, San
Francisco to Hong Kong in 59 days and Hong Kong to Cape Henry at the
mouth of Chesapeake Bay in 139 days. When she sailed from Dublin in
ballast on 14th October 1927 for Australia, she was still not fitted with
halyard winches, the only labour-saving device being a donkey engine for
the anchor windlass, and she still relied on flags to signal, having no radio
aboard.

Life aboard would have been familiar to a seaman fifty years earlier,
although the pay was quite good for the time, £9 a month for an able seaman,
more than I myself earned as a first and second year apprentice thirty years
later. The traditional effigy of the old dead horse would be paraded round
the ship at the end of the first month at sea, then hoisted to the yardarm and
cast into the sea. This signified the point at which the seamen had worked
off their first month's pay in advance, received when they signed on and
incidentally provides the origin of the expression about the pointlessness of
flogging a dead horse. With these advances on pay they would have needed
to buy a 'Donkey's Breakfast', that is a six-foot sack filled with hay which
passed as a mattress, plus eating utensils and some clothing. The heavy
canvas sails were changed for the light suit as they approached the north-
east trade winds, and then all the running cordage was coated with Stockholm
tar. As they reached the Equator and the trade winds died, the work load
increased, as the yards were trimmed for every catspaw of wind, and the
only break in this drudgery was the crossing-the-line ceremony. Then the
south-east trades began to be felt and, close hauled on the port tack, the
Garthpool picked up speed, making the wide sweep to the west that had
been in use by sailing ships in the South Atlantic since Vasco da Gama
pioneered it in the fifteenth century. The island of Tristan da Cunha was
sighted as she swept into the Southern Ocean.

Catching an albatross had been sport for seamen for centuries and the *Garthpool*'s crew were no exception. A discarded tin had a triangular hole cut into it with a piece of salt pork wedged inside before being thrown overside on a length of line. The albatross swooped down, poked its beak into the tin and seized hold of the meat but then found that with its beak open it could not pull clear of the tin. It was hauled aboard and photographed and then, because the deck of the vessel was too small to allow the huge bird to take off, it was held up in the air so that the wind caught it beneath its wings, and off it planed.

On 14th December Ordinary Seaman Maddock was loosing the port side of the mainsail when he slipped and fell into the sea. The dreaded cry, 'Man overboard', rang out through the ship, which was making a good 12 knots in a rising wind and considerable sea. The barque was swung immediately into the wind and the lifeboat lowered but its gunwale was stove in and one of the crew broke his ankle before the boat could reach the water. By this time the man was no longer in sight and the captain decided that it would only risk more lives if he were to try to lower the other boat so the course was resumed. No one doubted that the right decision had been made, but the empty bunk in the forecastle was a constant reminder of the loss and a caution to remember the old sailing ship adage, 'One hand for yourself, one for the ship'. Those square riggers, when brought head to wind with sails aback, drifted quickly to leeward and the man, even if still alive, might have been two or three miles away by the time the boat was in the water, which would have meant a hard and dangerous row and no guarantee that the boat would find the victim or her way back to the barque again. We were luckier fifty years later in the same vicinity when we lost a man overboard from the maxi-yacht *Condor*. Although we travelled almost a mile before we could get the spinnaker down, we had managed to throw a lifebelt and seen the man grab it. We also had the advantage of a motor to get back on a reciprocal bearing and although the seas were large, the wind was easing. We could not see our casualty from the low deck of the yacht, but we could see where he was from the birds circling him. Despite the fact that we were at 55° south and the temperature was close to freezing, we got him back alive about twenty minutes after he had gone into the sea, but he was already very cold.

The *Garthpool* arrived off Semaphore Island near Adelaide after a voyage of 91 days and waited for a cargo of wheat. Shore leave was given and the crew piled into the local bars to make up for five months' abstention. Two of the more sober members brought the remainder back on a trolley along the wharf and started to get them up the gangway when it collapsed, depositing everyone in the water. More by luck than anything else, since many of the men could not swim, no one was drowned, although one man was found to be missing. Even he was saved. After reaching shore he stripped off his wet clothes only to be picked up by the police and charged with exposing his person, but he was released uncharged when the truth was explained.

Loaded with 5,000 tons of wheat the *Garthpool* sailed, intending to make her passage home via the Cape of Good Hope, where they might collect supplies, since her crew were considered too few to take her round Cape Horn. The Great Australian Bight had other ideas, though, and a severe westerly storm persuaded the captain to turn the other way. This entailed at least an extra month at sea, for which supplies had not been bought, nor had any of the men prepared themselves for the winter in the Southern Ocean. The result was that they were permanently underfed, cold and wet, with water sluicing around the forecastle beneath their bunks. Being in the main young and fit they survived, but the conditions as the barque made her way down to 65° southerly latitude must have been horrendous. Frequently up to three men had to hold the six-foot wheel which kicked and threw them off, and oil was often streamed from bags astern to reduce the breaking tops of the seas. The weather worsened as they approached the Horn where hurricane-force winds engulfed them. Then the wind died, and in those huge and confused seas the vessel was somehow held on an easterly heading with waves crashing across the deck and rolling the yardarms into the water. On a large open-decked vessel the quantity of water trapped between the bulwarks could weigh nearly 1,000 tons, and have the effect of reducing the freeboard by as much as two feet. If the vessel were heavily loaded, her freeboard might thus be temporarily reduced from five to three feet and she would be even more vulnerable to a following wave.

When the wind returned it was with tremendous force out of the west and the strain was sufficient to part three bottlescrews on the fore shrouds. Often submerged, the crew struggled to replace them with chains before the mast fell. No one except the captain seemed to think that the vessel would survive, but somehow she held together and was headed north.

The scrawny pigs and some dolphins were the only fresh food available on the homeward voyage although wheat was brought up from the hold and ground down to make porridge or flapjacks fried in rancid pork fat. Weevils knocked out of the ship's biscuits would float to the top of a mug of tea or coffee, (the distinction meant little as both tasted the same), and were eaten as a delicacy. The main relaxations were trying to catch sharks and cockroach racing. Finally in August 1928 the vessel drifted into Queenstown harbour (County Cork), and the anchors were let go.

The *Garthpool* was lost two voyages later off the Cape Verde Islands when she followed what she thought was a steamer close inshore. Unfortunately the steamer was aground and the *Garthpool* joined her. The crew were saved but the barque slowly rusted away. She had not been back to the Horn since her last round-the-world voyage in 1928 and this voyage remains the last around the Horn by a square rigger under the Red Ensign.

In 1927 the sailing fleet numbered seventeen, mainly owing to a dispute in the steamship trade removing the competition. The vessels sailed as soon as they had completed loading but two, the *Archibald Russell* and the *Hougomont* found themselves together in the Tasman Sea and decided to make a race of it. They were evenly matched and sighted each other on the Equator and close to the Irish coast as they approached home, the *Hougomont* winning by four days. This was a bad year for ice at the Horn. The *Hougomont* ran through large fields and the *C. B. Pedersen* had difficulty getting through, sighting bergs as far from the Drake Passage as 48° 37' south and 44° 10' west. The *Winterhude*, homeward bound from Callao with nitrates, sailed through bergs for 850 miles, some over ten miles in length. The six-masted barquentine *E. R. Sterling*, which made the winter passage with Australian grain, only ran into heavy gales and icebergs once she had rounded the Horn and lost her second and third masts. She crawled as far as the West Indies before seeking repairs but since the facilities were not available, hired a tug to tow her to London. From loading to discharging ports her voyage took 286 days. She was not the only vessel to be damaged off the Horn that year as the *Greif* was swept by a giant wave, losing everything movable on deck including her lifeboats, which were hurled sixty metres away from the vessel. The *Fennia*, loaded with nitrates, was dismasted at the Horn, losing two of her crew. She struggled into Port Stanley but was condemned. The *William Mitchell*, the last square rigger registered in Britain, was sold for scrap at the end of that season.

A cup was presented in 1928 for a match between the *Herzogin Cecilie* and the *Beatrice,* so this might be called the year when the Great Grain Races can be said to have started. The two vessels sailed five hours apart from Port Lincoln in the Spencer Gulf, the *Herzogin Cecilie* taking the Horn route whilst the *Beatrice* went via the Cape of Good Hope. The *Herzogin* was the easy winner by eighteen days, though the *Beatrice* ran into a hurricane in the Indian Ocean which caused some damage. The *C. B. Pedersen*, which had sailed from Sydney a day earlier than the other two, was overhauled by the *Herzogin* just before the Equator but although she tried to make a race of it she arrived at Queenstown a week after the *Herzogin* reached Falmouth. These vessels made up only a third of the grain fleet that year, but an account of events by the Tasmanian Alan Villiers, who served as an AB aboard the *Herzogin*, caught the public imagination and the newspapers began to talk of the 'Grain Race'. Publicity for Alan Villiers' book was probably done no harm by the discovery of a female stowaway aboard the vessel shortly after she sailed.

The last of the square riggers were mostly in Finnish hands by now and young men, lured by the romance of Villiers' writing, began to volunteer to join their crews. Volunteer was the right word since Eriksen was not slow to take commercial advantage and signed them aboard as crew in return for the standard £50 apprenticeship fee! Of the fourteen vessels that sailed in 1929, eleven were Finnish-registered and two, the *Mozart* and the *Penang*, departed on the same day from Walleroo and arrived within a day of each other at Queenstown, the former being the winner. But the Horn was still taking its toll and Laeisz's lost a vessel, the *Pinnaes*, after she was dismasted by the combination of a heavy storm followed by a complete calm which rolled the masts out of her. No sooner had the masts gone than the wind rose again. She must have been caught by the centre of a cyclone and in these conditions there was little hope of response to her SOS. Nevertheless a small Chilean steamer did reach her and took off all twenty-five crew safely and not before time as she had only twenty miles of searoom left before she would have drifted ashore on Diego Ramirez to leeward. This reduced the Laeisz fleet to six four-masted barques, the *Pamir, Passat, Priwell, Padua, Peking* and *Parma*. Although the loss of the *Pinnaes* was unfortunate, a far greater tragedy occurred when the Danish school vessel, the five-masted barque *Kobenhaven* just disappeared in the Southern Ocean and no trace of her or her crew was ever found, despite a major search. Thus the potential grain fleet was reduced by three in one year, as this was the year the *Garthpool* went ashore as well.

The Depression was now beginning to take effect and world trade was drying up. Small sailing-ship companies with their limited financial resources could not hope to survive in a freight war with the more profitable steamship companies and many just faded away, their vessels being laid up or scrapped. The South American coast trade was on the decline anyway as Chile and Peru had at last developed their own basic industries and no longer required imports such as cement so there were no longer cargoes available for the outward voyage to help pay the running costs.

The depressed freight rates reduced the grain loadings to seven vessels in 1930, with one extra loading wool, and two, having been offered cargoes at less than 15/- (75 pence) per ton, sailing home in ballast. No one could make money at these sorts of rates as the costs of running a square rigger averaged at least 25/- (£1.25) per ton per year, assuming there was no damage sustained. The following year rates improved slightly and fourteen ships loaded grain at freights averaging 32/6 (£1.62½) which showed a profit for the owners. Although none of the fleet sailed together so there was no real race, sailing times were better. In fact it was the best yearly average, with 1935, between the wars. The fastest passage was made by the *Magdalene Vinnen*, built by Krupps in 1920, and still sailing today as the *Sedov*, a Russian Sail Training vessel, but she had an auxiliary engine which enabled her to motor through the calms. The fastest run by a pure sailing ship was again the *Herzogin Cecilie* with 93 days. The only difficulties experienced were aboard the *Hougemont*, which developed a leak on her run to the Horn that filled her bilges and put the men to the pumps in heavy seas. After drydocking on arrival home she was found to have sprung eight rivets near her stern. This was her last round-trip as the next year she was dismasted approaching Australia and although, miraculously, no lives were lost and she avoided a salvage claim, the costs of rerigging her in Australia were too high to be economic.

Lack of cargoes elsewhere in the world increased the participation in the grain trade to nineteen loadings in 1932. The nitrate trade only provided occasional cargoes by this time, but there was some business left for square-riggers carrying timber from the Baltic to South Africa on their way to load grain. That year all the grain ships between Australia and the Horn experienced a particularly widespread storm around 5th April, although none was lost. There was one close race between the *Pamir* and *Parma* who both sailed on 18th March and arrived on 29th June at Queenstown and Falmouth respectively, achieving the best time home apart from the auxiliary-engined *Magdalene Vinnen*. The next year saw a fascinating race between the *Herzogin* and the *Olivebank*, both now owned by Eriksen. The latter, one of Weir's ships which had seen many owners during her long life, was a big carrier which had never been known for fast passages. A new captain, however, was beginning to show her potential and she began to make respectable passages. She sailed ten days after the *Herzogin* but caught her before the Horn and the two vessels rounded together with everything they dared set although there were icebergs in sight. They were in sight of each other again in the South Atlantic but then the *Olivebank* got away and arrived home four days ahead. So much for the reputation of the 'invincible' *Herzogin*.

The theoretical speed of a vessel is between 1.25 and 1.5 times the square root of her waterline length, but those who wonder why the big square riggers did not achieve higher average speeds, closer to their theoretical potential, should remember that ships need calm water to reach high speeds and they were frequently heavily loaded. Even when there was a strong wind from the stern and the waves were running with the ship, the underlying swell would still cause her to slow. Also, on long ocean passages with small crews no master could afford to push his vessel until she broke gear since the manpower was not available to deal with the repairs quickly and this might endanger the vessel. Nevertheless there is one incredible run in calm conditions, which was between fixed marks and witnessed, so is not in fear of contradiction like some of the very high speeds claimed for the American clippers. It does indicate what might have been possible. When homeward bound in 1930 the *Herzogin Cecilie* rounded the Skaw light-ship off the northern tip of Denmark at 5 p.m. precisely, altered course to bring the strong wind further astern, heeled over to 32° and brought the Laeso Trindel light-ship abeam at 6.15 p.m. The distance was twenty-six nautical miles, so the average speed was 20 ¾ knots. This steady speed through the water, as opposed to a brief burst when surfing down a wave, was not achieved again until the big racing multi-hulls made their appearance in the 1970s

Nearly three-quarters of the grain fleet was now owned by the Finn Eriksen, based in the port of Mariehamn in the Baltic. He found most of his crews from his own island of Aland and a degree of rivalry existed between them and the remaining ships as a result, which perhaps explains their improved performances. Competition seldom has the opposite effect! In 1936 Eriksen bought the *Moshulu* from her San Francisco owners, his last purchase and also the largest square rigger left afloat. In that year he lost the *Herzogin Cecilie*, which had called at Falmouth for orders and was on her way up Channel when she sailed ashore onto the Hamstone Rocks inside Bolt Head. She was eventually floated off, but subsequently broke her back whilst beached awaiting a decision as to her future. The *Parma* came to the end of her career the same year when she rammed the quay at Glasgow and was deemed beyond economic repair. The following year the *Pedersen* was run down in the Channel on a clear moonlit night, one of many such losses between the wars as steamers failed to appreciate the speeds of these big square riggers or their lookouts, accustomed to looking for other steamers with their white masthead lights, failed to pick out the sailing ships, which are only required to carry sidelights and a sternlight.

In 1937 fifteen ships loaded grain, twelve of them owned by Eriksen and the following year the fleet was down to twelve. Second to sail in February was the German Sail Training ship *Admiral Karpfanger*, formerly *L'Avenir*. She radioed her position three weeks out and acknowledged a call eleven days later but was never heard of again. Wreckage came ashore on Navarino Island close to the Horn but this gave no clue as to the cause of her loss and she was assumed to have broached to and been overwhelmed. Laeisz was still running the *Padua* and *Priwell* on the nitrate run, round the Horn in both directions, and in that year on her outward voyage the *Priwell* doubled the Horn in the very fast time of 5 days 14 hours. Only Captain Learmont's rounding in the *Brenhilda* in 1902 in 5 days 1 hour was faster for a square rigger. The *Priwell* stayed on the nitrate trade and dropped anchor in Valparaiso the day before war broke out, the last square rigger to make the passage from Europe to Chile. She was interned and taken over when Chile entered the war after the Japanese attack on Pearl Harbor. She continued trading along the American west coast until her cargo of nitrates caught fire in 1945 and although she was beached she was a total loss.

The last year when a grain 'fleet' may be said to have sailed was 1939 which was to be the last time for many things. This was the last time so many trading sailing ships were ever to be seen together. The only real race was between the *Pommern* and the *Olivebank*, both of which took the Cape route since they ran into easterlies as they left Spencer Gulf. These two kept in close contact nearly all the way home, indeed so close that they nearly collided in the Southern Indian Ocean. The *Pommern* ran out the winner by two days whilst her unlucky rival struck a German mine off Jutland and only nine of her crew survived.

After the war the *Pamir* was the first to return to the Horn route, loading a general cargo in New Zealand which had operated her during the war. She was bound for London which she made in the respectable time of 80 days. The *Passat* and *Vinland*, both Eriksen vessels, took cargo out to South Africa once the mines were cleared from the Baltic, which enabled them to leave Mariehamn. Thence they both collected other cargoes but ended up in Port Victoria for grain at the end of 1947. Gustav Eriksen had died a few months earlier and without his determination to keep square riggers going, the very small fleet left was doomed to extinction, at least as cargo carriers. Both vessels sailed again in March the next year and made slow passages, 143 and 139 days respectively. The *Vinland* was withdrawn from service after this voyage and eventually finished up as a museum ship in Gothenburg. This left just two famous old 'Flying P' four-masted barques in service, the *Pamir* and the *Passat*, and both loaded grain again in 1949, the *Pamir* coming home in 127 days and the *Passat* in 110. This was the last grain voyage from Australia around the Horn, as both vessels were converted into training ships and sent on the River Plate grain route.

That might have been the end of the story but in 1957 the *Pamir* was homeward bound with grain in bulk from South America when she ran into a storm not far from the Azores. The weather was extremely bad, and I can remember that particular storm all too well as my ship, a motor cadet ship, the *Chindwara*, was coming home through the Bay of Biscay at the time. During the night I was on lookout on the forecastle with the ship nosing into the seas so that water was spurting up the hawse pipes just behind me and no one came to my relief. We picked up the *Pamir*'s SOS after she had gone over onto her beam-ends when her cargo shifted, but we were 500 miles away and other ships were closer. Only six out of a total complement of eighty-six survived.

The fault seemed to lie in the way the cargo was stowed. Grain was rarely loaded in bulk in sailing ships. It was usually bagged as bags did not easily shift. Loose grain is like water and will flow if it is tilted beyond about 27°. If the grain is loaded loose, shifting boards, fore and aft bulkheads are normally fitted down the centre line of a hold to prevent it moving too far and a form of hopper is built in the hatchway to provide grain to fill up the void as the cargo compresses. Instead of this tried and tested method, the *Pamir*'s grain had been loaded loose with possibly four layers of bagged grain on top to hold it in place but only in the hatchways. When the barque heeled heavily the grain must have shifted and held her down. One wonders what the masters of the square riggers from the Australian trade would have thought about it all and whether they would even have agreed to sail with such a stow. The *Passat*, which was also at sea at the time, flooded her deep tanks, which were loaded with bulk barley, and this gave additional stability although it ruined the cargo. Even so she had to be towed to Lisbon to have her cargo restowed before completing her voyage. This was the end of this particular experiment in training cadets as the *Passat* was laid up when she reached home. It is a pity that what was basically a sound idea, to give trainee officers an unequalled experience, should have failed, not because the idea was wrong, but because of casual loading and resulting public clamour, much of it ill-informed.

When the *Passat* laid up European square-rig commercial sail came to an end. Only on the west coast of South America did it linger on, but the last commercial sailing square-rigged vessel still in commission, the aptly named *Omega,* formerly the *Drumcliffe,* sank with 3,000 tons of cargo on 26th June 1958 between the Pachacamac Islands and Huacho. With her loss the great age of sail, of Cape Horners, hard passages and real seamen, came to an end. The voyages that attracted attention through loss, damage or fast passages are the ones that are remembered, but these are just a small fraction of many unremarkable trips that were made where the vessel got around the Horn without too much difficulty and the cargo was delivered safely. It was these ships and men who built up the reputation of Cape Horners. From 1949 onwards the only square-rigged sailing vessels to approach and round the Horn were sail training vessels, the most recent being the British-registered brigantine *Soren Larson* and the hermaphrodite brig *Eye of the Wind* on 9th and 10th December 1991 respectively, and by then the whole motivation for rounding Cape Stiff had changed irrevocably.

12

A Theatre of War

As we have seen, by 1939 few vessels were left using the Cape Horn route. The British and the Germans eyed it warily, little realising that it was to be the scene of their largest naval conflict outside European waters. As in 1914, the Horn still provided a route for German raiders to escape from the Atlantic to the Pacific as they attacked British commerce, and to the British it remained a choke point, which if blockaded, could restrict the raiders and make their elimination easier.

Limited by the Treaty of Versailles to building warships of no more than 10,000 tons, the German Navy had produced a design that was a triumph of compression, the pocket battleship. Into 10,000 tons, the size of a large light cruiser carrying 6-inch guns, had been designed a diesel-powered vessel, capable of 26 knots, well armoured and mounting 6 11-inch guns (the diameter of the shells they fired was 11 inches), heavier than anything except the armament of a battleship. These formidable vessels were capable of outgunning any British cruiser and their existence alone gave the British Admiralty an enormous problem as far as protecting merchant shipping was concerned.

When war was declared on 3rd September 1939, one of these ships, the *Deutschland*, was lurking near the Denmark Straits off Greenland and a second, the *Graf Spee*, was already on her way south through the Atlantic but her exact position was unknown. She showed herself on 30th September when she sank the British liner *Clermont* off Pernambuco. Since cruisers were not capable of dealing with the German ships on their own, more powerful hunting groups had to be formed. These comprised all available aircraft carriers, battleships and heavy cruisers mounting 8-inch guns, with light cruisers mounting 6-inch guns to act as scouts. These groups were strong enough in most cases either to sink the German ships or damage them and drive them into a neutral port where, as in the Great War, they could be interned for the duration.

The British flotilla nearest to Cape Horn was Commodore Harwood's Force G consisting of the two heavy cruisers *Exeter* and *Cumberland* and the two light cruisers *Ajax* and *Achilles*. The *Graf Spee* sank a vessel on the Cape Town to Freetown route on 7th December 1939 and, anticipating that she would strike near the River Plate next, Harwood disposed his flotilla, less the *Cumberland* which was refitting in the Falklands, across the middle of the shipping route. On the 13th his guess proved right. Smoke was sighted to the east and the pocket battleship quickly identified. The British tactics were simple. The force was split into two, the *Exeter* on her own and the two light cruisers acting as a pair in order to split the German fire control. The *Graf Spee* had 4 knots less speed than the British ships, but had she turned away at the moment of sighting she could have had ample time to destroy the British ships with her longer range of armament whilst they pursued in order to come within range with their own guns. Instead she held on and the two forces approached each other at a speed close to sixty miles per hour, the *Graf Spee* picking out the *Exeter* as the most dangerous opponent. Both vessels scored hits immediately, but whereas the British shells did modest damage to the German, the heavier German shells soon caused serious damage to the *Exeter*. Seeing that her fire was so effective, the German turned her attention to the two light cruisers who were plastering her with even lighter shots, but finding that she was sustaining too much damage, she turned away behind a smoke screen.

The action had started at 6.17 a.m. when the *Graf Spee* opened fire, the smoke screen was created at 6.36. By 6.46 the *Exeter* had her two forward turrets out of action but was continuing the fight with her remaining one aft. After the *Graf Spee* set course for Montevideo, all three British cruisers joined in the chase but the German turned briefly on her pursuers and hit the *Exeter*. Despite taking further damage the *Exeter* continued the fight until 7.30 a.m. when her last turret was put out of action. She now withdrew out of range to try and effect repairs, leaving the pursuit to the *Ajax* and *Achilles* which, being damaged as well, contented themselves with following the German to Montevideo, where she was intending to take advantage of the neutrality rules' permitted 72-hour respite to take on stores and land her dead and wounded.

On the British side there was frantic activity. Whilst the crippled *Exeter* made her way to the Falkands, her sister ship the *Cumberland* was racing northwards and joined the light cruisers on 14th December. Two more heavy cruisers were on the way from Cape Town and the battle cruiser *Renown*, armed with 15-inch guns, and so more than a match for the *Graf Spee*, was in Rio taking bunkers. She was accompanied by the aircraft carrier *Ark Royal*. There was a slight feeling of *déjà vu* about the impending action, a British battle cruiser chasing a *Graf Spee* again after a gap of twenty-five years. Further east, two more heavy cruisers and the aircraft carrier *Eagle* were bunkering in Durban ready to join the chase if necessary.

A single raider needs space and by tying herself down in one place the *Graf Spee* was losing her greatest asset, the ability to hide from searching ships and aircraft in the vastness of the oceans. The noose was drawing tight and her options were reduced to coming out and being nobly sunk, being interned until the end of the war, or going to sea and scuttling herself. Instructions were eventually received from Berlin to take the latter course. Most of the crew were put aboard a German merchant ship in Montevideo harbour and with a skeleton crew the *Graf Spree* steamed out of port at 6.15 p.m. At 8.45 p.m. the aircraft from the *Ajax* reported that the German ship had blown herself up.

This action exposed once again the practical difference between the two sides. Whereas the British could repair damage in ports scattered all over the world in colonies like the Falkland Islands and a vast Commonwealth, the Germans, apart from being allowed a 72-hour stopover in a neutral port, had nowhere to go except home, which meant running the gauntlet of the very powerful British Home Fleet.

Apart from submarines, the only other German raiders to penetrate towards the Horn were the disguised merchant ships, one of which, known as Raider E, fought an inconclusive action with the British armed merchant cruiser *Carnarvon Castle* off the Plate. None of these raiders hid in the channels of Tierra del Fuego although they did use the Kerguelen islands, which lie in the Southern Ocean between Africa and Australia, as a base.

Shipping using the Horn route hardly increased at all during the Second World War. The convoy system had proved the most effective method of escorting merchant vessels and so trade employed the shorter route via the Panama Canal. Both Chile and Argentina declared their neutrality at the outbreak of hostilities as both had ties with the belligerent countries. They were the last South American countries to expel the Axis representatives of

Germany, Japan, and Italy, and Argentina did declare war on the side of the Allies in March 1945 but took no part in the action.

Relations between the two southernmost nations in America have been strained by boundary disputes since the end of the nineteenth century. Arbitration by King Edward VII in 1902 over the boundary in Patagonia has never really settled the differences in the islands and both countries maintain a strong naval presence in Tierra del Fuego to this day. I had personal experience of this state of affairs in 1994 whilst passing round the Horn in the catamaran *Enza*. We had to hurry to complete the operation of transferring film footage by micro wave radio to an aircraft because we were sailing into Argentinian air space and our aircraft had come from Chile!

For more than 150 years a desultory argument between Argentina and Britain over who owned the Falkland Islands had rumbled along. Neither side ever really considered coming to blows over it, but the temptation for a nationalistic government to use a border dispute as a means to unite its population is always a danger, particularly when the rulers feel under threat. By the late 1970s Argentina was ruled by a military Junta which was becoming increasingly unpopular. To distract their people they resurrected claims to the Falkland Islands or Malvinas. The arguments on both sides had some historical merit, thus making a solution more difficult.

Richard Hawkins was probably the first person to sight the Falklands, Davis also saw them, but the first person to set foot there as far as is known was Captain John Strong in 1690 when driven back from the Cape by fierce winds whilst voyaging to Chile. He gave them the name of the First Lord of the Admiralty, Lord Falkland, found an abundance of fresh water, killed geese to replenish his stores, and sailed on. Lord Anson, who had experience of the Horn when he led his expedition around the world, was enthusiastic for a base to offer succour to English vessels sailing around the Horn, but nothing was done about it and the French were the first to found a colony there in 1764. The French explorer Antoine de Bougainville chose a site at Port Louis, just north of the present Port Stanley in East Falkland. A settlement was established and a small fort built. The next year, perhaps in response to the French, the British sent an expedition led by 'Foulweather' Jack Byron, grandfather of the Poet, who planted a small vegetable patch on West Falkland, hoisted the Union Jack, and sailed away. In 1776 a British resupply operation encountered the French settlers, who now numbered some 250 people. The British demanded that the French leave immediately, the French responded by insisting the British depart as they, the French, were established first.

The small islands now became the cause of a major diplomatic row. Spain claimed the islands as part of her traditional South American territories recognised by Britain and France under the Treaty of Utrecht in 1713 and demanded that both nations remove their settlements. The French agreed, once De Bougainville had been compensated, and their people were evacuated in 1767. In 1769 1,400 Spanish troops were sent to evict the British, who, hopelessly outnumbered, departed under protest. This created the first Falklands crisis, resolved by diplomacy which allowed the British back (they stayed for only three years) but with the Spanish understanding that the return was only temporary whereas the British always claimed the right was permanent. This agreement was replaced by the signing of the Nootka Sound Convention in 1790 by both nations under which Britain renounced all colonial rights to South America and its adjacent islands.

Spain established a colony at Port Louis, renamed Puerto Soledad, which was occupied until 1810, and ten years late the United Provinces of Rio del Plata, newly independent from Spain, claimed the islands as a part of their inheritance. A governor was appointed in 1823 and settlement commenced once more. During the tour of the second governor an American vessel, the *Harriet*, was arrested and her captain taken to Buenos Aires for trial. The American consul in Buenos Aires reacted strongly to this action and since there was an American warship in port, ordered it to Puerto Soledad to recover property belonging to the *Harriet* and make a display of force. Captain Silas Duncan of the USS *Lexington* interpreted his orders freely and not only recovered the confiscated property, but also sacked the settlement, spiked the guns of the fort and blew up the magazine. As he sailed away he declared the islands free of all government. Argentina, which was the successor to the United Provinces, sent another governor but he was murdered by convicts who had been freed and left unsupervised since the *Lexington* had sailed. An Argentine frigate was dispatched and was still restoring order when two British warships, the *Tyne* and the *Clio,* arrived with orders to take and hold the islands. Under protest, but outgunned, the Argentine captain agreed to haul down his flag and depart. The islands have been British ever since apart from a few months in 1982, their strategic value being as a coaling station for the Navy and a refuge for vessels damaged rounding Cape Horn, although the discovery of oil may add a new dimension.

The large and lawless whaling and sealing community that had grown up in the Falklands and given the Argentine government so much difficulty was brought under some semblance of control by the new British administration, but it was not until 1843 that a new town was begun at Port Stanley. For many years thereafter all needs for the colony had to be brought in by sea, although a chart and sailing directions for the port were not published until 1850. This appeared just in time for the sudden increase in traffic due to the development of the Californian gold fields and the Peruvian guano trade. Later, the Australian gold rush led to more ships taking the Cape Horn route and increased the number seeking assistance. This was the hey-day of the settlement, when scores of vessels damaged by their battle with Cape Horn struggled back to Port Stanley for repairs. Wages for shipwrights rose to such a level that many captains soon preferred to try and make their way to the River Plate rather than pay the extortionate charges being levied. Nor was this the only factor that militated against Port Stanley as a haven. All too often the vessels which called in for repairs were condemned by the port authorities, which meant they could not sail. Their value plummeted and as there was no one else to buy them the local traders benefited from knock-down prices. The vessels might be condemned but the cargoes and equipment still had a value.

Trade started to decline in the 1890s as Punta Arenas proved the more convenient coaling station for the steamers that were beginning to replace the sailing vessels. The opening of the Panama Canal, which gave the steamer the final advantage on the South American and antipodean runs, moved more traffic away from Cape Horn, and Port Stanley suffered accordingly. The last sailing ship to be condemned at Port Stanley was the *Fennia* in May 1927.

When the ship-servicing trade died the islanders concentrated on sheep farming and fishing. But if the islands were reduced to being a backwater in peacetime, they played an important part in the three sea actions between Britain and Germany in the First and Second World Wars and even more dramatic events were to unfold. The expulsion of the Argentine garrison in 1830 had not removed Argentina's claims to the islands and the squabble was carried on in a gentlemanly way for the next 150 years, with Britain retaining possession largely on account of the population being of British extraction, the powerfulness of the British fleet, and the Argentines' unwillingness to create a major dispute with an old trading partner. Attitudes changed after the Second World War. Prior to this, Argentina had opened its gates to a large flow of German, Spanish and Italian immigrants. Britain for her part had begun to withdraw from Empire, granting independence to nearly all of her erstwhile colonies and showing no firm intention or wish to continue to govern small islands dotted all over the world which had ceased to be of use now she no longer needed bases for her ships to safeguard the Empire.

Two signals that were misinterpreted by Argentina were transmitted by the British during the 1970s. Britain retired her two large aircraft carriers, thereby removing her ability to provide any mobile air defence or retribution in the event of an Argentine attack. The islands themselves had only a short temporary landing strip. Secondly, the British openly discussed the withdrawal of their Antarctic ice patrol ship HMS *Endurance*. The former action was seen as a continuation of the weakening of Britain militarily, the latter as a continuation of the intention to withdraw from colonial commitments. From Buenos Aires the perception was that Britain was no longer really interested in the islands, which were a drain on her exchequer and, furthermore, she no longer had the military capability to defend or recapture something so far from home. The nation that had been able to scatter large and powerful fleets around the world in 1940 no longer had any capital ships. Her only new carrier, *Invincible*, was being sold to Australia and she had one older vessel laid up, the *Hermes*, which India was negotiating to buy. In part the Argentines were right, Britain was losing interest, but the Argentine Junta made the classic mistake of assuming that after noisy protest Britain would accept a *fait accompli*. It was a calamitous mistake.

The belligerent attitude of Argentina and the obvious build-up of forces had alerted the British government to the potential risk and as a precaution three nuclear hunter killer submarines were dispatched south four days before the invasion. This was part of an overall plan to create a task force to protect the islands but the invasion changed this objective to the recovery of the islands.

Perhaps the greatest Argentine miscalculation concerned the nature of the British Prime Minister, Margaret Thatcher, and the Royal Navy's ability to find ships that were rumoured to be sold or laid up and bring them into commission remarkably quickly. The Prime Minister's reaction to the invasion in 1982 was one of anger and a determination to punish this clear breach of international law. So whilst Argentine forces landed near Port Stanley, attacked the Royal Marine barracks and forced the governor, Rex Hunt, to surrender, Britain was already preparing to fight back. The core of the force was to be two helicopter carriers, the old *Hermes* and the almost new but smaller *Invincible* which were both stored and sailed within a week. To provide air cover and a small strike capability, both vessels would carry Harrier aircraft, capable of vertical take-off and so able to use these smaller flight decks, but they paid for this ability by having only a small load capability and therefore a restricted time in the air. Only twenty could be taken, a minute number to deal with a modern airforce such as Argentina could deploy with seven times more combat aircraft and from air bases close to the conflict zone. The first objective was to reduce this air force by forcing it to attack the British Task Force and hope the missile systems aboard the ships, in conjunction with the Harriers, would prove up to the task.

This was a considerable risk as no one had ever fought a missile war at sea. Despite the sophistication of weapons that were, in many cases, being tested for the first time in anger, it was hard not to see the whole undertaking as a venture reminiscent of the colonial wars of the previous century rather than the mobilisation of a modern navy, trained and equipped for a highly technical war with the Soviet Bloc.

The first British objective was the retrieval of South Georgia, an island which had been a base for whaling and sealing from 1788 until 1965, and subsequently used as a research station. A contract granted to an Argentine company to remove the old whaling station had led to the Argentines hoisting their flag which they had been ordered to take down by the British. The island had been occupied by Argentina shortly after the Falklands. A small force of British ships was diverted for its relief. The campaign started badly with a series of accidents, including the loss of two helicopters and the near-loss of a Gemini dinghy containing three members of the SAS, which had drifted eastward with a stalled outboard motor and was nearly swept past the island into the Southern Ocean. Then the pendulum swung the other way. The Argentine submarine *Santa Fe* was attacked and forced to beach herself early in the morning of 25th April. A bombardment of the Argentine camp at Grytviken followed and then every available Marine and SAS trooper, only seventy-five in total, was landed and advanced on the Argentine base. White flags appeared immediately and the next morning, the smaller detachment at Leith, who had radioed defiance all night, surrendered. South Georgia had been recaptured just twenty-three days after the original Argentine invasion of the Falklands, providing the British with a base to repair and replenish ships if necessary. This should have sent a warning to the Junta that, if the British could manage to recapture an island so quickly so far from their bases, the occupation of the Falklands might be short lived.

The attack on the Falklands themselves commenced on 1st May with a bombing raid by the Royal Air Force which put one crater in Port Stanley airfield. The British Battle Group, thirteen ships strong, entered the Total Exclusion Zone established by Britain for an area 200 miles around the islands the same day and launched an immediate attack designed more to cause a reaction than actual damage. The objective was to force the Argentine forces to come out and fight so the way could be prepared for a landing by the 3rd Commando Brigade Royal Marines which was already practising landing procedures from the liner *Canberra* at Ascension Island. To increase the pressure, a bombardment group of a destroyer and two frigates closed Port Stanley and shelled Argentine positions. The ships did produce a reaction from four Argentine Mirage aircraft which attacked the group with rockets and cannon. There was only superficial damage but two of the Mirages were shot down by Harriers and a third shot down by the Argentines themselves. Later another Harrier shot down an Argentine Canberra light bomber as it approached the Battle Group. Its partner fled. First blood to the British, but the crews of the attacked ships, the first to be strafed in this manner since 1945, found the experience far from pleasant.

The following day the British submarine HMS *Conqueror* reported contact with the Argentinian 13,645-ton cruiser *Belgrano* escorted by two destroyers of the British Type 42 Class hovering some forty miles outside the total exclusion zone to the east of Staten Island. Permission was requested from London to attack which, after some deliberation, was agreed. In the light of subsequent reaction this decision must be placed in the context of the moment. The British were operating far from home with a stretched supply line. They had no high-performance fixed-wing aircraft, whereas the Argentines did, aboard an aircraft carrier whose position was not known. The *Belgrano* had been completed for the US Navy in 1939 as a light cruiser of the Brooklyn Class, in fact of the same vintage as the *Graf Spee* and British cruisers that fought off the River Plate in 1939. Nevertheless, armed with fifteen 6-inch guns, she posed a formidable threat as she completely outranged any gun the British had. A single salvo from the *Belgrano* was heavier than all the British Battle Group could fire at one time. Escorted by two air-defence destroyers, sister ships of the *Coventry*, *Sheffield* and *Gloucester* in the British fleet, and armed with the same Sea Dart anti-aircraft missile system, she was a dangerous nut to crack. The only weapon, apart from submarines, the British had that might deal with her were their Harrier aircraft. But what British leader was going to order their aircraft against their own missile systems? Both the Argentine cruiser and the aircraft carrier posed a really serious threat to the British, which had to be neutralised before they could consider bringing down the invasion force in its lightly armed amphibious vessels and hastily converted passenger liners. Here was an opportunity to halve the threat to the fleet and strike a blow against the aggressor and permission to attack was given.

HMS *Conqueror* closed to within 5,000 yards and fired a pattern of old-fashioned Mk8 torpedoes and then dived deep to avoid the expected counter measures from the destroyers. As she dived two explosions were heard.

Twenty minutes later she surfaced to take a look from a safe distance of eleven miles. The old cruiser was already low in the water and listing to starboard. Shortly afterwards she sank. The destroyers had disappeared and the survivors huddled together on life-rafts as the weather conditions worsened. By the time rescue arrived 368 of the crew had died. It was a devastating blow and caused shockwaves throughout the world, not least to the British who had intended to cripple the ship and were as surprised as anyone when she sank so quickly. The effect on the war was as dramatic. The Argentine navy, whose leader was the hardliner in the Junta, withdrew to its bases and never really emerged again. The war from now on was fought on the Argentine side by air force and army.

If the British thought the war would be a walkover after this sinking they were quickly disabused two days later when an Exocet missile, launched from an aircraft, struck the Type 42 air-defence destroyer *Sheffield* and opened her up amidships. Fire broke out and the vessel had to be abandoned. Later she was reboarded and taken in tow but sank on 10th May. Despite this loss, the British continued their policy of trying to entice the Argentine air force out in strength and at the same time whittle away at the morale of the occupiers in the Falklands. But it soon became clear that the air force, and perhaps the navy, were conserving their strength against the arrival of the amphibious fleet.

The problem facing the British was that there were at least 10,000 Argentine troops in the Falklands, according to elements of the SAS and SBS (British special forces who had been ashore observing the enemy since the beginning of May), whereas 3rd Commando Brigade, the designated assault force, consisted of just five battalions and their support. Instead of the three to one superiority usually required for an attacking force, the odds were almost reversed. A further brigade was added to the force, and the liner *Queen Elizabeth II* taken into service to carry them south, but the British never even had equality in numbers, let alone the usually accepted superiority.

Landing troops from ships in enemy territory far from home is a hazardous undertaking at the best of times and provides enormous scope for utter chaos; landing them without air superiority over the beaches is almost inviting disaster. Choosing a suitable landing site is fundamental and the task force was fortunate that it included Major Southby-Tailyour, a keen yachtsman, who had commanded the garrison a few years before. During his tour he had cruised the islands writing a cruising guide for yachtsmen for which he had failed to find a publisher as the number of yachts visiting the islands was very small. Now his manuscript was conscripted and marked 'Top

Secret', but in exchange for handing it over Southby-Tailyour wangled his way onto the Brigade staff. His actual command at the time was a flotilla of landing craft and his knowledge and experience were to prove invaluable.

The need for an area large enough to take the amphibious force and yet within reasonable striking distance of Port Stanley but easily defensible, eventually forced the planners to choose San Carlos Bay on East Falkland at the north end of the Falkland Sound between the two main islands. Although a considerable distance from the objective, Port Stanley, it provided a good anchorage and the hills around made it difficult for attacking aircraft to make a proper bombing run. During the morning of 21st May, the troop carriers, assault ships, supply ships and their escorts crept undetected into the sound and started to disembark the assault troops. There was no opposition. The first the inhabitants of the small settlement knew of the attack was when a British officer knocked at the door of a house and introduced himself.

There was no Argentine response until 10 a.m. when an aircraft flew over and saw below him what he thought must be the entire British fleet at anchor. The Argentine army did not try and counter-attack at the one time when any invasion force is at its most vulnerable – just as it is getting ashore and before it has dug in – but their air force did respond. Four ground support aircraft approached and strafed the troops but two were shot down and then the real air assault commenced. HMS *Argonaut* was strafed and later put out of action by two bombs, *Antrim* received rockets and two bombs, neither of which exploded. All the vessels in the force were strafed and late in the day, another frigate, *Ardent*, was struck by a number of bombs and had to be abandoned. Although the landing of more than 4,000 men was safely accomplished and stores were now being rushed ashore, it had been a sobering day for the British. One destroyer and a frigate were seriously damaged and another frigate sunk with the loss of twenty-four men for the price of sixteen aircraft destroyed.

It appeared that the Argentine air force was licking its wounds on 21st May, which allowed some redispositions of the British forces but they were back again on Sunday the 22nd. It began well for the British who shot down three helicopters, crippled one freighter and forced another ashore, but at midday the first aircraft appeared. Skyhawks hit the frigate *Antelope* with bombs just as she shot down one of them and another crashed into her mast. Neither bomb exploded immediately, but later, when one was being defused, it went off and started a huge blaze. The magazines blew up and the ship sank. In all eight Argentine aircraft were downed that day, a rate of attrition which could not be maintained for long. Nevertheless they continued to press home their attacks and the next day the missile systems aboard *Coventry* and *Broadsword* failed to acquire attacking aircraft and the latter was hit by a bomb that exploded amidships. She sank soon afterwards. Nor was this the only loss of the day as an Exocet hit the supply ship *Atlantic Conveyor* which caught fire. Although ten additional Harriers which this ship had brought out had been flown off, thirteen helicopters, vital to the planned movement of troops for the attack on Port Stanley, were lost when the ship went down. The plan to convey the troops by helicopter had to be cancelled and the advance would now have to be made on foot, across the sixty-mile breadth of West Falkland where the ground was wet moorland with little cover. Furthermore the men would have to carry nearly all their own kit.

Despite the British losses, 25th May can, with hindsight, be seen as the turning point of the war. Four days later 450 men of the 2nd Parachute Battalion attacked four times their own numbers at the settlement of Goose Green and after a vicious little battle, during which they lost their CO and sixteen others killed and thirty-five wounded, captured it for a loss to the Argentinians of at least 120 killed and 1,200 surrendered. It was an awesome demonstration of what highly trained and motivated soldiers could do against a conscript army even if better equipped and dug in.

The British forces, now reinforced by 5th Brigade, advanced towards the ultimate objective of Port Stanley. 3rd Commando Brigade marched, or 'yomped', as the Marines called it, across the island towards the ring of mountains encircling Port Stanley whilst 5th Brigade leaped up to Bluff Cove, taking advantage of a local telephone call to islanders there who advised them that the Argentinians had left. In fact, unbeknown to the British, the Argentine forces, apart from a small garrison on West Falkland which was being ignored for the time being, had withdrawn behind defences dug into the mountains around Port Stanley.

Reinforcing the detachment that had helicoptered to Bluff Cove was to cause one of the greatest tragedies to befall the British forces during the whole operation. Elements of the Welsh Guards had been sent round to Bluff Cove in the logistics ship *Sir Galahad* where her sister ship, the *Sir Tristram* was offloading ammunition. Landing the men at Fitzroy settlement where the vessels were anchored meant they would have a circuitous march of twelve miles to join the rest of their battalion and so the Guards demanded landing craft to take them there instead. Major Southby-Tailyour ordered a landing craft that was offloading ammunition to go and collect them but the Guards refused to board on the grounds that mixed loads of men and ammunition were against regulations. So they were, but the two vessels were lying in an open unprotected anchorage in broad daylight, a tempting target for the Argentine air force. Part of the problem was that the Guards were recent arrivals and had not been at San Carlos and experienced what the Argentine air force was capable of. Shortly after 1 p.m. four aircraft streaked into the anchorage and attacked both ships. The *Sir Galahad* was the most seriously hit and subsequently sank and in total 51 men died in the attack. Even whilst this tragedy was unfolding, HMS *Plymouth* was being attacked by five aircraft and although she shot down two, four of ten bombs aimed at her hit, setting off an explosion aft. She had to be withdrawn to San Carlos to effect repairs. Nor was this the end of the losses as one of the landing craft was attacked and sunk on her way from Goose Green to Bluff Cove, killing six.

Despite this loss the build-up for the attack on the mountains continued and went ahead as planned. Initially the fighting was hard and vicious but the Argentine will to fight suddenly broke. They had had enough of the violence the British were prepared to unleash and they fell back in their thousands on Port Stanley where General Menendez, their Commander, surrendered on 14th June. The Junta's gamble had failed and with it the Junta itself lost all credibility. All its leaders resigned or were removed from office within a month of the surrender at Port Stanley.

In the immediate aftermath of hostilities there could be no question of any negotiations to discuss the sovereignty of the islands, but the war had drawn attention to this isolated corner of the earth where the British have fought more often than any other nation – four battles this century. An airfield capable of landing the largest jets has been built to improve communications with the outside world and provide a means of reinforcing the garrison in the unlikely event of the threat of a further Argentine invasion.

Efforts have also been made to improve the Falklands economy. For example fishing has expanded largely through foreign craft which have to purchase an operating licence. Merchant vessels are using the Cape Horn route again as they find the economic advantages for large container ships of travelling from New Zealand to Europe via the Cape now outweigh the shorter distance through the Panama Canal.

The increased traffic going around the Horn is unlikely to have any immediate effect upon the islands but the development of techniques to operate at greater depths beneath the surface of the sea will ensure that research and later exploitation of the sea and its bed around the islands will be active for some considerable time into the future. Oil has been discovered in commercial quantities although this is certain to cause conflict with Argentina over the boundary of zones for exploitation. However, twelve years after what has become known as the Falklands War the British and

Argentine governments have at least restored some semblance of normal relations, although the sovereignty issue will always be a cause of friction as long as the islands remain British.

13

Racing the Greybeards

The appalling weather and chilling list of losses around Cape Horn make it an unlikely destination for those sailing for pleasure, especially in small fragile yachts. But the same pride that the seaman serving on the great square riggers felt at being a 'Cape Horner' applies just as much to the men of sail today. The craft are very different. But modern materials and equipment have provided some compensations for the loss of size. Design changes, too, have made the dangerous scramble aloft on an icy winter night in a gale a thing of the past since all sail trimming and reefing can be done from the deck and one only needs to go aloft in emergencies. But a wave can sweep a deck just as easily as it did 500 years ago and there is pitifully little shelter on the deck of a yacht from a rumbustious sea. The only compensation for the soaking clothing is that the accommodation, although more cramped, is usually a little better than the forecastle of a square rigger. The passage past Cape Stiff is still something to be reckoned with.

The first yachts to round the southern end of America did so in the heyday of commercial sail at a time when spreading wealth from the newly industrialised countries was creating more leisure time and a growing interest in the sport. Just which yacht came first is not definitely known but it may have been the 40-foot cutter *Tocca*, sailed by an American, J. M. Crenston in 1849. It is arguable whether the topsail schooner *Allen Gardiner* can be classified as a yacht, but she was only 64 feet long overall and definitely rounded the Horn east to west and west to east on 14th November 1885, captained by W. Parker, while engaged on bringing missionaries out to convert the Fuegians.

The first definite pleasure voyage into Fuegian waters was made by an English Member of Parliament, Thomas Brassey. His yacht was enormous by modern standards, 157 feet in length and displacing 531 tons. Rigged as a three-masted topsail schooner, the *Sunbeam* was also fitted with an auxiliary engine. The crew totalled forty-three, including servants and the owner's wife and children, and Lady Brassey wrote a Victorian best-seller, *The Voyage of the Sunbeam*, about their voyage around the world which was accomplished in less than eleven months. The expedition was full of adventures. Off the River Plate they came across the British barque *Monkshaven*, bound from Swansea to Valparaiso, with her cargo of coal on fire. The barque's crew of fifteen were taken aboard the yacht and transferred to a homebound mail steamer a week later, with one exception who was invited to join the yacht's crew. The *Sunbeam* took the route through the Magellan Strait from east to west rather than rounding the Horn. A stopover was made at Sandy Point en route, the name at that time for Punta Arenas, where Lady Brassey went ashore to observe three Fuegian women who had been rescued from an inter-tribal war. When they continued their leisurely cruise through the strait, exploring a number of channels and anchoring each night, they came across other Fuegians in a canoe, clothed in simple seal-skin robes. Sir Thomas Brassey found the passage comparatively easy and recommended that it should be used by large steamers and warships. He accepted, however, that without tugs the sailing ships of the day were too large to manoeuvre safely through the narrower parts in view of sudden squalls. The *Sunbeam* continued her voyage safely back to England via the new Suez Canal.

The yacht *Wanderer* owned by an Englishman called Lambert followed shortly afterwards, taking the same route in, but the Americans went one better in 1888 when the *Coronet*, a 133-foot schooner, sailed around the Horn east to west in May under Captain C. S. Crosby with passengers aboard. Whether she passed back to the east coast via the Horn on this voyage is unclear, but in February 1896 she passed east to west again, and in December the same year west to east. The yacht seems to have developed a taste for the Horn as twenty years after her first passage she again rounded east to west under Captain Lester Mackenzie.

This was not the only voyage to Tierra del Fuego in 1888 which was beginning to extend an attractive challenge to a few yachtsmen who could afford to indulge themselves. J. Cumming Dewar sailed through the Magellan

Strait, east to west, in his large engineless schooner *Nyanza*. They passed the recent wreck of a Pacific Steam Navigation Steamer on the rocks off Cape Isidro and a German steamer in the same condition in Indian Reach. For a while they were accompanied by an American schooner, *Mary H. Thomas*, bound from Boston to San Francisco, and passed numerous steamers including one which agreed to provide a tow for £10 a day since they had fallen behind schedule dealing with the opposite extremes of calms and storms that are a feature of the area. The *Nyanza* was wrecked off Panapi in 1889.

One of the most famous yacht voyages to Tierra del Fuego, in fact one of the greatest yacht voyages of all time, occurred in 1896. Joshua Slocum was a Yankee ship's captain, although originally from Canada, who was semi-retired when a friend gave him an old wreck named the *Spray*. He resolved to rebuild the boat and take her on a single-handed voyage around the world. His route took him across the Atlantic to Gibraltar, then down through the Atlantic islands to Brazil and from there through the Magellan Strait. Although it was February, summer in the Southern Hemisphere, the *Spray* ran into a gale as soon as she rounded Cape Virgins which lasted for thirty hours and delayed her arrival at Sandy Point (Punta Arenas). He found a Chilean frontier town of some 2,000 inhabitants, whose main trade was coaling ships, sheep farming, hunting and gold mining. The local governor had recently sent a party of men to wipe out a Fuegian native settlement for massacring the crew of a wrecked schooner, so Slocum was advised to ship a crew for his passage through the strait but he could find only one willing to join him and then only on condition that another man and a dog were shipped as well. Since no more volunteers could be found, Slocum cleaned and loaded his guns and resolved to sail on alone. Hearing of this, an Austrian captain gave Slocum a bag of carpet tacks telling him to avoid stepping on them himself! As a single-hander he could not continue sailing by night in such restricted waters and the tacks were to be spread on deck while Slocum was asleep.

Two days after leaving Punta Arenas Slocum found himself being pursued by two canoes, so to disguise the fact that he was alone he made a 'crew' out of an old piece of bowsprit and a spare set of oilskins to which he attached lines so the body would appear to move. The leader of the canoe party was a bearded man, therefore not a pure Fuegian, and well known for a number of massacres of shipwrecked seamen, but a well-judged shot sent the canoes away. It was a nervous Slocum who anchored that night on the opposite side of the strait to where the canoes were last seen. Perhaps for once the gales were on a seaman's side, however, as one arose almost immediately and made the strait too dangerous for the canoes to cross and reach him. So fierce were the williwaws that the *Spray* dragged her anchors and had to be sailed into a more sheltered landlocked bay called Three Island Cove where Slocum took the opportunity to gather firewood for his stove and replenish his water tanks. After another gale, the sloop set out again and, with the help of a tow from a Chilean gunboat, cleared Cape Pilar eleven days out from Punta Arenas.

Any relief that Slocum may have felt at clearing the strait evaporated when the *Spray* ran into a heavy gale which quickly swung round to the north-west. Progress was impossible and under bare poles, for all the sails had been torn, the *Spray*, like the *Golden Hinde* before her, was forced to run off towards Cape Horn. Four days later, thinking he was now coming up to the Horn, Slocum bent on a spare squaresail and headed towards land. As dusk fell he saw breakers ahead and wore round intending to hold off until daybreak only to find, alarmingly, breakers ahead on the new course. He had not rounded the Horn as he thought and was now surrounded by rocks in the middle of a gale, a totally horrifying position for any seaman but appalling for a single-hander who knows that there is no chance of a relief until safety can be found – or else the vessel goes onto the rocks. All night he remained at the helm keeping his little boat clear of rocks until the light improved and he recognised his whereabouts. He was to the west of Cape Horn in a mass of rocks and spray known as the Milky Way close to the entrance to the Cockburn Channel. There was no way he could beat out to sea so somehow he worked his way through and found a safe anchorage.

After such an experience Slocum was exhausted, but before he turned in he spread tacks around the decks. He was fast asleep towards midnight when the air was rent by screams of pain and the sound of Fuegians fleeing from his deck. The tacks had worked. A few shots from a rifle accelerated the retreat of their canoes. All was quiet the next day when Slocum settled down with canvas, palm and needle to make some new sails, keeping a lookout for Fuegians and wondering why there were no trees on the land around his anchorage. He soon found out. A williwaw blasted through the anchorage with sufficient power to blow the *Spray*, despite two anchors, straight out into deep water. This happened again and then again until the poor battered *Spray* was nearly blown back to Punta Arenas again.

Pressing on carefully, anchoring frequently, and sewing constantly, Slocum slowly created a new mainsail out of his square sail. At the sight of canoes he would weigh anchor, however tired, and be forced to sail across the other side of the strait for his own safety. Gales became an ally rather than something to be feared, for although they usually prevented any progress being made at least they kept the natives to the shore. He did not avoid the bearded Fuegian, who boarded for a short chat under the lee of Great Charles Island. Slocum kept his revolver in his hand and a rifle handy throughout the meeting. Later he came across the American steamer *Columbia*, which had come into the same anchorage for the night. This led to the food lockers of the sloop being replenished. There was little time to enjoy these delicacies, however, as the next day the wind went calm and more than twenty canoes came out and stood about eighty yards off, at what Slocum called his self-defence line. Fortunately the wind came back, scattering the canoes, but Slocum was forced to remain up for the next night and day whilst he beat his way north-west to safer waters. A brief rest in Borgia Bay, followed by a few hours' rest whilst anchored to kelp in twenty fathoms of water and a 3-knot tide; coming across wreckage and salvaging some barrels of tallow for resale further along, a typical Yankee skipper's commercial instinct; anchoring in Port Angosto and being narrowly missed by a Fuegian arrow: the story, published under the title *Sailing Alone Around the World* is one of the great sailing classics and provides a unique snapshot of attitudes and behaviour in Tierra del Fuego at the end of the nineteenth century. Slocum completed his voyage and eventually returned home to Newport, Rhode Island. He was lost at sea some years later in the *Spray*.

In 1911 when sailing vessels were still to be seen off the Horn in large numbers, a British gaff yawl, *Pandora*, skippered by George Blyth with one crewman, Pietro Arapakis, became the first of what might be recognised as a yacht in modern terms to pass around the Horn when she sailed from west to east on 16th January that year (Slocum of course had gone through the Magellan Strait). The *Pandora* was only 36' 9" long, about the same length as the *Spray*. A world war and thirteen years were to pass, by which time commercial sail was becoming a rarity, when Conor O'Brian followed in the 42-foot *Saoirse,* registered in the new republic of Eire. She made the rounding from west to east rigged as a brigantine with four crew.

Yacht numbers increased very slowly and the 1930s saw only two more pass south of the Horn. In April 1934 the Norwegian Al Hanson became the first single-hander in his 36-foot gaff sloop *Mary Jane*. Furthermore he went from east to west, against the currents. He was lost shortly afterwards when his boat went ashore on the coast of Chiloé. In November 1936 the American 85-foot gaff schooner *Wanderbird* went west to east skippered by the owner Warwick Tompkins with his wife, six crew and two children.

But if most yachtsmen preferred to take the Panama Canal route when making a round-the-world cruise, there was a growing acceptance that for a circumnavigation to matter it had to take a course south of Cape Horn. The example was set during the Second World War by the Argentinian Vito Dumas in his 32-foot Bermuda ketch *Legh II*. He set out alone in June 1942, winter in the Southern Hemisphere, from Buenos Aires taking a route west to east. He stopped at Cape Town, Wellington New Zealand, and Valparaiso where the generous Chilean navy refitted the boat for the passage round the Horn. He rounded in mid-winter, though a due was exacted for such temerity when he broke his nose in a fall. He returned home to a tumultuous reception.

Dumas had become the first person to circumnavigate the world alone south of Cape Horn and thereby set a standard which all future real circumnavigators would have to follow. In 1952 the French single-hander Marcel Bardiaux, in his 31-foot sloop *Les Quatre Vents*, passed round on May 12th and then there was a gap of thirteen years before Bill Nance of Australia went round in one of the smallest crafts ever to pass the Horn on a long voyage, the 25-foot *Cardinal Vertue* on 7th January 1965. But then things began to hot up. In 1966 Bernard Moitessier and his wife Françoise rounded in the 40-foot *Joshua* and three months later the Englishman Edward Allcard went east to west in his 36-foot ketch *Sea Wanderer*, as did the American 53-foot cutter *Awahnee II* skippered by R. L. Griffith, and his wife, son and various crew.

Within a year another single-hander had passed the Horn setting yet another record. Francis Chichester circumnavigated the world with only one stop in Australia sailing his 53'1" (length over all) Bermuda yawl *Gipsy Moth IV*. Chichester might be said to have sparked off the modern interest in sailing around the Horn. He encountered typical Horn weather. On 19th March 1967 his track inwards was between Isla Ildefonso and the Diego Ramirez group. A typical Southern Ocean front the day before he reached the Horn backed the wind quickly from the north-west to south with an increase to Force 9 within minutes and a rapidly rising barometer. Nine hours later the wind was averaging 15 knots but there were occasional gusts to 36 knots, a far from enjoyable situation for a yacht since the lesser winds meant that extra sail was required to keep the boat moving in the large seas whilst in a gust of 36 knots no one would want to carry more than storm sails. He compromised by putting up a larger staysail which increased his general speed slightly but did not overstrain the boat in gusts and then, since it was too dark to see anything, he went to sleep trusting that two recent sun sights had given him an accurate enough position and there was no land in his path.

At 0500 on the 20th he awoke to a cold, grey morning with a west by southerly wind and steady barometer. Shortly afterwards he found himself joined by the Royal Navy's ice patrol ship HMS *Protector*, which accompanied him around the Horn. The Horn was rounded shortly after 1100 hours as the wind began to rise again. From the *Protector*, the conditions were later described as tall heaving seas with 50-plus-knot winds tearing away the crests of the breaking waves and driving them forward as spindrift. The storm blew him quickly towards Staten Island which he cleared during the morning of the 21st.

Only ten days later the 30-foot Australian sloop *Carronade*, skippered by Andy Wall with two crew, also got around the Horn, but, as if to make light of the dangers, the same year Kees Bruynzeel took his 73-foot ketch *Stormvogel* round and found conditions so favourable he went into the lee of the Horn and went ashore for a picnic. Not satisfied that he could claim to have rounded the Horn unless in rough weather, he sailed back to the west and awaited the next storm to make what he called a proper rounding!

Alec Rose, another Briton, who had intended circumnavigation at the same time as Chichester, rounded the Horn on 1st April 1968 in his 36-foot yawl *Lively Lady*. Although rather late in the season, owing to a second stop in New Zealand to carry out repairs, he had a quiet passage with a light north-westerly wind and was accompanied by the British fleet tanker *Wave Chief*. A month later an even smaller yacht, *Sundowner*, only 24 feet overall, skippered by the Briton Tom Harrison, may have rounded from east to west. He called at the Falkland Islands and set off for the Horn but was never heard from again, perhaps overwhelmed by a large sea.

There is a point where a particular sea is just too large and it does not matter what action is taken, a wave will appear that will overwhelm a small yacht. Small vessels can survive amazingly in big seas by bobbing over the top of the waves. The danger comes when these waves are very large and breaking, then they can engulf a yacht. At best the wave will sweep the deck with incredible force, ripping away even substantial structures, at worst the whole boat can be broken and forced down, taking her crew with her. One huge greybeard swept my boat *Suhaili* in the Southern Ocean. Fortunately nothing too serious was broken and as I saw it coming and knew that there was no time to dive below for shelter I shinned up the rigging to avoid being swept away. The wave crashed aboard, hiding the boat for what seemed like an eternity and leaving me and two masts all that was visible until the gallant little boat shook herself and re-emerged. Unfortunately, the main hatch had been open and I spent the next three hours baling!

Less fortunate were Miles and Beryl Smeeton, sailing in their 46-foot ketch *Tzu Hang* with John Guzzwell as crew. In their first attempt to sail round the Horn their yacht was picked up and either somersaulted or broached

and rolled. Beryl, who was at the helm, had her lifeline broken and floated
to the surface 30 feet from the boat, which lost her doghouse, forehatch and
masts and was lying half full of water. Frantic baling and carpentry to
cover the gaping holes in the deck saved them and *Tzu Hang* limped into
Chile for repairs under jury rig. Almost a year later they set off again, this
time without John Guzzwell, and ran into another storm in which they
broached again, losing their new masts. This was enough and their battered
boat was shipped home. These were experienced yachtsmen of no mean
determination and yet the seas were just too big for their craft. Beryl and
Miles Smeeton persevered and were at last successful in doubling the Horn
in December 1968 in *Tzu Hang* with John Guzzwell again as their crew.
They passed from east to west on 16th December.

Chichester, now Sir Francis, was largely responsible for the next major
step in solo long-distance voyaging, an attempt to sail around the world
non-stop which of course entailed a voyage south of the Cape of Good
Hope and Cape Horn. The *Sunday Times* decided to present an award to be
called the Golden Globe for the first person to complete this achievement
who sailed from a British port between June and October 1968. In all, nine
people set out. Since no vessel had ever tried to sail such a distance without
refit or replenishment, there was considerable doubt as to whether the voyage
was possible and whether any of the contestants would be in a fit state to
round the Horn after some 20,000 miles of non-stop sailing, including some
15,000 in the Roaring Forties. Only three actually made it as far as the
Horn, myself in my 32' 5" Bermuda ketch *Suhaili* on 17th January 1969,
Bernard Moitessier of France sailing his faithful *Joshua* on 5th February
and Nigel Tetley in his trimaran *Victress* later on 18th March 1969.

I had intended to round the Horn about the beginning of January 1969,
but damage and three weeks of easterly winds in the Roaring Forties had
delayed me. By the 15th of that month I had some 200 miles to go, but was
coping with a broken main gooseneck, a torn jib, a spare mizzen that did not
fit its mast and no self-steering. The boat was not really capable of going to
windward in her present state and I dreaded the thought of being caught on
a lee shore if my navigation proved to be wrong. By this time my wet-
weather gear had become porous and my boots cracked and holed, but at
least it meant they let any incoming water out as quickly as it came in. I was
nervous as I had seen the fury of many Roaring Forties storms in the previous
five months and was all too aware that I was approaching the bottleneck
where things could be drastically worse. This close to the Horn, and heading
into north-easterly winds, the barometer began to drop a millibar an hour.
Like Chichester and Rose, my desired path was north of the Diego Ramirez

group. A front during that evening gave me a following wind and speed improved so the next day I was able to repair the main gooseneck and jib which gave me more manoeuvrability; windward work of a sort was now a possibility. That day the wind came in heavy, very cold squalls, sleet hammering at all exposed flesh, but the barometer became steadier and the squalls less frequent although the wind remained very cold as night drew on. The Diego Ramirez Islands were in sight on 17th January 1969 at daybreak, some fifteen miles to the south-east, close to where my position put us, and two hours later I sighted land to the north – Tierra del Fuego. The westerly wind eased throughout the day so speed slowed but we drifted eastward and finally passed Cape Horn in the evening. We lay for a few hours completely becalmed less than seven miles from the Cape over which huge dark clouds were suspended. Despite this I had all sail set to catch the slightest catspaw of wind to get away but poor *Suhaili* just pitched and rolled on the enormous swell which shook any wind that might have come along out of the idle sails. There was no Naval ship to keep me company. Since my radio had failed five months before, my only contact had been by sight with Australia and New Zealand. I kept watch that night, shielded as much as possible by the hatchway so that only my eyes were above the deck since the cold was penetrating but eventually a light north-easter came up and by the next day I was beating heavily with only a snatch of sail in a north-east gale. A gale before and a gale after, but whilst actually rounding the Horn a flat calm!

Nineteen days later, Bernard Moitessier in *Joshua* made his second rounding in hot pursuit. His problem was, like mine, not knowing where his competition was, but had he known he might well have been encouraged, as he had been reducing the distance between us steadily in his larger and sleeker vessel. Instead of the easterly gale east of the Horn, he found more favourable winds and took only four days to reach the Falklands, a distance which had taken me six. He pressed on after failing to find anyone to report his position although he was seen, a sighting that caused confusion as the figure 2 on his mainsail was confused with the S I had on mine until someone realised that *Joshua* had a red hull. Then on 8th March, when well into the Atlantic, he decided that he did not wish to return to Europe. He had lost interest in the race altogether and altered his course for the Cape of Good Hope. He eventually sailed round to Tahiti, through the Roaring Forties south of the Indian Ocean again.

The third of the nine starters to get as far as the Horn was Nigel Tetley in his trimaran *Victress*. Although his lighter multihull might have been expected to sail faster than *Joshua*, in fact it took two weeks longer to reach the Horn from Plymouth. *Victress* did not make her rounding until 18th March and her skipper complained of the cold and squalls he found this late in the season. Misled by reports of another contestant's progress – Donald Crowhurst was later discovered to have falsified his positions and sent in radio reports ostensibly from the Southern Ocean when in fact he never left the Atlantic – Tetley pressed onwards but his battered and strained vessel, the first multihull ever to complete a passage through the Southern Ocean or around the Horn, began to break up when level with the Azores. The brave sailor was rescued when he had less than 1,000 miles to go. Thus of the nine starters, only one boat, *Suhaili*, managed to complete the voyage in a time of 312 days. Arguably the last and greatest test for a man alone at sea had been successfully achieved.

Less than two years later, one of the nine starters, the young Briton Chay Blyth, who had been forced to pull into Cape Town, set off again. This time, however, since the non-stop voyage along the traditional route had been achieved, he resolved to attempt to sail in the opposite direction, westabout against the prevailing winds in the Southern Ocean. His boat, named after its sponsors *British Steel*, was 59 feet in length and completed the circumnavigation successfully in 292 days.

It was inevitable that minds would turn to a properly organised round-the-world race after three single-handers had sailed around within three years and the genesis of the first fully crewed yacht race around the world stems directly from the *Sunday Times* Golden Globe. In 1970 Guy Pearce and Anthony Churchill started talking about the project but failed to find a sponsor. The Royal Naval Sailing Association, known as the RNSA, which was closely involved with adventure sail training for the services in Britain, saw the whole idea as an extension of their sail training role and obtained a sponsor in the form of the large British brewer Whitbread and Company and the project was off the ground. The first race took place in 1973 with fourteen entries completing the course which started and finished in Portsmouth, England and had stops in Cape Town, Sydney and Rio de Janeiro. This was a handicap race, run under the International Offshore Rule which attempts to level out the differences between dissimilar yachts. The first race was won on handicap by the 65-foot Mexican entry *Sayula*. Inevitably the contestants were cautious, the reputation of the Roaring Forties ensured that the crews thought more of seamanship and survival than sailing flat out. Even so two men were lost from the yacht *Great Britain 2* which nevertheless sailed home first and with the fastest time.

The undoubted success of this race spawned another two years later known as the *Financial Times* Clipper Race which attracted four entrants and had only one stop in Sydney. However the next RNSA/Whitbread race had already been announced and it was quickly obvious from the standard of entries that it would be much more of a race than the first. Yachtsmen had read the accounts of the previous circumnavigations and now felt that with modern boats and equipment the Southern Ocean could be taken on and yachts pushed at full racing speed. Certainly this is what attracted me to this race, the opportunity to try and outrun the waves in a large racing yacht with a crew of sixteen rather than be forced in *Suhaili* to put the brake on in large waves to avoid broaching.

The 1977 race attracted fifteen entrants and I skippered *Heath's Condor* for legs two and four, so did not take her round the Horn. The competition was intense from the start. The loss of the mast on the first leg meant that we were out of the handicap race, but there were compensations in gaining line honours in the second and fourth legs. In the Southern Ocean it was possible to hold onto sail, even spinnakers, right up to gale conditions when the waves created magnificent surfs of more than 33 knots. When the boat was maintaining an average of close to 14 knots the moment a huge wave came up astern she would accelerate forward and downwards with the bow waves extending right past the stern and rising more than twelve feet above the deck on each side. Astern a huge rooster tail was dragged along in the wake. Steering in these circumstances required total concentration. If helm was not applied instantly when a cross wave came in at the wrong moment, the bow would be driven round, leaving the boat broadside onto the wave and losing speed. The same would happen if the boat was not kept going straight down the front of the wave and sometimes the cavitation created by the keel and skeg meant that the rudder was not biting into the water properly and the boat would not even respond to a full rudder. When this happened in a large breaking wave a knock-down was almost inevitable, the boat being smashed over onto her side so that the masts and sails were in the sea. Then as the wave passed the head had to be brought round again and the nearest equivalent to the Nantucket sleigh ride, as the old whalermen called being dragged by a harpooned whale, would start all over again. We learned as we went along. The spinnakers did not provide a good balance for the helmsman, it was far better in big seas to set poled-out headsails, one on each bow, than set a spinnaker of equal sail area. In fact we found this so well balanced that we were able to put inexperienced helmsmen on the wheel even in storm conditions knowing we were making better speed and at lesser risk.

Cape Horn provided a spectacular and memorable sight for the competitors. One by one they swept past, all recording squalls and snow, but aboard *Gauloise II* the conditions nearly became disastrous when her bow dug into a wave and the boat was pivoted round in a broach that put several feet of the mast under water. The turning moment of a spinnaker and its pole on the mast was such that the whole structure was twisted, but it stayed in one piece. Strong gusts continued to the east of the Horn and most of the yachts steered for the Le Maire Strait under boomed-out headsails. Aboard *King's Legend* they observed a light coming up fast from astern, so fast that they thought it must be the Royal Navy's patrol ship HMS *Endurance*. As the sky lightened they realised it was a spinnaker, that of the French yacht *33 Export* which was surfing ever closer. Eventually she surfed past but then broached right in the path of *King's Legend*. For a moment time stood still. The helmsman aboard *King's Legend* knew that if their boat began to surf now there was no way he could avoid running aboard the other yacht with dire results for both. Whether applying full rudder might have acted as a brake will never be known, probably it would have only reduced the force of the collision by a fraction, but fortunately the boat did not surf. The craft remained under control and the two boats were able to steer clear of each other. A narrow escape for both and a warning not to get too close in large seas where the sheer size and power of the waves can cancel out the effect of the rudder on even the best-balanced vessel.

It was inevitable that a regular series of single-handed around-the-world races would follow the fully crewed event and in 1982 the first of what became known as the BOC Challenges was organised, named after the sponsor, the British Oxygen Company. This race started and finished in Newport, Rhode Island with stops at Cape Town, Sydney and Rio de Janeiro. It attracted seventeen starters of which ten finished. The winner, Frenchman Philippe Jeantot, set a new record from Sydney to Cape Horn of 29 days 23 hours, a speed many of the clipper ships would have envied. His overall time was 159 days 2 hours and 26 minutes, almost half the time I had taken only fourteen years before in *Suhaili*, albeit in a 56-footer instead of a 32-foot cruiser.

If the competitors were drawn mainly from those who simply wanted to achieve a circumnavigation in 1982, by 1986 when the second race was organised the scene had changed. As with the Whitbread race, this time there were more entrants confident enough to want to race and such was the keenness of the competition that the boats went around Cape Horn in small groups almost in sight of each other. The South African John Martin pulled in to anchor inside Deceit Island for emergency repairs which took only an hour but this was enough to allow Guy Bernardin of France to catch up and the two boats raced in sight of each other right up through the Le Maire

Strait. Although they then lost sight of each other they arrived off Rio within an hour and Bernardin managed to hold onto a light breeze and finish ahead. The final winner of the race was again the Frenchman Philippe Jeantot in a time of 134 days 5 hours 23 minutes and 56 seconds. This was almost 25 days faster than the previous race, an improvement that cannot just be explained by a permitted increase in overall length to 60 feet, a length that had been agreed internationally between the two races as the upper limit for single-handed sailing events.

The urge to win can present the sailor with the difficult problem of deciding just to what point it is permitted to risk the boat to achieve a quicker time. During the 1990/91 race many of the competitors ran into ice at latitudes of 60° south, as they strove to cut the distance for the leg from Sydney to Cape Horn by taking a route closer to the shortest possible route, a composite Great Circle along the earth's surface which passes very close to Antarctica. Large bergs will show up on radar, now mandatory for the boats, but growlers, which float just at the surface, are not easily discernible, especially in rough weather or at night. John Martin, lying third, in *Allied Bank*, fell off a wave onto a growler which broke a stringer close to the keel when some 2,000 miles west of Cape Horn. A storm created further problems and the hull began to delaminate. There were three other competitors close behind but fellow South African Bertie Reed, one of the few to be taking part in his third BOC race, managed to get close and find Martin who had taken to his liferaft thirty minutes before. In the appalling conditions the raft had broken away from the stricken yacht and Reed had to search for it in 35-knot winds.

Other ice collisions, such as Philippe Jeantot having a large growler jammed between his boat's two rudders, subsequently led to a call to restrict the southing that could be made by competitors in future races, a decision that was shared with the Whitbread organisers. This will inevitably mean that future times cannot be fairly compared with those up to the 1990 race. But such has been the recent development in the 'Open 60-footer' class and the new Whitbread 60 class, (which, confusingly, is usually 64 feet in length) that it will probably not be long before the overall times are shortened even further. In the third BOC the winning time was down to 120 days, 22 hours, 36 minutes, and 35 seconds, set by Frenchman Christophe Auguin.

The only race that could possibly eclipse the BOC Challenge for the title of the toughest test of any human would be another solo non-stop event and it was not long in coming. Philippe Jeantot, winner of the first two BOCs, established the event, known as the Globe Vendée, to be raced every four years starting in November 1989. Thirteen boats set out, seven returned, the winner, a veteran of the BOC, was yet another Frenchman Titouan

Lamazou in a time of 109 days, 8 hours, 49 minutes and 54 seconds, a new record for a circumnavigation under sail of any sort. This time was good enough to be unthreatened four years later when this race was run a second time.

As ocean-going yacht design and speeds improved, it was inevitable that yachtsmen would seek to challenge the records of the great clipper ships. The yachts might be much smaller, but they were able to sail as close to their theoretical top speed much of the time whereas the sheer weight and size of the sailing cargo ships meant that few ever averaged more than 8 knots on a long voyage. One of the most enduring of these records was the 89-day run from New York to San Francisco set by *Flying Cloud* in 1851. Chay Blyth, who had already set the record for a non-stop circumnavigation east to west in 1971, made an attempt in 1984 in the 55-foot trimaran *Beefeater 2*. He was running some three days ahead of schedule when he and his crew, Eric Blum, ran into atrocious weather just to the west of Cape Horn. They decided to turn and run before the sea's streaming warps until they could get into shelter to the east of Cape Horn but, as Blyth described it, 'A huge 40-foot swell tossed the boat onto its side before it turned turtle'. Fortunately they were able to set off a satellite alarm and were discovered by an aircraft that brought a fish factory ship to pick up the men who were sitting on the upturned hulls. Whilst awaiting rescue the two men had been thrown into the water but were able to salvage some food and equipment. Lines were thrown from the rescue ship and they were hauled to safety suffering from nothing worse than hypothermia and a broken collar bone for Blyth caused when he was swung into the ship's hull.

There was some criticism that a trimaran was an unsuitable vessel to take into the waters of the Horn but this rather ignores Nigel Tetley's rounding in 1969 in a smaller vessel. The fact of the matter is, as shown by the experience of the much larger square riggers, the Southern Ocean can generate waves sufficiently large to overwhelm even the largest of ships. Blyth was unlucky, had he been a couple of days earlier, or perhaps later, he would probably have managed to get round without difficulty. A rounding from east to west has to be timed to coincide with the lulls between gales but when trying to beat a record there are no days to spare waiting for a weather window. This record did subsequently fall to the 60-foot American yacht *Thursday's Child* skippered by Warren Luhrs.

As recently as 22nd November 1990, the American 60-foot trimaran *Great American* was rolled over by waves in excess of fifty feet in height at a point some 350 miles north-west of Cape Horn. About an hour later as the two-man crew struggled inside the upturned boat to try and sort out the mess, another large wave rolled them back upright again. Fortunately the Emergency Position Indicating Radio Beacon had been activated by the accident and there were two ships close by. The first to respond was the 900-foot container ship *New Zealand Pacific*, bound from New Zealand to Holland. The captain, adding a further example of superb seamanship to the sagas of Cape Horn, deftly brought his enormous vessel alongside the waterlogged trimaran in conditions described as the worst he had seen in the area and enabled the crew to reach lines thrown to them.

The record from San Francisco to Boston had lasted from 1853 when the 1,021-ton clipper ship *Northern Light* covered the distance in 79 days. Setting off on 11th January 1993, Bill Biewenga and Rich Wilson in their 55-foot trimaran *Great American II* ran into heavy weather and lost part of their port float. They returned to San Francisco for repairs and were ready to try again on 27th January. This time they had better luck and it was not until they were running down the coast of Chile that they ran into serious weather. The smashing of the hulls into the seas as their boat was forced south gave little chance for rest or proper feeding and every action became a huge effort. If this was to be the weather north of the Horn what would the Horn itself have to offer them? In fact, as was to be seen by other craft over that winter period, the Horn itself seems to have had a fairly easy season and they rounded in safety. Once into the Atlantic the seas and swell that are so much a part of sailing along the southern west coast of America disappeared but the crew were faced with a hard push if they were to maintain their average. Despite a 70-knot storm forecast for the Gulf Stream they managed to reach Boston in 69 days. Yet another record had crumbled to the force of modern technology.

Reporting similarly easy conditions were the ten yachts of the British Steel fleet racing, with amateur crews, westabout. None had a real pasting off the Horn, indeed, they discovered that the Horn can be a bit of an anticlimax – but no one in their right mind would complain about that.

If the regular series of Whitbreads, BOCs and Globe Vendées had proved an interesting replacement to the tea, wool and grain races run by the square riggers, they were not the only around-the-world races that could excite interest whilst using the Cape Horn route. In 1992 a new prize was announced, the Trophée Jules Verne, for any sailing craft that could sail around the world, without outside assistance, in under 80 days. Three boats set out, two agreeing to comply with these simple rules, the 85-foot catamaran *Commodore Explorer,* skippered by Frenchman Bruno Peyron and the equal length *Enza New Zealand*, skippered jointly by the author and Peter Blake. The third boat, which refused to comply with the Jules Verne rules, was a

90-foot trimaran skippered by Olivier de Kersuason. In the event only *Commodore* completed the voyage, the other two being forced to pull out through damage sustained by freak collisions in the Southern Ocean. What might give a severe knock to a boat at 12 knots became a major risk at 24 knots, the speed that the boats were often doing. *Commodore*'s time was an incredible 79 days, 6 hours, 15 minutes and 56 seconds, an average speed of more than 14.5 knots and a world record for a fully crewed yacht.

Peyron's record was not to last a year. Both the *Enza* team and de Kersuason were convinced they could complete a circumnavigation in a faster time and returned for another attempt in January 1994, starting together to make a match of it. The Horn was not kind to *Enza*, leading at that point by two days. Seas of 60 feet whipped up by 55-knot winds forced her to heave to and run quietly under bare poles abeam to the seas but running off whenever a particularly large wave was encountered some 120 miles south of the Cape. With her lead reduced to 350 miles *Enza* headed north but it was not until the Azores that the result became safe to predict. *Enza* won in a new record time of 74 days, 22 hours, 17 minutes and 22 seconds, an average speed of 14.68 knots. De Kersuason finished just over two days later.

Although the yachts might appear to be the successors to the great square-riggers the significance of the rescue of the crew of the *Great American* in 1990 was not just superb seamanship by the container ship *New Zealand Pacific*, but the fact that she was in the area at all. This new generation of vessel, the very large container ships, are finding it more economic to take the route around Cape Horn between Europe and Australasia rather than through the Panama Canal. Their route thus follows that of the traditional sailing ships around the world and in commercial terms at least they can be fairly described as the true successors to the Clippers and Down Easters of 100 years ago.

Modern communications, enormous ships and high speeds may have made the passage around the Horn a hundred times safer but only a fool would go there to defy the power of the seas. Even on the huge container ships the great greybeards of the Southern Ocean can crash aboard and sweep the decks more than twenty metres above the sea.

Appendix
Cape Horn Records

None of these records can be proved by modern standards, such as the independent polling of a Global Positioning System aboard the boat by someone ashore, and many are the result of interpolation which is not allowed today. Nevertheless the times were claimed and not disputed at the time.

Doubling the Horn, ie the time taken between latitudes 50° S in the Atlantic to the same latitude in the Pacific, or vice versa.
Brenhilda, three-masted British barque. Skipper Captain Learmont. East to west passing east of Staten Island. 9th–14th July 1902. *5 days, 1 hour.*

New York to San Francisco
Flying Cloud, US clipper ship. 229 loa, 1,789 tons. Skipper Josiah Cressy. 1854. *18 days, 21 hours.*

New York to Cape Horn
Great Republic, US clipper ship. 1856–7. *45 days, 17 hours.*

Cape Horn to San Fransisco
Flying Cloud, US clipper ship. 1854. *39 days.*

Slowest around the Horn
Falls of Halladale, 275 loa, 2,026 tons. Skipper D.W. Thomson. Liverpool to San Francisco in 238 days between July 1903 and March 1904.

San Fransisco to Boston
Great American II, Richard Wilson and Bill Biewenga, 1993. *69 days, 19 hours.*

New York to San Francisco
Ecuriel Poitou-Charentes II (France). Skipper Isabelle Autissier. 1994. *62 days, 5 hours, 55 minutes.*

Non-stop Circumnavigation Yacht Records

1969 First single-handed non-stop by Robin Knox-Johnston (UK) in 32' Bermudian ketch *Suhaili* between 14th June 1968 and 22nd April 1969, thereby winning the *Sunday Times* Golden Globe. *313 days.*

1971 First single-handed non-stop east to west. Chay Blyth (UK) in 59 loa aux. ketch *British Steel*. *292 days.*

1989 Fastest single-handed completed by Titouan Lamazou (France) in 60' sloop *Ecuriel d'Aquitaine*, during the Globe Vendée Race. *109 days, 8 hours, 48 minutes, 50 seconds.*

1993 First in under 80 days, west to east, 82' catamaran *Commodore Explorer* skippered by Bruno Peyron (France), with a crew of five, between January and April. *79 day, 6 hours, 15 minutes, 56 seconds.*

1994 Fastest crewed west to east *Enza New Zealand*, catamaran skippered by Robin Knox-Johnston (UK) and Peter Blake (NZ), with a crew of eight, between January and April. *74 days, 22 hours, 17 minutes, 22 seconds.*

1994 Fastest single-handed non-stop east to west. Mike Golding (UK) in 65' sloop *Group 4* between November 1993 and May 1994. *161 days, 16 hours, 35 minutes, 24 seconds.*

Yacht Roundings of Cape Horn

1876 *Sunbeam* (UK) 531 ton, three-masted topsail schooner via

Magellan Strait. Owned by Sir Thomas and Lady Brassey. Lady Brassey wrote a Victorian bestseller as a result called *The Voyage of the Sunbeam.*

1888/1896 *Coronet* (USA) 133' schooner. Skipper C. S. Crosby. East to west, 8th May 1888; west to east 3rd February 1896; west to east 9th December 1896.

1896 *Spray* (USA) 36' yawl. Skipper Joshua Slocum. East to west single-handed via Magellan Strait, 11th February – 13th April.

1911 *Pandora* (UK) 36' 9" gaff yawl. Skipper George Blyth. West to east, 16th January.
1924 *Saoirse* (Eire) 42' gaff ketch. Skipper Conor O'Brian. West to east, 3rd December.
1934 *Mary Jane* (Norway) 36' gaff sloop. Skipper Al Hanson. First single-hander *and* east to west, April.

1936 *Wanderbird* (USA) 85' gaff schooner. Skipper Warwick Tompkins. East to west, 22nd November.

1943 *Legh II* (Argentina) 31' 2" Bermudian ketch. Skipper Vito Dumas. Single-handed west to east, 24th June.

1952 *Les Quatre Vents* (France) 30' 8" Bermudian sloop. Skipper Marcel Bardiaux. Single-handed west to east, 12th May 1952.

1958/1962 *Freedom* (UK) 40' Bermudian ketch. Skipper Bill Watson. Single-handed west to east, 15th December 1958; east to west and west to east, 25th December 1962.

1965 *Cardinal Vertue* (Australia) 25' 3" Bermudian sloop. Skipper Bill Nance. Single-handed west to east, 7th January.

1966 *Joshua* (France) 39' 6" Bermudian ketch. Skipper Bernard Moitessier. West to east, 10th January.

1966 *Sea Wanderer* (UK) 36' Bermudian ketch. Skipper Edward Allcard. Single-handed east to west, 12th April.

1966 *Awahnee II* (USA) 53' Bermudian cutter. Skipper R. L. Griffith. East to west.

1967 *Gipsy Moth IV* (UK) 53' Bermudian yawl. Skipper Francis Chichester. Single-handed west to east, 20th March.

1967 *Carronade* (Australia) 30' Bermudian sloop. Skipper Andy Wall. 30th March.

1967 *Stormvogel* (South Africa) 73' Bermudian ketch. Skipper Kees Bruynzeel. West to east and east to west, 1967.

1968 *Lively Lady* (UK) 36' Bermudian yawl. Skipper Alec Rose. Single-handed west to east, 1st April.

1968 *Tzu Hang* (UK) 46' 3" Bermudian ketch. Skipper Miles Smeeton. East to west, 16th December.

1969 *Suhaili* (UK) 32' Bermudian ketch. Skipper Robin Knox-Johnston. First non-stop circumnavigation, single-handed west to east, 17th January.

1969 *Joshua* (France) 39' 6" Bermudian ketch. Skipper Bernard Moitessier. Single-handed west to east, 5th February.

1969 *Victress* (UK) 40' trimaran. Skipper Nigel Tetley. Single-handed west to east, 18th March.

GLOSSARY

Bald Headed   A sailing vessel distinguished by carrying no sails above the topgallants, a combined jib-boom and bowsprit (known as a spike bowsprit), a square sail set on the crossjack and no fore and aft mizzen.

Barque   A vessel with three or more masts, square-rigged on all but the mizzen.

Barquentine   A vessel resembling a barque but square-rigged on the fore mast only.

Brig   A two-masted vessel square-rigged on both masts.

Brigantine   A two-masted vessel, square-rigged on the fore, fore and aft rigged on the main.

EPIRB   (Emergency Position Indicating Radio Beacon) An automatic distress buoy that transmits a distress signal on 121.5 or 406MHz (The latter now linked to satellite tracking).

Monitor   A low freeboard, shallow draft vessel which mounted one or two heavy guns used for coastal bombardment.

Nao   A big ship, usually one that was square-rigged with at
                     least three masts.

Pink   A small square-rigged vessel whose distinctive feature
                     was a narrow stern.

Pinnace   A small two-masted craft of about twenty tons, square-
                     rigged in the sixteenth century but later fore and aft
                     rigging was introduced. Used for taking messages from
                     the admiral to other vessels and for exploration.

Ship-rigged   A vessel with three or more masts, square-rigged on
                     all.

Tartan or Tartane A small, originally Mediterranean craft, lateen-rigged
                     on a single mast with a small foresail set on the
                     bowsprit.

INDEX